William Shakespeare

THE TAMING OF THE SHREW

Edited with a Commentary by G. R. Hibbard
Introduced by Margaret Jane Kidnie

PENGUIN BOOKS

PENGUIN BOOKS

Published by the Penguin Group
Penguin Books Ltd, 80 Strand, London WC2R ORL, England
Penguin Group (USA) Inc., 375 Hudson Street, New York, New York 10014, USA
Penguin Group (Canada), 90 Eglinton Avenue East, Suite 700, Toronto, Ontario, Canada M4P 2Y3
(a division of Pearson Penguin Canada Inc.)
Penguin Ireland, 25 St Stephen's Green, Dublin 2, Ireland (a division of Penguin Books Ltd)
Penguin Group (Australia), 250 Camberwell Road, Camberwell, Victoria 3124, Australia
(a division of Pearson Australia Group Pty Ltd)
Penguin Books India Pvt Ltd, 11 Community Centre, Panchsheel Park, New Delhi – 110 017, India
Penguin Group (NZ), cnr Airborne and Rosedale Roads, Albany, Auckland 1310, New Zealand
(a division of Pearson New Zealand Ltd)
Penguin Books (South Africa) (Pty) Ltd, 24 Sturdee Avenue, Rosebank 2196, South Africa

Penguin Books Ltd, Registered Offices: 80 Strand, London WC2R ORL, England

www.penguin.com

This edition first published in Penguin Books 1968
Reprinted with revised Further Reading 1995
Reissued in the Penguin Shakespeare series 2006

1

This edition copyright © Penguin Books, 1969
Account of the Text and Commentary copyright © G. R. Hibbard, 1968
General Introduction and Chronology copyright © Stanley Wells, 2005
Introduction, The Play in Performance and Further Reading copyright © Margaret Jane Kidnie, 2006

Designed by Boag Associates
Set in 11.5/12.5 PostScript Monotype Fournier
Typeset by Palimpsest Book Production Limited, Polmont, Stirlingshire
Printed in England by Clays Ltd, St Ives plc

ISBN-13: 978-0-141-01551-4
ISBN-10: 0-141-01551-9

Contents

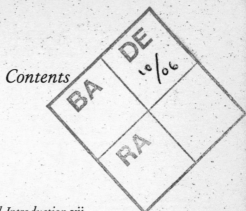

General Introduction

Every play by Shakespeare is unique. This is part of his greatness. A restless and indefatigable experimenter, he moved with a rare amalgamation of artistic integrity and dedicated professionalism from one kind of drama to another. Never shackled by convention, he offered his actors the alternation between serious and comic modes from play to play, and often also within the plays themselves, that the repertory system within which he worked demanded, and which provided an invaluable stimulus to his imagination. Introductions to individual works in this series attempt to define their individuality. But there are common factors that underpin Shakespeare's career.

Nothing in his heredity offers clues to the origins of his genius. His upbringing in Stratford-upon-Avon, where he was born in 1564, was unexceptional. His mother, born Mary Arden, came from a prosperous farming family. Her father chose her as his executor over her eight sisters and his four stepchildren when she was only in her late teens, which suggests that she was of more than average practical ability. Her husband John, a glover, apparently unable to write, was nevertheless a capable businessman and loyal townsfellow, who seems to have fallen on relatively hard times in later life. He would have been brought up as a Catholic, and may have retained

Catholic sympathies, but his son subscribed publicly to Anglicanism throughout his life.

The most important formative influence on Shakespeare was his school. As the son of an alderman who became bailiff (or mayor) in 1568, he had the right to attend the town's grammar school. Here he would have received an education grounded in classical rhetoric and oratory, studying authors such as Ovid, Cicero and Quintilian, and would have been required to read, speak, write and even think in Latin from his early years. This classical education permeates Shakespeare's work from the beginning to the end of his career. It is apparent in the self-conscious classicism of plays of the early 1590s such as the tragedy of *Titus Andronicus*, *The Comedy of Errors*, and the narrative poems *Venus and Adonis* (1592–3) and *The Rape of Lucrece* (1593–4), and is still evident in his latest plays, informing the dream visions of *Pericles* and *Cymbeline* and the masque in *The Tempest*, written between 1607 and 1611. It inflects his literary style throughout his career. In his earliest writings the verse, based on the ten-syllabled, five-beat iambic pentameter, is highly patterned. Rhetorical devices deriving from classical literature, such as alliteration and antithesis, extended similes and elaborate wordplay, abound. Often, as in *Love's Labour's Lost* and *A Midsummer Night's Dream*, he uses rhyming patterns associated with lyric poetry, each line self-contained in sense, the prose as well as the verse employing elaborate figures of speech. Writing at a time of linguistic ferment, Shakespeare frequently imports Latinisms into English, coining words such as abstemious, addiction, incarnadine and adjunct. He was also heavily influenced by the eloquent translations of the Bible in both the Bishops' and the Geneva versions. As his experience grows, his verse and prose become more supple,

the patterning less apparent, more ready to accommo-
date the rhythms of ordinary speech, more colloquial in
diction, as in the speeches of the Nurse in *Romeo and
Juliet*, the characterful prose of Falstaff and Hamlet's
soliloquies. The effect is of increasing psychological
realism, reaching its greatest heights in *Hamlet*, *Othello*,
King Lear, *Macbeth* and *Antony and Cleopatra*. Gradually
he discovered ways of adapting the regular beat of the
pentameter to make it an infinitely flexible instrument for
matching thought with feeling. Towards the end of his
career, in plays such as *The Winter's Tale*, *Cymbeline* and
The Tempest, he adopts a more highly mannered style,
in keeping with the more overtly symbolical and emblem-
atical mode in which he is writing.

So far as we know, Shakespeare lived in Stratford till
after his marriage to Anne Hathaway, eight years his
senior, in 1582. They had three children: a daughter,
Susanna, born in 1583 within six months of their marriage,
and twins, Hamnet and Judith, born in 1585. The next
seven years of Shakespeare's life are virtually a blank.
Theories that he may have been, for instance, a schoolmaster, or a lawyer, or a soldier, or a sailor, lack evidence
to support them. The first reference to him in print, in
Robert Greene's pamphlet *Greene's Groatsworth of Wit*
of 1592, parodies a line from *Henry VI, Part III*, implying
that Shakespeare was already an established playwright.
It seems likely that at some unknown point after the birth
of his twins he joined a theatre company and gained
experience as both actor and writer in the provinces and
London. The London theatres closed because of plague
in 1593 and 1594; and during these years, perhaps recog-
nizing the need for an alternative career, he wrote and
published the narrative poems *Venus and Adonis* and *The
Rape of Lucrece*. These are the only works we can be

certain that Shakespeare himself was responsible for putting into print. Each bears the author's dedication to Henry Wriothesley, Earl of Southampton (1573–1624), the second in warmer terms than the first. Southampton, younger than Shakespeare by ten years, is the only person to whom he personally dedicated works. The Earl may have been a close friend, perhaps even the beautiful and adored young man whom Shakespeare celebrates in his *Sonnets*.

The resumption of playing after the plague years saw the founding of the Lord Chamberlain's Men, a company to which Shakespeare was to belong for the rest of his career, as actor, shareholder and playwright. No other dramatist of the period had so stable a relationship with a single company. Shakespeare knew the actors for whom he was writing and the conditions in which they performed. The permanent company was made up of around twelve to fourteen players, but one actor often played more than one role in a play and additional actors were hired as needed. Led by the tragedian Richard Burbage (1568–1619) and, initially, the comic actor Will Kemp (d. 1603), they rapidly achieved a high reputation, and when King James I succeeded Queen Elizabeth I in 1603 they were renamed as the King's Men. All the women's parts were played by boys; there is no evidence that any female role was ever played by a male actor over the age of about eighteen. Shakespeare had enough confidence in his boys to write for them long and demanding roles such as Rosalind (who, like other heroines of the romantic comedies, is disguised as a boy for much of the action) in *As You Like It*, Lady Macbeth and Cleopatra. But there are far more fathers than mothers, sons than daughters, in his plays, few if any of which require more than the company's normal complement of three or four boys.

The company played primarily in London's public playhouses – there were almost none that we know of in the rest of the country – initially in the Theatre, built in Shoreditch in 1576, and from 1599 in the Globe, on Bankside. These were wooden, more or less circular structures, open to the air, with a thrust stage surmounted by a canopy and jutting into the area where spectators who paid one penny stood, and surrounded by galleries where it was possible to be seated on payment of an additional penny. Though properties such as cauldrons, stocks, artificial trees or beds could indicate locality, there was no representational scenery. Sound effects such as flourishes of trumpets, music both martial and amorous, and accompaniments to songs were provided by the company's musicians. Actors entered through doors in the back wall of the stage. Above it was a balconied area that could represent the walls of a town (as in *King John*), or a castle (as in *Richard II*), and indeed a balcony (as in *Romeo and Juliet*). In 1609 the company also acquired the use of the Blackfriars, a smaller, indoor theatre to which admission was more expensive, and which permitted the use of more spectacular stage effects such as the descent of Jupiter on an eagle in *Cymbeline* and of goddesses in *The Tempest*. And they would frequently perform before the court in royal residences and, on their regular tours into the provinces, in non-theatrical spaces such as inns, guildhalls and the great halls of country houses.

Early in his career Shakespeare may have worked in collaboration, perhaps with Thomas Nashe (1567–c. 1601) in *Henry VI, Part I* and with George Peele (1556–96) in *Titus Andronicus*. And towards the end he collaborated with George Wilkins (*fl.* 1604–8) in *Pericles*, and with his younger colleagues Thomas Middleton (1580–1627), in *Timon of Athens*, and John Fletcher (1579–1625), in *Henry*

VIII, *The Two Noble Kinsmen* and the lost play *Cardenio*. Shakespeare's output dwindled in his last years, and he died in 1616 in Stratford, where he owned a fine house, New Place, and much land. His only son had died at the age of eleven, in 1596, and his last descendant died in 1670. New Place was destroyed in the eighteenth century but the other Stratford houses associated with his life are maintained and displayed to the public by the Shakespeare Birthplace Trust.

One of the most remarkable features of Shakespeare's plays is their intellectual and emotional scope. They span a great range from the lightest of comedies, such as *The Two Gentlemen of Verona* and *The Comedy of Errors*, to the profoundest of tragedies, such as *King Lear* and *Macbeth*. He maintained an output of around two plays a year, ringing the changes between comic and serious. All his comedies have serious elements: Shylock, in *The Merchant of Venice*, almost reaches tragic dimensions, and *Measure for Measure* is profoundly serious in its examination of moral problems. Equally, none of his tragedies is without humour: Hamlet is as witty as any of his comic heroes, *Macbeth* has its Porter, and *King Lear* its Fool. His greatest comic character, Falstaff, inhabits the history plays and *Henry V* ends with a marriage, while *Henry VI, Part III*, *Richard II* and *Richard III* culminate in the tragic deaths of their protagonists.

Although in performance Shakespeare's characters can give the impression of a superabundant reality, he is not a naturalistic dramatist. None of his plays is explicitly set in his own time. The action of few of them (except for the English histories) is set even partly in England (exceptions are *The Merry Wives of Windsor* and the Induction to *The Taming of the Shrew*). Italy is his favoured location. Most of his principal story-lines derive from printed writings; but the structuring and translation of these narratives into dramatic terms is Shakespeare's own, and he invents much additional material. Most of the plays contain elements of myth and legend, and many derive from ancient or more recent history or from romantic tales of ancient times and faraway places. All reflect his reading, often in close detail. Holinshed's *Chronicles* (1577, revised 1587), a great compendium of English, Scottish and Irish history, provided material for his English history plays. The *Lives of the Noble Grecians and Romans* by the Greek writer Plutarch, finely translated into English from the French by Sir Thomas North in 1579, provided much of the narrative material, and also a mass of verbal detail, for his plays about Roman history. Some plays are closely based on shorter individual works: *As You Like It*, for instance, on the novel *Rosalynde* (1590) by his near-contemporary Thomas Lodge (1558–1625), *The Winter's Tale* on *Pandosto* (1588) by his old rival Robert Greene (1558–92) and *Othello* on a story by the Italian Giraldi Cinthio (1504–73). And the language of his plays is permeated by the Bible, the Book of Common Prayer and the proverbial sayings of his day.

Shakespeare was popular with his contemporaries, but his commitment to the theatre and to the plays in performance is demonstrated by the fact that only about half of his plays appeared in print in his lifetime, in slim paperback volumes known as quartos, so called because they were made from printers' sheets folded twice to form four leaves (eight pages). None of them shows any sign that he was involved in their publication. For him, performance was the primary means of publication. The most frequently reprinted of his works were the nondramatic poems – the erotic *Venus and Adonis* and the more moralistic *The Rape of Lucrece*. The *Sonnets*, which appeared in 1609, under his name but possibly without his consent, were less successful, perhaps because the vogue for sonnet sequences, which peaked in the 1590s, had passed by then. They were not reprinted until 1640, and then only in garbled form along with poems by other writers. Happily, in 1623, seven years after he died, his colleagues John Heminges (1556–1630) and Henry Condell (d. 1627) published his collected plays, including eighteen that had not previously appeared in print, in the first Folio, whose name derives from the fact that the printers' sheets were folded only once to produce two leaves (four pages). Some of the quarto editions are badly printed, and the fact that some plays exist in two, or even three, early versions creates problems for editors. These are discussed in the Account of the Text in each volume of this series.

Shakespeare's plays continued in the repertoire until the Puritans closed the theatres in 1642. When performances resumed after the Restoration of the monarchy in 1660 many of the plays were not to the taste of the times, especially because their mingling of genres and failure to meet the requirements of poetic justice offended against the dictates of neoclassicism. Some, such as *The Tempest* (changed by John Dryden and William Davenant in 1667 to suit contemporary taste), *King Lear* (to which Nahum Tate gave a happy ending in 1681) and *Richard III* (heavily adapted by Colley Cibber in 1700 as a vehicle for his own talents), were extensively rewritten; others fell into neglect. Slowly they regained their place in the repertoire, and they continued to be reprinted, but it was not until the great actor David Garrick (1717–79) organized a spectacular jubilee in Stratford in 1769 that Shakespeare began to be regarded as a transcendental genius. Garrick's idolatry prefigured the enthusiasm of critics such as Samuel Taylor Coleridge (1772–1834) and William Hazlitt (1778–1830). Gradually Shakespeare's reputation spread abroad, to Germany, America, France and to other European countries.

During the nineteenth century, though the plays were generally still performed in heavily adapted or abbreviated versions, a large body of scholarship and criticism began to amass. Partly as a result of a general swing in education away from the teaching of Greek and Roman texts and towards literature written in English, Shakespeare became the object of intensive study in schools and universities. In the theatre, important turning points were the work in England of two theatre directors, William Poel (1852–1934) and his disciple Harley Granville-Barker (1877–1946), who showed that the application of knowledge, some of it newly acquired, of early staging conditions to performance of the plays could render the original texts viable in terms of the modern theatre. During the twentieth century appreciation of Shakespeare's work, encouraged by the availability of audio, film and video versions of the plays, spread around the world to such an extent that he can now be claimed as a global author.

The influence of Shakespeare's works permeates the English language. Phrases from his plays and poems – 'a tower of strength', 'green-eyed jealousy', 'a foregone conclusion' – are on the lips of people who may never have read him. They have inspired composers of songs, orchestral music and operas; painters and sculptors; poets, novelists and film-makers. Allusions to him appear in pop songs, in advertisements and in television shows. Some of his characters – Romeo and Juliet, Falstaff, Shylock and Hamlet – have acquired mythic status. He is valued for his humanity, his psychological insight, his wit and humour, his lyricism, his mastery of language, his ability to excite, surprise, move and, in the widest sense of the word, entertain audiences. He is the greatest of poets, but he is essentially a dramatic poet. Though his plays have much to offer to readers, they exist fully only in performance. In these volumes we offer individual introductions, notes on language and on specific points of the text, suggestions for further reading and information about how each work has been edited. In addition we include accounts of the ways in which successive generations of interpreters and audiences have responded to challenges and rewards offered by the plays. The Penguin Shakespeare series aspires to remove obstacles to understanding and to make pleasurable the reading of the work of the man who has done more than most to make us understand what it is to be human.

Stanley Wells

The Chronology of Shakespeare's Works

A few of Shakespeare's writings can be fairly precisely dated. An allusion to the Earl of Essex in the chorus to Act V of *Henry V*, for instance, could only have been written in 1599. But for many of the plays we have only vague information, such as the date of publication, which may have occurred long after composition, the date of a performance, which may not have been the first, or a list in Francis Meres's book *Palladis Tamia*, published in 1598, which tells us only that the plays listed there must have been written by that year. The chronology of the early plays is particularly difficult to establish. Not everyone would agree that the first part of *Henry VI* was written after the third, for instance, or *Romeo and Juliet* before *A Midsummer Night's Dream*. The following table is based on the 'Canon and Chronology' section in *William Shakespeare: A Textual Companion*, by Stanley Wells and Gary Taylor, with John Jowett and William Montgomery (1987), where more detailed information and discussion may be found.

The Two Gentlemen of Verona	1590–91
The Taming of the Shrew	1590–91
Henry VI, Part II	1591
Henry VI, Part III	1591

Henry VI, Part I (perhaps with Thomas Nashe)	1592
Titus Andronicus (perhaps with George Peele)	1592
Richard III	1592–3
Venus and Adonis (poem)	1592–3
The Rape of Lucrece (poem)	1593–4
The Comedy of Errors	1594
Love's Labour's Lost	1594–5
Edward III (authorship uncertain, not included in this series)	not later than 1595 (printed in 1596)
Richard II	1595
Romeo and Juliet	1595
A Midsummer Night's Dream	1595
King John	1596
The Merchant of Venice	1596–7
Henry IV, Part I	1596–7
The Merry Wives of Windsor	1597–8
Henry IV, Part II	1597–8
Much Ado About Nothing	1598
Henry V	1598–9
Julius Caesar	1599
As You Like It	1599–1600
Hamlet	1600–1601
Twelfth Night	1600–1601
'The Phoenix and the Turtle' (poem)	by 1601
Troilus and Cressida	1602
The Sonnets (poems)	1593–1603 and later
Measure for Measure	1603
A Lover's Complaint (poem)	1603–4
Sir Thomas More (in part, not included in this series)	1603–4
Othello	1603–4
All's Well That Ends Well	1604–5
Timon of Athens (with Thomas Middleton)	1605
King Lear	1605–6

Introduction

The Taming of the Shrew, for perhaps obvious reasons, is a play that readers and spectators can find offensive. It advocates the subjection of a wife to her husband, it implies that Katherina, under duress, learns this lesson for her own good, and then in the final scene it puts an assertion of the duty women owe to men into the mouth of the converted, or 'tamed', female protagonist. For a modern age that has witnessed and continues to debate restructured gender roles within both home and workplace, the drama's politics are provocative, if not indeed incendiary. Despite, or perhaps in part because of, this ability to invite controversy, it remains one of Shakespeare's most enduring comedies.

Curiously, though, *The Taming of the Shrew* begins, not with a shrew or a tamer, but with an elaborate practical joke. A lord out hunting with his dogs comes across the tinker, Christopher Sly, asleep on the stage. Sly's evident poverty – he is described as a 'beggar' and 'simple peasant' (Induction 1.39, 133) – prompts the lord to try to trick him into believing he is a nobleman who for the past fifteen years has madly thought he is a tinker. The deception is managed through the careful provision of costume, set, narrative and role-play, the devices of theatre. Sly will be 'Wrapped in sweet clothes' and carried to the lord's 'fairest chamber' where the walls are hung with 'wanton pictures' (36, 44–5); when he wakes, he will be waited on with music, food and rose water, with the page Bartholomew, dressed as a woman, taking the part of Sly's supposed wife.

The only difference between this enacted spectacle and theatre is that the star actor, finally persuaded he is 'nothing but a mighty lord' (Induction 1.63), remains unaware that it is just a performance. The actual lord – functioning throughout these early scenes as playwright, stage-manager, director and actor – presents to his servants as sport the incongruous gap between what Sly is and what, duped by the pretence, Sly tries to perform. Another layer to this already complex ruse is added when a group of travelling actors is brought in to perform for Sly's entertainment a play set in Italy. This inset drama, or play within the play, tells the story of Baptista and his two daughters, the modest and virtuous Bianca and the fiery Katherina. Shakespeare's title, *The Taming of the Shrew*, guides one's attention not to Sly, but to this inset drama, and specifically to the plot thread involving the marriage of Katherina to Petruchio.

So when the actor playing Lucentio enters explaining that he has arrived in Padua, the theatre audience understands that, with the sole exception of the tinker in costume as a nobleman, every character onstage (the Lord, Bartholomew, the playing troupe) is self-consciously play-acting. Sly, of course, is also acting, but wrongly believes that his role as the Lord, unfamiliar to him though it seems, is one to which he was born. It seems curious that in such confused circumstances the potential for comic disruption is located exclusively with Sly. While the lord is confident that Bartholomew, cross-dressed as a lady, 'will well usurp the grace, | Voice, gait, and action of a gentlewoman', he expects that just the sight of Sly in costume will cause his men only with difficulty to 'stay themselves from laughter' (Induction 1.129–30, 132). It seems that boys dressed as women is theatrical convention, but beggars dressed as lords is farce.

PERFORMANCE AND DEGREE

This fascination with social status as a form of theatrical game is sustained when attention shifts from the so-called Induction scenes to the play within the play. Baptista is quickly established as the conventional 'blocking' father of romantic comedy, the parent who, like Egeus in *A Midsummer Night's Dream*, gets in the way of his child's marriage. By removing his desirable younger daughter from Paduan society until a husband is found for the elder, Baptista not only sets in motion the taming plot, with Bianca's suitors presenting the newcomer Petruchio as a likely husband for Katherina, but also prompts Lucentio and Hortensio, two suitors to Bianca, to disguise themselves as servants in order to gain illicit access to Baptista's home.

Lucentio takes the part of Cambio, a Latin tutor. Tranio, a servant, in turn agrees to assume his master's identity in order to cover for Lucentio's expected arrival in Padua, the switch passing undetected since they are as yet both strangers to the city. Their scheme is planned with care, but the instance of Hortensio, the next character to appear in disguise, demonstrates how realist effect is a possible, but by no means necessary, condition of Shakespearian comedy. When the music tutor Licio is introduced to Baptista by Petruchio, Hortensio's competitors for Bianca's hand in marriage neither comment on their neighbour's sudden absence from the pool of suitors, nor suspect Licio's true identity. The artistic priority here is not realism but dramatic structure. As Licio, Hortensio provides direct competition for Lucentio-as-Cambio, and so balances in the disguise plot the rivalry for Bianca pursued elsewhere by Gremio and Tranio-as-Lucentio.

This early comedy, probably written around 1590 when Shakespeare was still establishing his career as a professional playwright, is caught up in debates about social status and its performance. Sumptuary proclamations – laws that sought to regulate the clothing worn by different ranks of people – were passed by the English government throughout the sixteenth century. This legislation attempted to stabilize distinctions of degree and wealth by reserving certain fabrics, fashionable styles and types of decorative trim for the exclusive use of the nobility. Sly's poor performance in the role of the lord is therefore significant as it seems to confirm as innate the one-to-one relation asserted by law between costume and identity. Dressed in rich robes, but constantly betraying his low birth by addressing his wife in inappropriate terms and calling for small ale instead of sack, he becomes for his onstage audience an object of ridicule. Cast as a lord, Sly always remains a tinker.

Tranio, by contrast, is a superb actor. This character of the 'clever servant' harks back to a stock figure of *commedia dell'arte*, a form of highly conventionalized Italian theatre popular in the sixteenth century. Tranio is the brains behind Lucentio's bid to win Bianca – he negotiates the financial contracts with Baptista, he finds a supposed father to bequeath his fortune to a supposed son and he counsels Lucentio finally to elope with his bride. The disguise plot exactly reverses the relation between master and servant, giving Tranio the high status he lacks in the opening scene. As though to make the point that Tranio is the man indeed, the master's name, Lucentio, is withheld from the theatre audience until the moment it is emphatically appropriated, along with his clothes, by his servant:

> In brief, sir, sith it your pleasure is,
> And I am tied to be obedient . . .
> I am content to be Lucentio,
> Because so well I love Lucentio. (I.1.208–14)

Tranio's biggest test is probably his first appearance in disguise (I.2), when he joins onstage all of the other suitors to Baptista's daughters. Keen at first to assert their priority over this newcomer, the assembled competitors are forced by the end of the scene to accept him as one among their number. Tranio-as-Lucentio never falters. He is consulted by Baptista on Katherina's wedding day when it appears her 'mad-brain' groom (III.2.10) has shamed the family, and a double-time effect in the same scene suggests he has established a close personal alliance with Petruchio (in fact there is no time for this friendship to have evolved, but this is probably noticed by only the most attentive of spectators). Two scenes later, Biondello, calling 'O master, master' (IV.2.59), enters to Lucentio and Tranio to announce the arrival of a traveller suitable to play the part of the supposed father. While it is impossible to determine with certainty from the text to whom Biondello addresses his lines, it is Tranio who replies – even among those who know the deception, the categories of master and servant can seem porous and blurred.

Tranio is thus an actor who 'passes' as the part he plays. His ability to challenge the supposed link between rich costume and high status by (mis)matching rich costume to low status speaks powerfully to an irony already implicit in the early modern sumptuary laws. If every disguised commoner in England seemed as ludicrous a spectacle as Sly, there would be no need for royal proclamations to enforce dress codes. The impulse to legislate a fixed correlation between apparel and identity suggests, on the contrary, that clothing – the supposed sign and guarantor of degree – is always the stuff of performance. The character of Tranio-as-Lucentio, standing for a radically theatricalized notion of identity, thus brings to life an ideological concern peculiar to early modern England. For Tranio, if not Sly, costume makes, rather than marks, the man.

Tranio's performance is potentially unsettling to a sixteenth-century audience because it raises questions about who else (whether onstage, or sitting in the theatre audience) is doing the same thing. If one accepts that a character can 'pass', it then follows that identity is not reliably legible through signs of costume. It becomes impossible, in short, to know for certain who is really the part he or she plays. This is particularly a problem in a play like *The Taming of the Shrew* that is preoccupied with wealth and good breeding. The lord who encounters Sly prides himself on his excellent hounds and luxurious furnishings; even in disguise as a servant, he remains secure in his identity as the play's real lord, presumably in part because of his power to end the game at will. Baptista, in the play within the play, is no less attentive to social hierarchies than the lord of the Induction scenes as he seeks to broker financially advantageous matches for his two daughters.

MARRIAGE NEGOTIATIONS:
FATHERS AND HUSBANDS

The women's dowries are negotiated in Act 2, scene 1, and the emphasis in each instance is on wealth. In return for marrying Katherina and assuring her in her widowhood 'all [his] lands and leases whatsoever' (125), Petruchio is given half of Baptista's lands after his death and in ready money twenty thousand crowns. Bianca's dowry, by comparison, goes unspecified, while Gremio and Tranio-as-Lucentio enter into a bidding war for permission to marry her. What an audience witnesses in this scene is a case of supply and demand: Katherina goes to the only bidder, while Bianca goes to the highest. Conduct books from the period argue forcefully against enforced marriage – as Baptista puts it, his daughter's love, not the money, should be 'all in all' (129). But what the drama shows, and as the suitors to Bianca and Katherina seem already to know, is that a successful marriage bargain comes down in the end to successful financial negotiations among men.

This emphasis on Baptista's immense wealth raises questions, in particular, about the character of Petruchio. Is this newcomer to Padua independently rich or a crude opportunist? As Petruchio claims, and as his servant Grumio confirms, he comes 'to wive it wealthily in Padua; | If wealthily, then happily in Padua' (I.2.74–5). Evidence of Petruchio's financial means is limited to a short speech in which he reminds Baptista that he 'knew my father well, and in him me, | Left solely heir to all his lands and goods, | Which I have bettered rather than decreased' (II.1.116–18). Baptista and the theatre audience, however, only have Petruchio's word for it that he has 'bettered' his inheritance, and his determination to marry strictly for money seems to raise at least the possibility that he is a social climber seeking to consolidate his position through a prudent match. Another possibility, of course, is that what Baptista knows about Petruchio's father, and so his son, is that the family has nothing. Is Petruchio, like Tranio, merely 'passing' as a man of substance? What does Baptista risk in order to see his eldest daughter married?

Each production of the play provides a provisional answer to these questions at the beginning of Act 4, scene 1 when the action moves from Padua to Verona. Modern sets and lighting, in particular, can indicate quite precisely whether Petruchio lives in a well-appointed mansion or a ramshackle dump, and so allow an audience to discern whether Baptista, as he fears, has 'venture[d] madly on a desperate mart' (II.1.320). The importance of this shift in location is not limited to post-Restoration stages. There were no sets or lighting effects at the earliest, open-air productions, but spectators would have scanned servant liveries and stage properties instead to determine the financial security of the household into which Katherina has married. Major discrepancies between what Petruchio promises in Act II and what his new bride encounters in Act IV carry the potential for comic – or perhaps tragic – effect.

INSET SPECTACLES

From the outset then *The Taming of the Shrew* dramatizes unruly relations of degree. But as the action develops, issues of degree quickly become linked to related issues of gender and sexuality. Not long after his gamut of love is rejected by Bianca, Hortensio, his suspicions raised, persuades Tranio-as-Lucentio to spy with him on Bianca and Lucentio-as-Cambio. The scene witnessed by this hidden onstage audience is the unwelcome sight of the Latin tutor courting Hortensio's mistress. The still-disguised Hortensio at first pretends to be indignant on his companion's behalf, but then eventually sets aside the part of Licio to reveal that he also has a personal interest in the scene continuing to unfold before them. What dismays Hortensio is not that Bianca would disobey her father to entertain an illicit suitor – this is precisely what he himself was counting on, after all, when he approached her in disguise as the music tutor. Rather, Hortensio abandons her as 'one unworthy all the former favours | That I have fondly flattered her withal' (IV.2.30–31) because he wrongly believes she has lowered herself to favour a Latin teacher, a mere servant. More disturbing than the spectacle of Bianca's disobedience and sexual licence is the idea that she is 'such a one as leaves a gentleman | And makes a god of such a cullion' (19–20; 'cullion' was another word for 'testicle', and so came to be used at this time as a term of insult). The dramatic irony implicit in Hortensio's moral judgement is twofold: the Latin teacher Hortensio despises is really a gentleman, and Bianca's seemingly false exterior is exposed while she shares the stage with three other characters, *all* of whom have fashioned for themselves false exteriors either above or below their degree.

This plot thread involving the marriage of Bianca derives from an Italian drama called *I Suppositi* (in English, 'The Substitutes') written by Ludovico Ariosto in 1509, and translated by George Gascoigne in 1566 as *The Supposes*. Shakespeare heavily adapted this material. Most notably, he introduced to the story a headstrong older sister, thus building into a romantic disguise-comedy a 'shrew-taming' narrative, the general outlines of which had a long history in English and continental European folktale. The closest analogue to the story of Katherina and Petruchio is a fairly crude anonymous narrative poem called 'A Merry Jest of a Shrewd and Curst Wife Lapped in Morel's Skin, for Her Good Behaviour' (first published around 1550). The details of the two stories, however, vary enough to suggest strongly that Shakespeare was indebted not to this particular tale of a disobedient wife brought under her husband's control but, more generally, to the genre of which it is just one example. Shakespeare then situates these two stories within a third narrative, a sort of Rip van Winkle tale about a sleeper who awakes to find himself in a strange and unfamiliar world (complications surrounding the Sly plot, and the relation to Shakespeare's play of the anonymous *Taming of A Shrew*, first published in 1594, are discussed in The Play in Performance).

In borrowing material from *The Supposes*, Shakespeare also rearranges events and changes names. Most notably, Gascoigne's play (written entirely in prose) opens with Polynesta, the Bianca character, pregnant, and Erostrato her lover, the Lucentio character, already in place in her father's home as a disguised servant; *The Taming of the Shrew* omits the pregnancy altogether, and begins instead with their first encounter and the conceit of love at first sight. Shakespeare further invents the figure of Hortensio as a fourth rival for Bianca (alongside Gremio, Tranio-as-Lucentio and Lucentio). Hortensio is a useful, because immensely flexible, dramatic innovation. In the first half of the play, as a second disguised tutor, Hortensio provides a comic obstacle to Lucentio's secret suit to Bianca; much later, entering the closing banquet scene married in his own person, he serves to round out to three the number of newlywed grooms.

The scene in Act IV when he abandons Bianca in Padua to join Petruchio at his 'taming-school' in Verona is therefore structurally necessary as it not only sets Hortensio in pursuit of another bride, the wealthy widow, but frees him from the disguise plot to act as a bridge between the temporarily separate fortunes of the two sisters (the stories come together again in Act V when the family gathers for Bianca's wedding). The danger that this transition scene might seem too obviously functional is diminished by the decision to stage it as a play within an inset play: Hortensio and Tranio-as-Lucentio watch the spectacle of Bianca with her servant lover. This technique suggests visual and thematic links to Induction 2, in particular, and implicitly sets the performance of disruptive sexuality alongside the performance of disruptive degree. As the unsuspecting Sly embodies disorderly social relations for an onstage audience consisting of the Lord and his servants, so Bianca unwittingly enacts for her own onstage audience the part of 'unconstant womankind' (IV.2.14).

This device of the play within the play within the play is used as early as Act I, scene 1; the focus here, however, is Katherina, who enters with her family and her sister's suitors. Tranio, entertained by the 'show' provided by a woman threatening to 'comb [Hortensio's] noddle with a three-legged stool', comments that 'here's some good pastime toward. | That wench is stark mad or wonderful froward' (I.1.64, 68–9). Lucentio, by contrast, absorbed with a different show, finds in her sister's silence 'Maid's mild behaviour and sobriety' (71). The performance given by Katherina among her neighbours, like that given by Sly in the lord's chamber, and by Bianca in Act IV while seemingly courted by her servant Cambio, is marked by onstage spectators as transgressive; in each case, a self-contained display of behaviour presented as deviant either amuses or shocks its onlookers. Shakespeare would return to this sort of metatheatrical commentary – one level of action mediating another as the theatre audience watches and assesses it all – in plays as varied as *Much Ado About Nothing* and *Hamlet*, both written about a decade later. What sets *The Taming of the Shrew* apart as remarkable is the insistent repetition of such intertwined layers of theatrical spectacle, Shakespeare seeming in this early drama to test and play with the limits of the device.

Very occasionally the play within the inset play happens 'offstage', when the scene is related after the fact for the onstage and theatre audiences through narrative description. Gremio, for instance, enters to Tranio and Lucentio in the middle of Act 3, scene 2, as though coming from the church where he has witnessed the marriage of Katherina and Petruchio. Calling Petruchio a 'mad-brained bridegroom' and 'very fiend' (162, 154), Gremio describes an episode of utter chaos in which Petruchio at the altar swears 'by gogs-wouns' (159; 'God's wounds'), cuffs the priest, quaffs off all the communion wine, throws the dregs in the sexton's face and roundly kisses his bride 'with such a clamorous smack | That at the parting all the church did echo' (177–8). The potential comedy of a passage such as this can be irresistible. Franco Zeffirelli, for instance, in his film version of 1967, recasts Gremio's lines as dialogue and enacted spectacle in order to allow his audience to see the marriage ceremony for themselves. Narrative in the theatre, however, is an effective dramatic technique in its own right – it is pacey and imaginatively suggestive, yet shapes a clear standpoint on the action by means of the storyteller's bias and onstage listeners' responses. Removed from the scene of marriage, a theatre audience views the ceremony as it were through Gremio's eyes, thus at least provisionally having no choice but to see Katherina as 'a lamb, a dove, a fool' by comparison to the 'devil' Petruchio (156, 154).

Sometimes such passages of narrative anticipate a key entrance. After negotiating the terms of Katherina's marriage dowry with Baptista, Petruchio brags that he will easily obtain her love since he is 'as peremptory as she proud-minded' (II.i.131). Likening himself to a strong gust that blows out a small flame, or a mountain, impervious to blowing winds, Petruchio assures Baptista that he will make Katherina bow to his will. At this moment Hortensio, still in disguise as the music tutor, enters *'with his head broke'* (141) to relate to his onstage audience the progress of Katherina's first music lesson. The scene he describes is of a pupil, unwilling to take instruction, smashing the lute over her tutor's head while calling him 'rascal fiddler | And twangling Jack, with twenty such vile terms, | As had she studied to misuse [him] so' (157–9). The narrative of the music lesson intrudes into the dowry negotiations, with Hortensio's astonishment and wounds seeming to offer by proxy Katherina's silent reply to Petruchio's threat that he is 'rough and woo[s] not like a babe' (137). The onstage juxtaposition of Petruchio's and Katherina's violent characters just prior to their first encounter, handled in part through the device of narrative description, prompts a sense of eager expectation as spectators wait to see which of these two will prevail over the other.

MARRIAGE NEGOTIATIONS:
HUSBANDS AND WIVES

Petruchio, left alone onstage, seems as uncertain as the theatre audience about the outcome of their impending 'chat' (II.1.162). His plan to exercise a form of weak strength, misconstruing everything Katherina says to its opposite sense, is learned from his servant, Grumio. Grumio frustrates Petruchio's will upon their arrival in Padua by repeatedly mistaking the command to 'knock me here soundly' (I.2.8) – that is, to knock at the gate – as an order to hit his master, an order he dare not obey. The scene, while raising questions about Petruchio's authority by showing him driven to violence and still not able to command performance from a servant, at the same time demonstrates the slipperiness of language. Petruchio applies this lesson to changed circumstances:

> If she do bid me pack, I'll give her thanks,
> As though she bid me stay by her a week.
> If she deny to wed, I'll crave the day
> When I shall ask the banns, and when be married.
>   (II.1.177–80)

There is no opportunity, however, immediately to effect this plan – Katherina's and Petruchio's seamless transition into a form of intense competitive wordplay demonstrates instead that they understand each other only too well. Petruchio wins their first verbal bout by transforming an allusion to tongue and tales into a crude oral sex joke; evidently left without reply, Katherina strikes him, so surrendering the match. This type of stichomythic repartee – two characters using wit as a weapon – can be a highly sexualized form of dialogue. The banter's content may suggest mistrust or loathing, but its regimented formal structure consisting of one-line and half-line exchanges locks the two characters (and the actors playing them) into an intensely exclusive interaction. It seems curious then that a second bout is initiated by Katherina with a pun on the (heraldic) arms of a gentleman. If one ignores the editor's stage directions cueing her to struggle in Petruchio's arms (II.1.216–45), one perhaps sees instead that far from besting his opponent a second time, Petruchio, like Katherina earlier, is himself finally left without a reply. He begins a new line, 'Nay, hear you, Kate', only to hesitate, evidently at a loss for words, and to concede the contest in the next breath with the assertion 'In sooth, you scape not so' (234). Tellingly, this is the moment he finally switches tactics and acts on his initial plan to misinterpret deliberately her hostility; when her father enters shortly afterwards, this strategy transforms her promise to 'see [him] hanged on Sunday' (292) into vows of love.

Petruchio ultimately wins his bride by narrating to her father and her sister's suitors the spectacle of love she displayed to him in private:

> O, the kindest Kate!
> She hung about my neck, and kiss on kiss
> She vied so fast, protesting oath on oath,
> That in a twink she won me to her love. (II.1.300–303)

This speech is the inverse counterpoint to Hortensio's description of Katherina's brutality heard just over one hundred lines earlier. The difference between the two

passages rests in the effect of dramatic irony. Made privy
to the second encounter, the theatre audience – for once
set at an interpretative distance from the onstage audience – knows for certain that the scene of kindness
described by Petruchio never took place. A key point
easily overlooked by readers and spectators today is that
betrothals in early modern England could be nearly as
binding as actual marriage. If the promise between two
people remained conditional on the fulfilment of some
stipulation – Tranio-as-Lucentio, for instance, must have
his inheritance in hand, not promised – then it could be
broken off with relative ease. But in the case of an uncon-
ditional promise sworn with an oath, and without mutual
consent on both sides to annul the contract, each party
was legally compelled to marry the other. Katherina and
Petruchio enter into this kind of binding agreement when
Baptista joins their hands (311–12). Petruchio's description of Katherina 'protesting oath on oath' is therefore
a crucial turning-point since it is a lie that Bianca's suitors,
calling themselves 'witnesses' to the match (313), are
prepared to believe and swear to. Petruchio's account of
Katherina's behaviour, while not the factual truth, in this
way becomes the legal truth.

This is why it is such a problem when it seems in Act
3, scene 2 that Petruchio will not turn up to his own
wedding. Not only is it humiliating for Katherina and
her family but, already betrothed to Petruchio, Katherina
cannot with ease enter into another contract of marriage.
The news that he is indeed on his way is handled by
means of the now familiar device of narrative description. Biondello enters the stage ahead of the groom with
a long description of his outlandish, beggarly appearance
on the back of a diseased and ragged horse:

Why, Petruchio is coming in a new hat and an old jerkin; a pair of old breeches thrice turned; a pair of boots that have been candle-cases, one buckled, another laced . . . his horse hipped – with an old mothy saddle and stirrups of no kindred – besides, possessed with the glanders and like to mose in the chine, troubled with the lampass, infected with the fashions . . . with a half-cheeked bit and a headstall of sheep's leather, which, being restrained to keep him from stumbling, hath been often burst and new-repaired with knots . . . (43–58)

And so on. The form of Biondello's prose, heavily marked by excess, mirrors the thing it serves to describe. By the time Petruchio actually enters the stage, the wedding party (and theatre audience) have been conditioned to expect nothing less than a nine-day wonder, and they gaze on him as if 'they saw some wondrous monument, | Some comet, or unusual prodigy' (94–5).

Petruchio's wedding apparel, the report of his outrageous behaviour during the marriage ceremony and his startling announcement that he will not stay to share the bridal dinner can be interpreted as an exercise in image-making. As Tranio passes in this scene as a nobleman, Petruchio passes as an unpredictable, volatile clown whose actions and appearance are a figure of fun for everyone except Katherina, to whom he might instead feasibly represent danger. As Bianca puts it, her sister, 'being mad herself, [is] madly mated' (III.2.243). The difference between Tranio and Petruchio, however, is that whereas the theatre audience always knows that Tranio is playing a part, albeit a part for which he seems remarkably well suited, they have as little idea as the wedding party in this scene as to whether this is the 'real' Petruchio or 'just' a performance. At this point in the

play, in only his second scene, Katherina's groom remains
something of an unknown quantity to everyone.

It is not until the end of Act 4, scene 1 that the theatre
audience is given any assurance that Katherina is not, in
fact, married to a 'mad-brain rudesby' (III.2.10). After
arriving home to Verona only to abuse his servants, to
throw away as burnt the meal waiting for them and to
make at the end of the evening 'a sermon of continency'
to his wife, Petruchio finally re-enters the stage alone to
explain, 'Thus have I politicly begun my reign, | And
'tis my hope to end successfully' (IV.1.169, 174–5). Using
an extended metaphor that likens his wife to a wild bird
of prey, Petruchio confides in the theatre audience that
he plans to tame Katherina as he would any animal,
by continuing to deny her food and sleep. One of
Shakespeare's twists on the conventional shrew-taming
material is that throughout the taming process Petruchio
always presents himself as a caring husband, seeming to
refuse his wife the basic means to support life out of
concern, paradoxically, for her well-being. 'This is a way
to kill a wife with kindness,' Petruchio concludes, 'And
thus I'll curb her mad and headstrong humour' (194–5).

The theatre audience is now in a position to recon-
sider the wedding scene, and to interpret as deliberate
policy what they may have at first taken as madness. But
this insight into Petruchio's motivation and methods is
offered by means of soliloquy, no other character being
present onstage. For Katherina, then, Petruchio's behaviour remains inexplicable – 'What, did he marry me to
famish me?' she asks two scenes later (IV.3.3). She is
powerless, however, to remedy her situation. Not only
is she resident in a household in which she has no
authority, unable even to persuade Petruchio's servants
to give her food, but she is denied the words to

articulate any opinion that is at odds with her husband. They never disagree, but only because Petruchio always cheerfully misconstrues her plain meaning. 'Love me or love me not,' Katherina states in the tailor's scene, with heavy metrical emphasis, 'I like the cap, | And it I will have, or I will have none.' 'Thy gown?', Petruchio replies, dismissing the haberdasher, 'Why, ay. Come, tailor, let us see't' (84–6). Katherina, tellingly, falls increasingly silent in face of her husband's mastery; words to her, after all, are of no avail. She is goaded once again into speech, however, when Petruchio, unprompted and evidently wrongly, insists at the end of the scene that it is seven in the morning, not two in the afternoon.

LANGUAGE AND POWER

The language game has suddenly changed and the stakes have been raised. Whereas before he seemed to mishear or misunderstand her words, Petruchio now overtly tests his wife's subjection by demanding that she concede to his views even when they are demonstrably unreasonable. The lesson is that Petruchio has the absolute authority to rename their world, and the prize for learning it is the opportunity to escape from Verona to attend Bianca's wedding. This moment foreshadows in their next scene a more extensive test, when Petruchio will pretend that the sun is the moon and an old man, a beautiful young woman. It also foreshadows Katherina's capitulation, finally, to her husband's will.

The 'sun-moon scene', Act 4, scene 5, is the turning-point in the taming plot. On the road back to Padua, Petruchio reprises his display of poor time-telling with the comment, 'Good Lord, how bright and goodly shines the moon!' (2). He and Katherina then briefly fall into the pattern of fast-paced and competitive repartee heard at their first encounter. 'I say it is the moon that shines so bright,' Petruchio says again, Katherina contradicting him just as emphatically by repeating his claim with small but crucial changes, 'I *know* it is the *sun* that shines so bright' (4–5, emphasis added). This nascent word match is abruptly terminated, however, after only two lines. Introducing a pun on 'sun/son', yet his tone smacking of exasperated dogmatism rather than play, Petruchio insists that what he 'says' must take priority over what Katherina 'knows':

> Now by my mother's son, and that's myself,
> It shall be moon, or star, or what I list,
> Or e'er I journey to your father's house.
> Go on and fetch our horses back again.
> Evermore crossed and crossed, nothing but crossed! (6–10)

Katherina figures out Petruchio's seeming madness without benefit of soliloquy, realizing, with Hortensio, that they 'shall never go' until she agrees to 'Say as he says' (IV.5.11). Armed with this new insight, she and Petruchio rehearse again the dialogue with which the scene opened. 'I say it is the moon', he begins, Katherina replying, 'I know it is the moon' (16). Her concession, however, only leads to a further demonstration of Petruchio's power to control the arbitrary link between things and their names: 'Nay, then you lie. It is the blessèd sun' (17). Katherina finally puts into words – words her husband is willing to take in their right meaning – the lesson she has learned at Petruchio's 'taming-school':

Then, God be blessed, it is the blessèd sun.
But sun it is not, when you say it is not,
And the moon changes even as your mind.
What you will have it named, even that it is,
And so it shall be so for Katherine. (18–22)

Katherina proves herself an obedient wife – a tamed
falcon, to pick up Petruchio's metaphor – by agreeing
always to concede to her husband's will. His language
games, for her, are the only ones that count; and as they
change, so she is required to adapt to them. The encounter
with Vincentio later in the scene reinforces through comic
excess the realization that Petruchio's will takes priority
even in the presence of a stranger who is unfamiliar with
the peculiar terms of their relationship.

Unless one assumes that she has become will-less, an
automaton incapable of thought independent of her
husband, it seems Katherina has learned to function simultaneously within two distinct language games: the one
used by such characters as the tailor and Vincentio, and
the endlessly changeable one occasionally imposed on
her by Petruchio. Petruchio's topsy-turvy language game,
in which the sun is the moon and then again the sun, is
always about power, specifically, a husband's absolute
authority over his wife. Crucially, though, it can communicate this meaning only if one understands that all its
users are implicitly marking where and how it departs
from conventional language games. Hortensio, for
instance, has the language skills to understand that
Katherina's identification of the sun as the moon means
'the field is won'; Vincentio, by contrast, untutored in the
language and so 'amazed' by her description of him as
a 'Young budding virgin, fair and fresh and sweet'

(IV.5.23, 54, 37), can make no sense at all of her words. To look ahead briefly to the final act with its banquet scene and Katherina's show-stopping lecture, the question there is which language she is speaking – the one shared by all the wedding guests, or the one she has learned since marriage? If the latter, the words she speaks are knowingly detached, as they were in the sun-moon scene, from any point of reference beyond the limits of Petruchio's language game; in such a context, Katherina's extended address to women on wifely duty becomes no less, or more, meaningful than her 'merry' interaction with Vincentio, serving purely to demonstrate her personal subjection to her husband's power.

SHAKESPEARE'S HISTORY/ MODERN POLITICS

C. S. Lewis, writing as early as the second quarter of the twentieth century, frankly accepts that the vision of 'awful rule, and right supremacy' Petruchio presents as 'sweet and happy' (V.2.108–9) will seem 'very startling' to a modern audience. His opinion, however, is that 'those who cannot face such startling should not read old books'. Perhaps he has a point. The wordplay, for example, surrounding Gremio's claim that he is more likely to 'cart' than court Baptista's daughter (I.1.55), presupposes a world largely intolerant of headstrong women. His pun, which alludes specifically to the practice of leading women through the streets, on or behind a cart, in order to shame and so dissuade them from behaviour perceived as antisocial, offers a glimpse into commonplace sixteenth-century disciplining methods. A related and particularly vicious punishment was to place a metal bridle

around the head of a woman accused of garrulous or
nagging behaviour, to which was attached a metal bit that
fitted into her mouth. So silenced, she would then be
'carted' through the community. An image of a bridled
woman carved into the misericord (a supporting ledge
on the underside of a hinged seat in the choir stall) still
survives in Shakespeare's home town of Stratford-upon-
Avon in the church in which he is buried.

Clearly Shakespeare's earliest audiences would have
brought to the theatre attitudes and lifestyles that would
seem unfamiliar to many spectators today. However, this
is not necessarily to conclude that the play was uncon-
troversial. After all, it prompted John Fletcher to write in
1611 a comic sequel called *The Woman's Prize, or Tamer
Tamed* in which the gender roles are reversed: Petruchio,
Katherina now dead, marries again only to find his second
wife even more rebellious. Unable to control her and
finding his taming tactics frustrated repeatedly by a wife
in league with the other townswomen, he becomes in the
end a convert to the spirit of compromise and accom-
modation within marriage. Fletcher's epilogue, tellingly,
concludes that the men in the audience have nothing to
complain about 'when | They fitly do consider in their
lives | They should not reign as tyrants o'er their wives';
neither can the women claim supremacy over the men,
since the play was 'aptly meant | To teach both sexes due
equality, | And, as they stand bound, to love mutually.'
This idea of right rule was an important doctrinal issue.
Rachel Speght published a pamphlet in 1617 – an unusual
and striking achievement at that time for a woman – in
which she challenged as ungodly a fellow writer's attack
on wives, and women in general, as talkative, expensive
to keep and sexually licentious. Accepting the position
that wives are subordinate to their husbands, Speght yet

insists that women have a responsibility independently to assess the moral and religious propriety of their husbands' demands, obeying only those commands that are just:

Thus if men would remember the duties they are to perform in being heads, some would not stand a tip-toe as they do, thinking themselves Lords and Rulers, and account every omission of performing whatsoever they command, whether lawful or not, to be matter of great disparagement and indignity done them; whereas they should consider that women are enjoined to submit themselves unto their husbands no otherways than as to the Lord; so that from hence, for man, ariseth a lesson not to be forgotten, that as the Lord commandeth nothing to be done, but that which is right and good, no more must the husband; for if a wife fulfill the evil command of her husband, she obeys him as a tempter.

For Speght, and presumably for other members of Shakespeare's audience, Petruchio's assertion of absolute and arbitrary dominion over Katherina – affording to himself the power to rename their world, like a little Adam in another Garden of Eden – might seem a theologically problematic, and in its own way unruly, domestic arrangement.

The 'take it or leave it' attitude presented by Lewis also seems to ignore, perhaps disingenuously, the politics always implicit in the continued study and performance of Shakespeare's drama. Certain plays, *The Taming of the Shrew* among them, are rarely long out of the school curriculum and theatrical repertoire. It therefore seems relevant, even crucial, to consider how such iterations of a play about male authority and female subordination speak, and can be made to speak, to the experiences and expectations of readers and audiences who remain products of their own, not Shakespeare's, moment. In what specific ways does this particular 'old book' energize existing and continuing debates about marriage and sexuality, the role of women in the work-place and domestic violence? These are, undoubtedly, not the same issues the play raised for Shakespeare's earliest historical audiences, but British classrooms and Canadian theatres in the twenty-first century, to give just two national examples among many, have their own histories to take care of.

There have emerged typically three dominant ways of interpreting the politics of the taming plot. The first is to make even more evident, and often more physically violent, the way Katherina is forced to submit to Petruchio's will. The insight here is that Katherina, trapped in Verona without hope of outside aid, denied food and sleep and surrounded constantly by jarring clamour, is subjected to what are now well-documented forms of psychological torture. While perhaps more sophisticated, such abuse is no less damaging than the crude violence found, for example, in 'A Merry Jest of a Shrewd and Curst Wife' (*c.* 1550), a poem that features a disobedient wife beaten unconscious in a cellar and wrapped in a salted horsehide. In 1975 Charles Marowitz, perhaps most famously, reworked Shakespeare's play as *The Shrew* in order to foreground in performance the play's inherent brutality. In this version Katherina is trans-formed into a physically, mentally and sexually abused victim, a broken heroine with 'wide and blank' eyes who recites as though by rote her speech of female duty. Such critical and theatrical interpretations find in the play nothing amusing or light-hearted, and align it instead with *The Merchant of Venice* as a deeply troubling, even potentially tragic, 'comedy'.

A very different approach recuperates the play's comic effect by reading it within the conventions of farce. In the manner of a cartoon character who falls from great heights or picks up exploding bombs only to walk away unharmed, Katherina bounces back unscathed from her experiences with Petruchio. Far from breaking his wife's spirit, Petruchio frees her for her own good from the narrow mediocrity of life in Padua, teaching her to exchange a barren, self-destructive anger for fertile creativity. Their relationship from the outset is premised on wordplay and games, and the watershed moment in the sun-moon scene when Katherina willingly embraces a spirit of pretence and make-believe functions both to establish her as an expansive and inventive player in her own right, and to mark her and Petruchio's growth as a couple from a relationship of non-productive rivalry to loving mutuality.

This type of critical reading encourages one to find in Katherina and Petruchio early prototypes for the seemingly unmarriageable and therefore perfectly matched characters of Beatrice and Benedick in *Much Ado About Nothing*. The power dynamics of the two plays, however, are completely different. Beatrice and Benedick are gulled by their family and friends to confess a love for the other that both, once the deception is revealed, are willing to own. By contrast, while one may infer sincerity when Petruchio (as yet unacquainted with his future wife) calls Katherina 'a lusty wench' and swears he 'love[s] her ten times more than e'er [he] did' (II.1.160–61), it remains the case that Katherina, for her part, has only ever limited options. The textual evidence would suggest she is married against her will; after marriage, she is free to 'choose' between a life of misery and a game of Petruchio's, rather than her own, making. Shakespeare writes for Katherina speeches of wit and sparkle in the sun-moon scene, and so brilliantly transforms an enforced conformity to powerful gender hierarchies into the strong perception that she actually makes a choice. It becomes easy, or perhaps convenient, to believe this character loves her husband, and to forget that if she refuses to participate in his game, she is powerless to continue the journey to Padua.

A third potential interpretative strategy is to argue that Katherina escapes the 'taming-school' through pragmatism and irony – she tells Petruchio what he wants to hear, but she doesn't mean what she says. Katherina, in effect, passes as an obedient wife in the same way Tranio passes as a gentleman, any sense of a 'true' identity coming to seem less relevant than the sustained delivery of a good performance. This reading, emphasizing the successful manipulation of word, image and performance, speaks powerfully to issues of identity explored in such a sustained way in both of the other plot lines. In performance this option tends to have the effect of making Petruchio seem a dupe, since he comes across as a controlling, overbearing husband who is unable in the end to see how he is being manipulated by his wife. Some readers object that such an interpretation demeans Petruchio, and thus detracts from the protagonists' mutual achievement as a couple; others argue that it would be unbearable in performance to listen in the play's closing moments to over forty lines of irony (but see the discussion of Katherina's speech in The Play in Performance). Games, evidently, are only fun when played by a husband on, or with, his wife, not when played by a wife on her husband.

Readers and theatrical audiences tend to find what they want to find in the play. Perhaps this is because one's interpretation of the taming action, in particular, is coloured by personal assumptions about the politics of marriage and male–female power relations. No final answer to what Katherina's submission means or how it should be read is likely to emerge any time soon, and as far as the fortunes of *The Taming of the Shrew* are concerned this is probably a good thing. The play's core indeterminacy – the sense that there remains something left to debate and resolve – saves the comedy from reductive moralizing, stimulating argument even as it polarizes opinion.

SEEKING A COMIC RESOLUTION

By the end of the fourth act, Katherina's and Bianca's stories of marriage have come to seem largely estranged. Shakespeare brings them together again by allowing it to emerge that the old man Katherina and Petruchio happen to encounter on the road to Padua is Lucentio's father, on his way to visit his son. The dialogue that follows, like Tranio's unlikely but repeated claim in the wedding scene to be long familiar with Petruchio's strange habits, is an example of Shakespeare prioritizing dramatic effect over realist situation. Hearing that this is Lucentio's father, Petruchio tells Vincentio at length that his son by this time is married to Bianca, news Hortensio confirms is the truth. Sharp readers and spectators will realize, however, that there is no way for either of these characters to possess this information. If Petruchio knows Bianca has been promised to Tranio-as-Lucentio, then he should also, presumably, know that the marriage is conditional on Vincentio assuring her dowry; Hortensio, even more remarkably, thinks he knows he heard Lucentio (really Tranio in disguise as Lucentio) swear an oath with him 'Never to marry with [Bianca] though she would entreat' (IV.2.33).

The long explanation of Lucentio's marriage, ponderously drawn out yet seemingly plucked from the air, serves the function of dramatic irony. It urges audience members whose attention after four acts might be flagging to realize, not just that this new character is Lucentio's *real* father, but that he is about to arrive in Padua where he will find not just a false Lucentio and a false Cambio, but a false Vincentio. At the beginning of the next scene, as Lucentio and Bianca slip away to elope, Petruchio and Katherina deliver the real Vincentio to the false Lucentio's door, thus elegantly reconnecting the two plots and bringing together all the key characters for the final act.

The farcical comedy of the moment when the Pedant-as-Vincentio confronts and turns away the real Vincentio is thus carefully engineered. One of them must be lying but there is no way for Baptista and the rest to know for certain which one. This inability securely to identify which is the rich gentleman and which the impostor is a point on which the scene dwells. 'Take heed, Signor Baptista,' old Gremio warns, 'lest you be cony-catched [tricked] in this business' (V.1.89–90). And yet, when dared by the Pedant to swear that this newcomer is the real Vincentio, Gremio backs down, persuaded, ironically, by the reassuring certainty that Tranio-as-Lucentio is the real Lucentio. The theoretical implications of Vincentio being hauled to prison, unable to seem more like himself than the Pedant, are dizzying. The Lord who found Sly asleep on the ground was confident enough about the gap between innate and assumed identity to play games with it; Sly is a joke, rather than a threat, precisely because he can never fully inhabit the part he plays. Here, however, the inherent differences between a gentleman and a commoner, if they can any longer be thought to exist at all, seem indiscernible, and Baptista, seeking to single out and punish the fraudster, chooses the wrong man: 'Away with the dotard,' he says of Vincentio, 'to the gaol with him!' (96). The joke with which the play began has come full circle.

The deception, in fact, is only finally revealed when Lucentio, safely married to Bianca, chooses to surrender his assumed identity. The two fathers, their authority flouted in different ways by the now evident ruse, exit demanding retribution. Vincentio vows 'to be revenged for this villainy' and Baptista 'to sound the depth of this knavery' (V.1.124–5). Although Lucentio opens the next and final scene by assuring his wedding guests, the audience and perhaps himself that 'At last, though long, our jarring notes agree, | And time it is when raging war is done | To smile at scapes and perils overblown' (V.2.1–3), the tone of the banquet remains an open question. Shakespeare often ends his comedies with the moment or promise of marriage. When he develops the action into married life – one thinks, for instance, of *The Comedy of Errors*, *The Merry Wives of Windsor*, *All's Well That Ends Well* or *The Winter's Tale* – the plays tend to portray and resolve, at best uneasily, the discord generated by discontented wives and/or jealous and sometimes brutal husbands. *The Taming of the Shrew* is no exception.

As the guests sit to partake of the banquet (the last course of a rich feast consisting of fruit, wine and delicate and expensive confectionery), the 'jarring notes' are sounded once again. 'Nothing but sit and sit, and eat and eat!' (V.2.12) Petruchio complains, his vague tone of dissatisfaction and ingratitude quickly escalating among the newlyweds into pointed accusations of marital strife. Hortensio is goaded as a coward, the widow as overbearing and Katherina as a shrew, Hortensio and Petruchio spurring on from the sidelines an argument between their wives like punters with money on a dogfight. Bianca enters the fray with a barbed cuckold joke directed at Gremio, one of her former suitors, only to exit at once with the other wives before Petruchio can take aim at her with a 'bitter jest' (45). The episode presents much wit but little good will.

In such a context Hortensio's decision to marry a widow seems especially significant. This character is never addressed by a personal name and only rarely as 'wife'; significantly, even after remarriage, her identifying characteristic remains her status as a widow. Widows were figures of immense anxiety in early modern England because they were one of the few types of women who could possess money and property independently of men. If she married again, the widow's inheritance would typically pass to her second husband (unless it was entailed, in which case it would either return to her first husband's family estate or devolve to her children), but so long as she remained single she was legally free to manage her own finances and sexuality. The wedding banquet thus rounds off the play's examination of gender roles in courtship and marriage by staging a competition among three extreme types of unruly stage female, a shrew, a widow and a runaway, any one of which might seem to an early modern imagination the very embodiment of male fears about ungoverned womanhood.

GAMBLING ON OBEDIENCE

The wager is proposed by Petruchio, and he sees the stakes raised from twenty to one hundred crowns. As in

Cymbeline, another drama to feature a husband betting on his wife's virtue, the key issue here is the way female performance serves to enhance a male character's authority among his peer group. Low-status men have ill-trained hawks and hounds and disobedient wives; powerful men, by contrast, hazard on their prized possessions and win. This display of wifely (dis)obedience thus simultaneously functions as a display of (failed) masculinity, with male prestige, no less than the hundred crowns, riding on the wager's uncertain outcome. Tests in groups of three feature in other Shakespeare plays: the three suitors to Portia in _The Merchant of Venice_ are required to choose among gold, silver and lead caskets, and King Lear's three daughters rise in turn to put into words their love for their father. The device heightens suspense, training eyes expectantly on the third, and final, competitor. Bianca sends word she cannot come; the widow sends word she will not come. The anticipation among the onstage spectators of a third defeat makes Katherina's ready entrance to ask her husband's will appear nothing short of a miracle. Katherina seems no less an object of wonder at Bianca's wedding than Petruchio had seemed at his own wedding two acts earlier. The difference this time, of course, is that the spectacle conforms to prevailing political attitudes and is therefore welcomed. 'Another dowry to another daughter,' Baptista gives his son-in-law, 'For she is changed, as she had never been' (V.2.113–14).

Katherina's display of wifely obedience confirms Petruchio's pre-eminence among the group and allows him to collect two hundred crowns in winnings and a second dowry worth a hundred times that much. It seems strange, then, the wager won, that Petruchio should insist on staging an elaborate encore. Katherina is commanded

to tread on her cap, a sight that prompts outraged objec-
tions from both Bianca and the widow, and then charged
to instruct them in their duty to their husbands. This long
speech – the longest by any character in the play – argues
by analogy to the duty a subject owes his king that a wife
is bound to serve her husband as lord and master. As the
sovereign cares and provides for his people, so a husband
labours for his family, 'crav[ing] no other tribute at thy
hands | But love, fair looks, and true obedience'
(V.2.151–2). Good rule at the domestic and national levels
thus become mutually reinforcing principles, with the
unruly woman who challenges hierarchical order within
the household seeming directly comparable to 'a foul
contending rebel | And graceless traitor' (158–9).

Katherina's assertion of biological difference later in
the speech offers subtly different grounds on which to
support male dominion over women. The pragmatic point
that women's bodies are too physically weak to undertake men's work is couched within an almost aesthetic
sense of correspondence between inner and outer parts,
a rhetorical strategy that emphasizes as natural the view
that women's temperaments should be as mild as their
bodies weak. However, this line of reasoning takes a not
entirely orthodox turn towards the end of the monologue
when Katherina counsels obedience, not because open
warfare is wrong, but because wives lack the weapons
and resources to rebel and win:

Come, come, you froward and unable worms,
My mind hath been as big as one of yours,
My heart as great, my reason haply more,
To bandy word for word and frown for frown.
But now I see our lances are but straws,
Our strength as weak, our weakness past compare,

> That seeming to be most which we indeed least are.
> Then vail your stomachs, for it is no boot [use],
> And place your hands below your husband's foot.
>   (V.2.168–76)

Submission, in other words, is not necessarily the preferable, but rather the only, option. Late sixteenth-century theological and medical discourse constructed as inevitable female weakness relative to men, since to exceed expectations was to prompt a category shift (the former woman would be transformed in language into either a man or a monster). And yet, as increased literary and popular attention in Shakespeare's time to the phenomena of the 'womanish man' and 'mannish woman' suggests, such rigid attitudes were coming under increasing pressure. Katherina's implicit conclusion that duty is conditional and that women are bound to obey only so long as men are able to enforce deference thus marks an unexpected slippage that threatens to unravel the ideological foundations on which the assertion of male privilege depends.

There are other ways in which this speech, with what the twentieth-century playwright George Bernard Shaw derided as its 'lord of creation moral', can come to seem on closer inspection surprisingly vulnerable to revisionist readings. Earlier in the final scene there seemed a possibility that Katherina's performance might simply baffle the men rather than communicate to them a willing acceptance of wifely duty. 'I wonder what [this wonder] bodes' (106) Hortensio asks Lucentio as Katherina enters the room to ask her husband's will. This potential failure of meaning is avoided through Petruchio's careful gloss on her actions: 'Marry, peace it bodes, and love, and quiet life' (107). Indeed, it is precisely this initial interpreta-

tive hesitation on the parts of the other two husbands
that seems to prompt Petruchio to provide 'more sign of
her obedience' (116) by commanding her to stamp on
her cap and lecture the other wives. But multiplying signs
is not always to render more certain their meaning, and
there seems an inherent contradiction in the scene's treatment of female speech. If Katherina's behaviour is
supposed to signify, as Petruchio claims, a 'quiet life',
then it seems strange that such quietness should take the
form of an extended harangue, the tone of which is not
appreciably different from the sort of speech Petruchio
characterized in their first scene together as 'wasp[ish]'
and 'angry' (II.1.209). Virtuous female behaviour,
defined in Induction 1 as a 'soft low tongue and lowly
courtesy' (112), and later by Lucentio as 'mild behaviour
and sobriety [moderation]' (I.1.71), is necessarily
performed through restraint – through, in effect, the
non-performance of its headstrong opposite. Petruchio,
desiring to prove his authority, thus stage-manages a show
of female obedience that in its very excess can only be a
paradox, as Katherina, scolding and rebuking her sister
and the widow on their wedding night, dutifully engages
in a form of active agency that implicitly undermines
the principle of compliant submission she sets out to
advocate.

As so often occurs in this play – one thinks of Sly the
nobleman, Tranio the master, Petruchio the madman and
Bianca either the modest, or unruly, lover – the onstage
and theatre audiences watch characters make spectacles
of themselves. These previous scenes of overt and implied
role-play open so decisively the gap between inner
substance and external show that it becomes difficult to
know what to believe or how to interpret it. In this
instance, where the formal structure and sheer length

of the speech is so at odds with its articulation of the principle of female submission, it seems hard to know for certain what, exactly, this show of sincerity masks — perhaps a dutiful and loving wife, or perhaps a player acting the part of a dutiful and loving wife.

It is no surprise then that the play resists firm closure. Petruchio interprets his wife's performance as an unqualified victory:

> Come, Kate, we'll to bed.
> We three are married, but you two are sped.
> 'Twas I won the wager, though you hit the white [bull's-eye],
> And being a winner, God give you good night!
>   (V.2.183–6)

Bianca and the widow, however, the characters at whom the lecture on wifely obedience is explicitly directed, make no reply. Silence in drama, as evidenced by Isabella's problematic silence in the closing moments of *Measure for Measure* or Antonio's and Sebastian's silence at the end of *The Tempest*, is always difficult to interpret. Are the women chastened by, or dismissive of, Katherina's lecture? Might they even make an early exit, leaving Katherina to preach, as it were, to the converted? Their response is indeterminate, and can find, at best, a provisional answer in the theatre. The male characters, by contrast, given lines with which to comment on the speech, still seem not entirely sure what to make of it. Lucentio freely concedes that Petruchio has won the wager, yet the final two lines of the play, nearly but not quite a rhyming couplet, nearly but not quite affirm belief in Katherina's performance. 'Now go thy ways, thou hast tamed a curst shrew', Hortensio remarks as Petruchio exits. But Lucentio's reply hangs in the air, and his over-length verse line (six feet instead of the usual five) fails to match neatly either his friend's poetic metre or his confidence: ''Tis a wonder, by your leave, she will be tamed so'. Like all good theatre, Katherina's performance prompts, but exceeds, interpretation.

Margaret Jane Kidnie

The Play in Performance

There is a curious and textually inexplicable silence in *The Taming of the Shrew* that falls at Act II, scene 1.295–317. Easy to overlook on the page, it seems to demand in performance some sort of extra-textual justification. Petruchio and Katherina have just been joined onstage by Baptista, Tranio-as-Lucentio and Gremio, all of whom are eager to learn how Petruchio has thrived in his suit of marriage. Petruchio claims that he and Katherina have resolved to marry on Sunday, a promise that is quickly contradicted by Katherina who announces that she will 'see [him] hanged on Sunday first' (292). What follows is a sixteen-line monologue in which Petruchio explains that despite her great love for him, Katherina wishes to continue to seem 'curst in company'. On the basis of this lie, the contract of marriage is confirmed.

Why does Katherina not speak again? Why does she not avoid this seemingly unwanted marriage by telling her father the truth of her encounter with Petruchio? The moment depends in large part on pragmatic considerations of plot: Katherina and Petruchio must be married if the taming narrative is to develop any further. The challenge in performance, however, is to make sense of Katherina's seemingly tacit acceptance of her father's decision to marry her to Petruchio. The ways this can be achieved rely entirely on the imagination and resources of the company staging the play. Katherina might be somehow silenced by Petruchio, an interpretation adopted, for instance, by the Franco Zeffirelli film (1967) where Elizabeth Taylor's Katherina can say nothing because she is locked in a room by Richard Burton's Petruchio; her attention might be somehow distracted at a crucial moment; or she might seem to trust her father to reject Petruchio's story as ludicrous, learning only too late that her confidence in Baptista is misplaced. In *The Taming of A Shrew* (*A Shrew*), an anonymous play printed in 1594, with marked similarities to Shakespeare's play, the motivation for this difficult moment is found in an aside spoken by Katherina: 'But yet I will consent and marry him, | For I methinks have lived too long a maid, | And match him too, or else his manhood's good.'

A Shrew thus provides motivation where *The Shrew* offers silence by making it clear that Katherina, for her own reasons, chooses Petruchio for her husband. *A Shrew* and *The Shrew*, although dramatizing similar stories and evidently written within a few years of each other, are not the same play. There are characters in one version not found in the other, all but two of the characters are given different names, and the Sly material, not sustained by Shakespeare after Act I, scene 1, punctuates the other version throughout. Scholars have been unable to determine the relationship between these two texts with any certainty: *A Shrew* might be a source-text, a reconstruction of *The Shrew* from memory, or perhaps both plays imperfectly reproduce a now lost Shakespearian original. However, and partly as a result of this doubtful textual provenance, studies of *The Shrew* remain haunted by the existence of *A Shrew*.

Nowhere is the influence of this ghostly double seen more persistently than in performance where there is a long stage history of grafting passages from *A Shrew* onto *The Shrew*. A consideration of some of the differences between these texts raises important interpretative questions about the play in performance. Both plays close with a wedding banquet in which Petruchio wins his wager and Katherina delivers a long speech on duty to the other wives. What follows in *A Shrew*, however, has no parallel in Shakespeare's comedy. The players' performance over, the sleeping Sly is returned, in his own clothes once again, to the ground outside the alehouse. When he wakes, he tells the tapster that he has had 'The bravest dream tonight that ever thou | Heardest in all thy life', and promises immediately to go home and tame his own wife (for all the Sly passages in *A Shrew*, see The Sly Scenes in *The Taming of A Shrew*, pp. 109–12).

The appeal of this final scene is almost irresistible on the stage precisely because it transforms the Induction scenes into a fully developed framing device able to mediate and comment extensively on the inset narrative. Moreover, whereas Shakespeare's play as printed in the First Folio of 1623 leaves the Sly narrative unresolved – are Sly and the other spectators supposed to remain onstage after their final lines at Act I, scene 1 silently marking the play? when, if ever, does Sly return to being a tinker? – the anonymous version brings all of its plot lines to a firm closure. Some textual scholars, dissatisfied with the Sly material in *The Shrew*, argue that Shakespeare's play is somehow corrupt, and that there must have existed at some point in the play's history more Sly scenes. Tellingly, all major editions of the play in recent years, including the Penguin, reprint the Sly scenes from *A Shrew* as additional passages.

Theatre practitioners, in some ways freer than editors in the way they shape the text, regularly flesh out the framing device in performance in order to present the story of Katherina and Petruchio as Sly's waking dream, a form of wish-fulfilment. Sly stands between the theatre audience and the action set in Padua as a mediating layer providing interpretative distance from the action as it unfolds. In such productions, the theatre audience is implicitly asked to consider whether it agrees with, or rather distances itself from, Sly's reading of the narrative. Even if a production resists drawing on *A Shrew* for extra dialogue, it is still possible to leave Sly and his companions onstage to watch the play within the play. A theatre audience, in effect, watches Sly watching the play, with the onstage audience serving as a constant visual reminder that the story of Baptista and his daughters is an inset fiction, a drama mounted for the entertainment of a tinker dressed as a lord.

If, however, this onstage audience slips away shortly after its final dialogue at the end of Act I, scene 1, interesting doubling opportunities become available which serve to suggest thematic links between the Induction scenes and the play within the play. The actor playing Sly, for instance, could exit at the end of Act I, scene 1 to re-enter immediately at the beginning of the next scene as Petruchio, thus underscoring a reading of the taming narrative as the fantasy of a disempowered male. Alternatively, Petruchio could be played by the lord of the Induction scenes, a very different casting choice that might encourage spectators to draw parallels between Sly and Katherina as characters variously subjected to the authority of a male ruling class. In such instances, the curtailed framing device begins to make sense as yet another instance of the play's many theatrical transformations: the Induction scenes bleed into the inset narrative, leaving the theatre audience not entirely certain where to place the boundary dividing the play from the play within the play.

Yet another performance option is to cut the Induction scenes altogether. Zeffirelli, building a witty in-joke into the film's opening montage, shows Sly pilloried as a drunkard in the streets of Padua but otherwise omits all reference to this part of the text; the BBC/Time-Life television version (1980), starring John Cleese as Petruchio, strips away the Sly scenes without comment. Such treatments of the text in effect remove the device of the play within a play, shortening the play's running-time and simplifying the narrative by removing one metatheatrical layer. The Bianca–Lucentio disguise story is another thread that is frequently trimmed in performance. *The Taming of the Shrew* is perhaps most notorious for the plot line involving Katherina and Petruchio. By cutting the Induction and compressing the scenes of intrigue around the marriage of Baptista's youngest daughter, the taming plot can seem to take over the action as the primary, or even exclusive, focus. This was the interpretative approach adopted by David Garrick in 1754, and this version, entitled *Catharine and Petruchio*, dominated the English stage well into the nineteenth century. *10 Things I Hate About You* (1999), an American film directed by Gil Junger, in other ways a striking film modernization that transforms comedy into high-school romantic drama, preserves Shakespeare's balanced juxtaposition of the two sisters' fortunes in courtship.

10 Things I Hate About You offers a key insight into ways of playing *The Taming of the Shrew* by portraying Katherina (Julia Stiles) as an intelligent, non-conformist feminist. The comic energy of Shakespeare's play in performance often depends on a slapstick physicality. Actors playing Katherina might throw furniture around in their first scene, as though ready indeed to 'comb [Hortensio's] noddle with a three-legged stool' (I.1.64), and it is not unusual for Hortensio to relate the story of Katherina's music lesson with the lute she broke over his head still wrapped around his neck. By minimizing the slapstick humour associated with 'Kat', *10 Things I Hate About You* aligns the audience's sympathies with the so-called 'shrew' rather than with the ridiculous male suitors she refuses to entertain. In this way she is presented not as farcically violent, but as quick to defend herself verbally in face of sexist attack. A resistance to the expectations of farce thus helps to shape in performance a very different perception of the play's gender politics.

The nature of the evolving relationship between Katherina and Petruchio is a delicate issue for any production of the play. Attention tends to fall on the delivery of Katherina's long speech in the final scene simply because it is such a theatrical tour de force, but the interpretative groundwork for it is laid in the previous act. At the moment Katherina agrees to call the sun the moon, a rush-candle, or anything else Petruchio may please (IV.5.12–15), non-textual signs such as tone of voice, physical gesture, lighting shifts and music cues will prompt spectators to read this concession as a shared game between Petruchio and Katherina, as a sincere conversion to the principle of female subordination to male authority within marriage, or perhaps even as a brutalizing defeat for Katherina. This scene sets the stage, as it were, for Katherina's final speech, by far the most challenging moment for any theatrical or filmic production.

The question of what to do with this final speech has become a major theatrical issue. Like Hamlet preparing to deliver the 'To be or not to be' soliloquy, or Portia about to launch into 'The quality of mercy' monologue during the trial scene in *The Merchant of Venice*, the actor playing Katherina can expect that a significant proportion of the audience is waiting to see how she will handle *that* speech. Whereas a Hamlet or a Portia has the problem of trying to make overly familiar lines seem fresh, the player enacting Katherina faces the realization that many spectators will seek to discern from the speech's delivery a larger gender politics, extrapolating from this key moment the production's attitude towards issues of love, power and marriage. Does she really mean what she says? Do her words seem enforced?

Even worse for an actor, it is impossible in this instance to please everyone. For every spectator who objects to the lord of creation moral put in the mouth of the female protagonist, there is another who celebrates the triumph of romantic love. The speech can be played 'straight', as in the Zeffirelli and BBC/Time-Life productions, with the actor delivering an argument for female subjection within marriage on which Petruchio places his seal of approval with the simple one-line reply, 'Why, there's a wench! Come on, and kiss me, Kate' (V.2.179). However, the history of this play in performance offers a catalogue of stage interpretations that have troubled, one way or another, a perception of Katherina's words as sincere. Yücel Erten's staging in Turkey in 1986, for example, presented a Katherina who was literally suicidal, her speech brought to a close with slit wrists and a spreading pool of blood into which she collapses. Such approaches unsettle a perception of romantic love and mutuality in marriage by signalling that Katherina's emotional and/or physical well-being is the price at which Petruchio claims victory over his wife and the other bridegrooms.

Another alternative are those stagings that suggest that Katherina does not, in fact, mean what she says. Mary Pickford canonized this interpretation in a film version of 1929 when she winked broadly at the camera in the middle of her speech, thus reassuring both Bianca and the film audience that she is just saying what Douglas Fairbanks' Petruchio wants to hear; Petruchio, in this version, remains smugly and comically oblivious to his wife's ruse. This sort of interpretation is aided by the very length of Katherina's speech. Katherina's submission is so complete and unqualified, and yet staged with such command, that it can seem hard not to suspect a hidden agenda. When she then concludes by offering to place her hand beneath her husband's foot in order to demonstrate symbolically her subordinate position, her performance of wifely duty can come to seem exactly that – a performance. Productions in which the actor playing Petruchio seems to be made uncomfortable by his wife's rhetorical and theatrical excess further disrupt a sense that Katherina's speech should be taken at face value, as can the introduction of extra-textual stage business. A Leicester Haymarket production in 1995, for example, opened a clear gap between what Katherina says and what she thinks by punctuating her speech with cuckold's horns descending from the flies to rest over Petruchio's head. The closing stage picture, with the husband and wife looking with satisfaction at each other and the audience, was one of female empowerment (and sexual unruliness) sustained through marital deception.

This range of responses to the taming plot suggests the immense value of playing the Induction scenes. Whether or not Sly actually remains onstage to the end of the play, the early scenes set in England firmly contextualize the Italian action as 'just' a story. With Sly in

place, the theatre audience is better able to sustain a critical distance from the story of Baptista and his daughters. If Sly, however, is cut from the action, the repertoire
of interpretative options for both actors and audience –
at least at the moment – seems limited to willing conversion to the Petruchian creed, irony or brutality. Michael
Billington, theatre reviewer for the *Guardian*, famously
called in 1987 for a moratorium on new productions of
The Shrew after seeing Michael Bogdanov's production
at the Royal Shakespeare Company, arguing that a play
so offensive to modern sensibilities 'should be put back
firmly and squarely on the shelf'. More recently, the
problem is not just the play's troubling politics, but rather
a perception of predictability, the sense that the debates,
both on the stage and page, seem to have reached something of an impasse. It will be interesting to see whether
and how performance of *The Taming of the Shrew* in the
twenty-first century will advance further criticism on this
early comedy.

Margaret Jane Kidnie

Further Reading

An important strand of criticism around *The Taming of the Shrew* centres on its provenance and possible relation to an anonymous play published in 1594 called *The Taming of A Shrew*. The texts share intriguing points of contact, particularly in relation to the Christopher Sly material, but in other key respects seem entirely different plays. The Oxford editors, in *William Shakespeare: A Textual Companion* (1988), provide an excellent summary of the textual problems that dog this early comedy. *The Taming of A Shrew* has been edited by Stephen Miller (1988), and is also available in Geoffrey Bullough's *The Narrative and Dramatic Sources of Shakespeare*, vol. 1 (1957). Miller offers a very readable comparison of the plays and the theories devised to account for their similarities and differences (contributing a new one of his own), in '*The Taming of a Shrew* and the Theories; or, "Though this be badness, yet there is method in't"' (in *Textual Formations and Reformations*, ed. Laurie E. Maguire and Thomas L. Berger, 1998, pp. 251–63). He argues that editors have been too quick to dismiss *A Shrew* as corrupt, a view Leah Marcus provocatively explores in terms of editorial gender politics in *Unediting the Renaissance: Shakespeare, Marlowe, Milton* (1996).

Useful starting points for further reading into textual

and other interpretative issues are the scholarly single-volume editions: Ann Thompson's New Cambridge (1984) and H. J. Oliver's Oxford (1982) editions offer reliable texts and full introductions. Many of the essay collections aimed at school and undergraduate audiences are likewise excellent and easily available. Frances E. Dolan's *The Taming of the Shrew: Texts and Contexts* (1996) introduces in an interesting and accessible manner a handy collection of early modern documents relating to *The Shrew*; this material is reprinted alongside a text of the play edited by David Bevington. *Much Ado About Nothing and The Taming of the Shrew*, edited by Marion Wynne-Davies for the New Casebooks series (2001), offers a collection of five outstanding essays on *The Shrew*; also worth mention is Harold Bloom's *William Shakespeare's The Taming of the Shrew* (1988), a reprint of eight slightly more dated but nonetheless key essays on the play. Dana Aspinall's *The Taming of the Shrew: Critical Essays* (2002) and Laura Marvel's *Readings on 'The Taming of the Shrew'* (2000) sample a longer history of the play's critical reception. Most of the essays discussed below are available in one or other of these student-oriented collections (relevant cross-references are provided).

The spectacle of an unruly wife finally subjected to her husband's will has captured the attention and imagination of critics and spectators alike. Writers have been quick to point out, drawing on Jan Harold Brunvald's meticulous study of the shrew-taming folktale tradition ('The Folktale Origin of *The Taming of the Shrew*', *Shakespeare Quarterly* 17 (1966), pp. 345–59), that Shakespeare omits the cruel physical abuse typical of the genre. As Linda Woodbridge notes, however, Petruchio's strategies of hunger and sleep deprivation hardly count as progressive feminist politics: 'it does not speak well of a hero that the best thing to be said in his favor is that he neither beats his wife senseless nor wraps her in a salted horsehide' (*Women and the English Renaissance: Literature and the Nature of Womankind, 1540–1620* (1984)). Lynda Boose's historical research into actual shaming practices from the period, such as bridles for transgressive women – really a form of torture – makes for chilling reading ('Scolding Brides and Bridling Scolds: Taming the Woman's Unruly Member', *Shakespeare Quarterly* 42 (1991), pp. 179–213; see also Wynne-Davies, Aspinall).

In a slightly later essay, '*The Taming of the Shrew*, Good Husbandry, and Enclosure', Boose further troubles views of Petruchio's generosity by arguing that he is typical of the upwardly mobile but cash-hungry gentlemen who would have been familiar to many in Shakespeare's earliest audiences (*Shakespeare Reread: The Texts in New Contexts*, ed. Russ McDonald (1994), pp. 193–225; see also Marvel). Natasha Korda picks up this theme of liberality through a focus on women's education. Bianca and Katherina are taught very differently and to different effect by their suitor–tutors. Korda discerns in this the emergence of an economic order in which the housewife has to learn how to advance her husband's symbolic credit without breaking him financially – a lesson Katherina, but not Bianca, is forced to internalize by the end of the play (*Shakespeare's Domestic Economies: Gender and Property in Early Modern England* (2002); see also Wynne-Davies, Aspinall). Emily Detmer, by contrast, reads the taming plot in light of modern psychology, finding in Katherina's transformation the typical response of a victim of domestic violence ('Civilizing Subordination: Domestic Violence and *The Taming of the Shrew*', *Shakespeare Quarterly* 48 (1997), pp. 273–94; see also Marvel).

Woodbridge, Boose and Detmer mount a challenge to Shakespeare's vision of male supremacy within marriage, but do so at the price of finding anything at all comic in this early comedy. '*The Taming of the Shrew*: Inside or Outside of the Joke?' endorses this view. For Shirley Nelson Garner, *The Shrew* evinces little interest apart from marking a particular historical moment both in Shakespeare's career and in traditions of misogynist attitudes towards women: 'As someone who does not share [its patriarchal] values, I find much of the play humorless . . . If I went to see it, it would be out of curiosity, to find out how someone in our time would direct it' (*'Bad' Shakespeare: Revaluations of the Shakespeare Canon*, ed. Maurice Charney (1988), pp. 105–19).

Richard B. Heilman seeks to recuperate the play by arguing that in farce nobody is ever 'really' hurt, and that to interpret the play otherwise is to misread generic conventions ('The *Taming* Untamed, or, The Return of the Shrew', *Modern Language Quarterly* (1966); see also Aspinall, Marvel). This position is developed by Peter Saccio in 'Shrewd and Kindly Farce' (*Shakespeare Survey* 37 (1984), pp. 33–40), an essay marred by universalizing assumptions that Katherina's shrewdness is 'natural' to woman's 'fallen nature', and that her eventual kindness 'belong[s] properly' to woman's entry into socialized 'human relationships'. Since *The Shrew* was typically filled with slapstick gags well into the twentieth century, such discussion of literary genre is usefully contextualized through reference to Tori Haring-Smith's *From Farce to Metadrama: A Stage History of 'The Taming of the Shrew'*, *1594–1983* (1985). This valuable book offers insight into the theatrical traditions out of which a critical understanding of the play as farce evolved.

A very different critical tactic interprets the taming

plot as an initiation into games, Katherina learning from Petruchio how to escape Padua's numbing conformity through imagination. Alexander Leggatt offers an early and seminal statement of this position in *Shakespeare's Comedy of Love* (1974); Leggatt's analysis of the play's treatment of marriage is especially interesting for the way it gives full attention to the disguise plot surrounding Bianca. Marianne L. Novy, in *Love's Argument: Gender Relations in Shakespeare* (1984; see also Bloom), develops this thesis in a provocative direction, arguing that the games played between husband and wife function to explore alternative constructions of power at a moment in history when marriage relations were being contested. J. Dennis Huston likens a capacity for spontaneous invention to theatrical improvisation, arguing that Petruchio provides the disruptive, unpredictable force able to free Katherina from an otherwise mechanical existence. This lesson extends from Katherina to those spectators who, knowing 'that man is an actor, freely choose and change their roles in order to avoid the narrow, imprisoning roles society would impose on them' (*Shakespeare's Comedies of Play* (1981); see also Marvel).

An emphasis on metatheatre likewise informs the work of Michael Shapiro ('Framing the Taming: Metahistorical Awareness of Female Impersonation in *The Taming of the Shrew*', *Yearbook of English Studies* 23 (1993), pp. 143–66; see also Aspinall). Shapiro's point is that Shakespeare's earliest audiences realized they were watching not actual women but male actors performing stereotypes of femininity derived from theatrical convention and morality literature. Karen Newman similarly argues that the ideological force of Katherina's final speech is undermined by the way the play 'call[s] attention to the constructed character of the representation'

(*Fashioning Femininity and English Renaissance Drama* (1991); see also Wynne-Davies). Holly A. Crocker, in 'Affective Resistance: Performing Passivity and Playing A-Part in *The Taming of the Shrew*' (*Shakespeare Quarterly* 54.2 (2003), pp. 142–59), concludes that Katherina undermines Petruchio's authority through the realization that she can perform passivity more convincingly than the other women. In this way she escapes from one performance (that of a shrew) to another (that of the obedient wife).

As Coppélia Kahn notes, however, the problem with readings that locate empowerment in Katherina's performance – in a female voice that changes its tune but not its stridency – is that Kate 'is trapped in her own cleverness. Her only way of maintaining her inner freedom is by outwardly denying it, which thrusts her into a schizoid existence' (*Man's Estate: Masculine Identity in Shakespeare* (1981); see also Bloom). Kahn instead advocates reading the closing scene as ironic, a view supported by the perception that Katherina's speech is excessive both in tone and length. Wayne A. Rebhorn, documenting the unease generated historically by rhetorical oratory, argues that the irony is not merely contextual but built into the very structure of the speech with which Katherina ostensibly subjects herself to her husband. This fascinating article argues that Katherina, authorized by her husband to play the orator, 'deconstruct[s] the right rule/tyranny opposition maintained within the discourse of rhetoric' ('Petruchio's "Rope Tricks": *The Taming of the Shrew* and the Renaissance Discourse of Rhetoric', *Modern Philology* 92 (1995), pp. 294–327).

Richard A. Burt, taking issue with scholars who find in the play a celebration of love and marriage, yet countering claims that layers of artifice and role-play are plainly evident in the final scene, works through a constructionist argument at the level of the theatre audience ('Charisma, Coercion, and Comic Form in *The Taming of the Shrew*', *Criticism* 26 (1984), pp. 295–311; see also Bloom). It is we, not the character of Katherina, who are worked on to believe that male coercion of female will is acceptable – beneficial, even – by the way the play conceals inflexible power structures behind a façade of romantic love. Burt's discussion of ideological manipulation accounts for Sly's non-appearance at the end of the drama, not as redundant – and so, unnecessary – but as 'symptomatic of the play's social function'.

The Shrew remains controversial because its treatment of authority and power speaks to perceptions of continued social injustices. The play therefore has a vital life in the theatre and on screen which has been well served by recent criticism. Graham Holderness examines the play's cultural politics through an analysis of four late twentieth-century productions, as part of the Shakespeare in Performance Series (*The Taming of the Shrew* (1989)). Holderness's discussion of Jonathan Miller's staging is complemented by Carol Rutter's interview with Fiona Shaw, in *Clamorous Voices: Shakespeare's Women Today* (1988). Diane E. Henderson argues that *The Shrew* tended to reappear on film in those decades of the twentieth century when the 'woman question' seemed most pressing ('A Shrew for the Times', in *Shakespeare, The Movie: Popularizing the Plays on Film, TV, and Video*, ed. Lynda E. Boose and Richard Burt (1997), pp. 148–68; see also Wynne-Davies). An astute analysis of performing bodies in film and stage productions is offered by Barbara Hodgdon in *The Shakespeare Trade: Performances and Appropriations* (1998; see also

Aspinall), while Carol Chillington Rutter discusses the way film frames ideological interpretations of female character ('Looking at Shakespeare's Women on Film', in *The Cambridge Companion to Shakespeare on Film* (2000), pp. 241–60). Elizabeth Schafer's edition for the Shakespeare in Production series (2002), a volume that annotates key production choices in the English-speaking world since the Restoration, has become standard reading for performance-oriented study.

Margaret Jane Kidnie

THE TAMING OF
THE SHREW

The Characters in the Play

INDUCTION

CHRISTOPHER SLY, a drunken tinker
The HOSTESS of a country alehouse
A LORD
HUNTSMEN
PAGE
SERVINGMEN attending on the Lord
A company of strolling PLAYERS

THE TAMING OF THE SHREW

BAPTISTA Minola, a wealthy citizen of Padua

KATHERINA, the Shrew, elder daughter of Baptista
PETRUCHIO, a gentleman of Verona, suitor for the hand
   of Katherina
GRUMIO, Petruchio's personal lackey
CURTIS, Petruchio's servant, in charge of his country house
A TAILOR
A HABERDASHER
Five other servants of Petruchio (NATHANIEL, PHILIP,
   JOSEPH, NICHOLAS, PETER)

BIANCA, the Prize, younger daughter of Baptista

GREMIO, a wealthy old citizen of Padua, suitor for the hand of Bianca

HORTENSIO, a gentleman of Padua, suitor for the hand of Bianca

LUCENTIO, a gentleman of Pisa, in love with Bianca

TRANIO, Lucentio's servant and confidant

BIONDELLO, Lucentio's second servant

VINCENTIO, a wealthy citizen of Pisa, father of Lucentio

A PEDANT of Mantua

A WIDOW, in love with Hortensio

SERVANT attending on Baptista

INDUCTION

Enter Christopher Sly and the Hostess   I

SLY I'll pheeze you, in faith.

HOSTESS A pair of stocks, you rogue!

SLY Y'are a baggage, the Slys are no rogues. Look in the
Chronicles, we came in with Richard Conqueror.
Therefore *paucas pallabris*, let the world slide. Sessa!

HOSTESS You will not pay for the glasses you have burst?

SLY No, not a denier. Go by, Saint Jeronimy, go to thy
cold bed and warm thee.

He lies on the ground

HOSTESS I know my remedy, I must go fetch the third-
borough.   *Exit*   10

SLY Third, or fourth, or fifth borough, I'll answer him by
law. I'll not budge an inch, boy. Let him come, and
kindly.

He falls asleep

Wind horns. Enter a Lord from hunting, with his train

LORD

Huntsman, I charge thee, tender well my hounds.
Breathe Merriman, the poor cur is embossed,
And couple Clowder with the deep-mouthed brach.
Saw'st thou not, boy, how Silver made it good

At the hedge corner, in the coldest fault?
I would not lose the dog for twenty pound.

FIRST HUNTSMAN

20   Why, Belman is as good as he, my lord.
He cried upon it at the merest loss,
And twice today picked out the dullest scent.
Trust me, I take him for the better dog.

LORD

Thou art a fool. If Echo were as fleet,
I would esteem him worth a dozen such.
But sup them well, and look unto them all.
Tomorrow I intend to hunt again.

FIRST HUNTSMAN

I will, my lord.

LORD

What's here? One dead, or drunk? See, doth he
    breathe?

SECOND HUNTSMAN

30   He breathes, my lord. Were he not warmed with ale,
This were a bed but cold to sleep so soundly.

LORD

O monstrous beast, how like a swine he lies!
Grim death, how foul and loathsome is thine image!
Sirs, I will practise on this drunken man.
What think you, if he were conveyed to bed,
Wrapped in sweet clothes, rings put upon his fingers,
A most delicious banquet by his bed,
And brave attendants near him when he wakes,
Would not the beggar then forget himself?

FIRST HUNTSMAN

40   Believe me, lord, I think he cannot choose.

SECOND HUNTSMAN

It would seem strange unto him when he waked.

LORD
    Even as a flattering dream or worthless fancy.
    Then take him up, and manage well the jest.
    Carry him gently to my fairest chamber,
    And hang it round with all my wanton pictures.
    Balm his foul head in warm distillèd waters,
    And burn sweet wood to make the lodging sweet.
    Procure me music ready when he wakes,
    To make a dulcet and a heavenly sound.
    And if he chance to speak, be ready straight   50
    And with a low submissive reverence
    Say 'What is it your honour will command?'
    Let one attend him with a silver basin
    Full of rose-water and bestrewed with flowers,
    Another bear the ewer, the third a diaper,
    And say 'Will't please your lordship cool your hands?'
    Some one be ready with a costly suit,
    And ask him what apparel he will wear.
    Another tell him of his hounds and horse,
    And that his lady mourns at his disease.   60
    Persuade him that he hath been lunatic,
    And when he says he is Sly, say that he dreams,
    For he is nothing but a mighty lord.
    This do, and do it kindly, gentle sirs.
    It will be pastime passing excellent,
    If it be husbanded with modesty.

FIRST HUNTSMAN
    My lord, I warrant you we will play our part
    As he shall think by our true diligence
    He is no less than what we say he is.

LORD
    Take him up gently and to bed with him,   70
    And each one to his office when he wakes.
                         Sly is carried away

A trumpet sounds

Sirrah, go see what trumpet 'tis that sounds —

Exit Servingman

Belike some noble gentleman that means,
Travelling some journey, to repose him here.

Enter Servingman

How now? Who is it?

SERVINGMAN   An't please your honour, players
That offer service to your lordship.

LORD

Bid them come near.

Enter Players

Now, fellows, you are welcome.

PLAYERS

We thank your honour.

LORD

Do you intend to stay with me tonight?

FIRST PLAYER

80   So please your lordship to accept our duty.

LORD

With all my heart. This fellow I remember
Since once he played a farmer's eldest son.
'Twas where you wooed the gentlewoman so well.
I have forgot your name; but, sure, that part
Was aptly fitted and naturally performed.

FIRST PLAYER

I think 'twas Soto that your honour means.

LORD

'Tis very true, thou didst it excellent.
Well, you are come to me in happy time,
The rather for I have some sport in hand
90   Wherein your cunning can assist me much.
There is a lord will hear you play tonight;
But I am doubtful of your modesties,

Lest over-eyeing of his odd behaviour –
For yet his honour never heard a play –
You break into some merry passion
And so offend him, for I tell you, sirs,
If you should smile, he grows impatient.

FIRST PLAYER

Fear not, my lord, we can contain ourselves,
Were he the veriest antic in the world.

LORD

Go, sirrah, take them to the buttery,   100
And give them friendly welcome every one.
Let them want nothing that my house affords.

Exit one with the Players

Sirrah, go you to Barthol'mew my page,
And see him dressed in all suits like a lady.
That done, conduct him to the drunkard's chamber,
And call him 'madam', do him obeisance.
Tell him from me – as he will win my love –
He bear himself with honourable action,
Such as he hath observed in noble ladies
Unto their lords, by them accomplishèd.   110
Such duty to the drunkard let him do,
With soft low tongue and lowly courtesy,
And say 'What is't your honour will command,
Wherein your lady and your humble wife
May show her duty and make known her love?'
And then with kind embracements, tempting kisses,
And with declining head into his bosom,
Bid him shed tears, as being overjoyed
To see her noble lord restored to health,
Who for this seven years hath esteemèd him   120
No better than a poor and loathsome beggar.
And if the boy have not a woman's gift
To rain a shower of commanded tears,

An onion will do well for such a shift,
Which in a napkin being close conveyed,
Shall in despite enforce a watery eye.
See this dispatched with all the haste thou canst,
Anon I'll give thee more instructions.

                                        Exit a Servingman

I know the boy will well usurp the grace,
130   Voice, gait, and action of a gentlewoman.
I long to hear him call the drunkard husband,
And how my men will stay themselves from laughter
When they do homage to this simple peasant.
I'll in to counsel them. Haply my presence
May well abate the over-merry spleen,
Which otherwise would grow into extremes.   *Exeunt*

2   *Enter aloft Sly, with attendants; some with apparel,*
            basin and ewer, and other appurtenances; and Lord
SLY For God's sake, a pot of small ale.

FIRST SERVINGMAN
    Will't please your lordship drink a cup of sack?

SECOND SERVINGMAN
    Will't please your honour taste of these conserves?

THIRD SERVINGMAN
    What raiment will your honour wear today?

SLY I am Christophero Sly, call not me 'honour' nor 'lord-
    ship'. I ne'er drank sack in my life. And if you give me
    any conserves, give me conserves of beef. Ne'er ask me
    what raiment I'll wear, for I have no more doublets than
    backs, no more stockings than legs, nor no more shoes
10 than feet – nay, sometimes more feet than shoes, or such
    shoes as my toes look through the overleather.

LORD
    Heaven cease this idle humour in your honour!

O, that a mighty man of such descent,
Of such possessions, and so high esteem,
Should be infusèd with so foul a spirit!

SLY What, would you make me mad? Am not I Christopher Sly, old Sly's son of Burton-heath, by birth a ped-
lar, by education a cardmaker, by transmutation a
bear-herd, and now by present profession a tinker? Ask
Marian Hacket, the fat ale-wife of Wincot, if she know   20
me not. If she say I am not fourteen pence on the score
for sheer ale, score me up for the lyingest knave in
Christendom.

A Servingman brings him a pot of ale
What! I am not bestraught. Here's —
He drinks

THIRD SERVINGMAN
O, this it is that makes your lady mourn.

SECOND SERVINGMAN
O, this is it that makes your servants droop.

LORD
Hence comes it that your kindred shuns your house,
As beaten hence by your strange lunacy.
O noble lord, bethink thee of thy birth,
Call home thy ancient thoughts from banishment,   30
And banish hence these abject lowly dreams.
Look how thy servants do attend on thee,
Each in his office ready at thy beck.
Wilt thou have music? Hark, Apollo plays,
Music
And twenty cagèd nightingales do sing.
Or wilt thou sleep? We'll have thee to a couch
Softer and sweeter than the lustful bed
On purpose trimmed up for Semiramis.
Say thou wilt walk; we will bestrew the ground.
Or wilt thou ride? Thy horses shall be trapped,   40

Their harness studded all with gold and pearl.
Dost thou love hawking? Thou hast hawks will soar
Above the morning lark. Or wilt thou hunt?
Thy hounds shall make the welkin answer them
And fetch shrill echoes from the hollow earth.

FIRST SERVINGMAN

Say thou wilt course, thy greyhounds are as swift
As breathèd stags, ay, fleeter than the roe.

SECOND SERVINGMAN

Dost thou love pictures? We will fetch thee straight
Adonis painted by a running brook,
50   And Cytherea all in sedges hid,
Which seem to move and wanton with her breath
Even as the waving sedges play wi'th'wind.

LORD

We'll show thee Io as she was a maid,
And how she was beguilèd and surprised,
As lively painted as the deed was done.

THIRD SERVINGMAN

Or Daphne roaming through a thorny wood,
Scratching her legs that one shall swear she bleeds,
And at that sight shall sad Apollo weep,
So workmanly the blood and tears are drawn.

LORD

60   Thou art a lord, and nothing but a lord.
Thou hast a lady far more beautiful
Than any woman in this waning age.

FIRST SERVINGMAN

And till the tears that she hath shed for thee
Like envious floods o'errun her lovely face,
She was the fairest creature in the world —
And yet she is inferior to none.

SLY

Am I a lord and have I such a lady?

Or do I dream? Or have I dreamed till now?
I do not sleep. I see, I hear, I speak.
I smell sweet savours and I feel soft things.   70
Upon my life, I am a lord indeed,
And not a tinker nor Christophero Sly.
Well, bring our lady hither to our sight,
And once again a pot o'th'smallest ale.

SECOND SERVINGMAN
Will't please your mightiness to wash your hands?
O, how we joy to see your wit restored!
O, that once more you knew but what you are!
These fifteen years you have been in a dream,
Or when you waked, so waked as if you slept.

SLY
These fifteen years! By my fay, a goodly nap.   80
But did I never speak of all that time?

FIRST SERVINGMAN
O, yes, my lord, but very idle words,
For though you lay here in this goodly chamber,
Yet would you say ye were beaten out of door,
And rail upon the hostess of the house,
And say you would present her at the leet,
Because she brought stone jugs and no sealed quarts.
Sometimes you would call out for Cicely Hacket.

SLY
Ay, the woman's maid of the house.

THIRD SERVINGMAN
Why, sir, you know no house, nor no such maid,   90
Nor no such men as you have reckoned up,
As Stephen Sly, and old John Naps of Greece,
And Peter Turph, and Henry Pimpernell,
And twenty more such names and men as these,
Which never were nor no man ever saw.

SLY

Now Lord be thankèd for my good amends.

ALL Amen.

> *Enter Page as a lady, with attendants. One gives Sly a pot of ale*

SLY I thank thee, thou shalt not lose by it.

PAGE How fares my noble lord?

100 SLY Marry, I fare well, for here is cheer enough.

> *He drinks*

Where is my wife?

PAGE

Here, noble lord, what is thy will with her?

SLY

Are you my wife, and will not call me husband?

My men should call me 'lord', I am your goodman.

PAGE

My husband and my lord, my lord and husband,

I am your wife in all obedience.

SLY I know it well. What must I call her?

LORD Madam.

SLY Al'ce madam, or Joan madam?

LORD

110 Madam and nothing else, so lords call ladies.

SLY

Madam wife, they say that I have dreamed

And slept above some fifteen year or more.

PAGE

Ay, and the time seems thirty unto me,

Being all this time abandoned from your bed.

SLY

'Tis much. Servants, leave me and her alone.

> *Exeunt Lord and Servingmen*

Madam, undress you and come now to bed.

PAGE

    Thrice-noble lord, let me entreat of you
    To pardon me yet for a night or two,
    Or, if not so, until the sun be set.
    For your physicians have expressly charged,   120
    In peril to incur your former malady,
    That I should yet absent me from your bed.
    I hope this reason stands for my excuse.

SLY Ay, it stands so that I may hardly tarry so long. But I
    would be loath to fall into my dreams again. I will there-
    fore tarry in despite of the flesh and the blood.

    Enter the Lord as a Messenger

LORD

    Your honour's players, hearing your amendment,
    Are come to play a pleasant comedy;
    For so your doctors hold it very meet,
    Seeing too much sadness hath congealed your blood,   130
    And melancholy is the nurse of frenzy.
    Therefore they thought it good you hear a play
    And frame your mind to mirth and merriment,
    Which bars a thousand harms and lengthens life.

SLY Marry, I will. Let them play it. Is not a comonty a
    Christmas gambold or a tumbling-trick?

PAGE

    No, my good lord, it is more pleasing stuff.

SLY What, household stuff?

PAGE It is a kind of history.

SLY Well, we'll see't. Come, madam wife, sit by my side   140
    and let the world slip, we shall ne'er be younger.

    They sit
    A flourish of trumpets to announce the play

*

I.I   *Enter Lucentio and his man Tranio*

LUCENTIO

Tranio, since for the great desire I had
To see fair Padua, nursery of arts,
I am arrived for fruitful Lombardy,
The pleasant garden of great Italy,
And by my father's love and leave am armed
With his good will and thy good company,
My trusty servant well approved in all,
Here let us breathe and haply institute
A course of learning and ingenious studies.
Pisa renownèd for grave citizens
Gave me my being and my father first,
A merchant of great traffic through the world,
Vincentio come of the Bentivolii.
Vincentio's son, brought up in Florence,
It shall become to serve all hopes conceived
To deck his fortune with his virtuous deeds.
And therefore, Tranio, for the time I study
Virtue, and that part of philosophy
Will I apply that treats of happiness
By virtue specially to be achieved.
Tell me thy mind, for I have Pisa left.
And am to Padua come as he that leaves
A shallow plash to plunge him in the deep,
And with satiety seeks to quench his thirst.

TRANIO

Mi perdonato, gentle master mine.
I am in all affected as yourself,
Glad that you thus continue your resolve
To suck the sweets of sweet philosophy.
Only, good master, while we do admire
This virtue and this moral discipline,
Let's be no stoics nor no stocks, I pray,

Or so devote to Aristotle's checks
As Ovid be an outcast quite abjured.
Balk logic with acquaintance that you have,
And practise rhetoric in your common talk,
Music and poesy use to quicken you,
The mathematics and the metaphysics
Fall to them as you find your stomach serves you.
No profit grows where is no pleasure ta'en.
In brief, sir, study what you most affect.   40

LUCENTIO
Gramercies, Tranio, well dost thou advise.
If, Biondello, thou wert come ashore,
We could at once put us in readiness,
And take a lodging fit to entertain
Such friends as time in Padua shall beget.

Enter Baptista with his two daughters Katherina and
Bianca; Gremio, a pantaloon, and Hortensio, suitor
to Bianca. Lucentio and Tranio stand by

But stay awhile, what company is this?

TRANIO
Master, some show to welcome us to town.

BAPTISTA
Gentlemen, importune me no farther,
For how I firmly am resolved you know;
That is, not to bestow my youngest daughter   50
Before I have a husband for the elder.
If either of you both love Katherina,
Because I know you well and love you well,
Leave shall you have to court her at your pleasure.

GREMIO
To cart her rather. She's too rough for me.
There, there, Hortensio, will you any wife?

KATHERINA *(to Baptista)*
I pray you, sir, is it your will

To make a stale of me amongst these mates?

HORTENSIO

Mates, maid, how mean you that? No mates for you
Unless you were of gentler, milder mould.

KATHERINA

I'faith, sir, you shall never need to fear.
Iwis it is not halfway to her heart.
But if it were, doubt not her care should be
To comb your noddle with a three-legged stool,
And paint your face, and use you like a fool.

HORTENSIO

From all such devils, good Lord deliver us!

GREMIO

And me too, good Lord!

TRANIO (aside to Lucentio)

Husht, master, here's some good pastime toward.
That wench is stark mad or wonderful froward.

LUCENTIO (aside to Tranio)

But in the other's silence do I see
Maid's mild behaviour and sobriety.
Peace, Tranio.

TRANIO (aside to Lucentio)

Well said, master. Mum! And gaze your fill.

BAPTISTA

Gentlemen, that I may soon make good
What I have said – Bianca, get you in.
And let it not displease thee, good Bianca,
For I will love thee ne'er the less, my girl.

KATHERINA

A pretty peat! It is best
Put finger in the eye, an she knew why.

BIANCA

Sister, content you in my discontent.
Sir, to your pleasure humbly I subscribe.

My books and instruments shall be my company,
On them to look and practise by myself.

LUCENTIO (*aside*)
Hark, Tranio, thou mayst hear Minerva speak.

HORTENSIO
Signor Baptista, will you be so strange?
Sorry am I that our good will effects
Bianca's grief.

GREMIO   Why will you mew her up,
Signor Baptista, for this fiend of hell,
And make her bear the penance of her tongue?

BAPTISTA
Gentlemen, content ye. I am resolved.   90
Go in, Bianca.   *Exit Bianca*
And for I know she taketh most delight
In music, instruments, and poetry,
Schoolmasters will I keep within my house
Fit to instruct her youth. If you, Hortensio,
Or Signor Gremio, you, know any such,
Prefer them hither; for to cunning men
I will be very kind, and liberal
To mine own children in good bringing-up.
And so farewell. Katherina, you may stay,   100
For I have more to commune with Bianca.   *Exit*

KATHERINA
Why, and I trust I may go too, may I not?
What, shall I be appointed hours, as though, belike,
I knew not what to take and what to leave? Ha? *Exit*

GREMIO You may go to the devil's dam. Your gifts are so
good here's none will hold you. There! Love is not so
great, Hortensio, but we may blow our nails together,
and fast it fairly out. Our cake's dough on both sides.
Farewell. Yet, for the love I bear my sweet Bianca, if I
can by any means light on a fit man to teach her that   110

wherein she delights, I will wish him to her father.

HORTENSIO So will I, Signor Gremio. But a word, I pray. Though the nature of our quarrel yet never brooked parle, know now, upon advice, it toucheth us both – that we may yet again have access to our fair mistress and be happy rivals in Bianca's love – to labour and effect one thing specially.

GREMIO What's that, I pray?

HORTENSIO Marry, sir, to get a husband for her sister.

120 GREMIO A husband? A devil.

HORTENSIO I say a husband.

GREMIO I say a devil. Think'st thou, Hortensio, though her father be very rich, any man is so very a fool to be married to hell?

HORTENSIO Tush, Gremio. Though it pass your patience and mine to endure her loud alarums, why, man, there be good fellows in the world, an a man could light on them, would take her with all faults, and money enough.

GREMIO I cannot tell. But I had as lief take her dowry
130 with this condition – to be whipped at the high-cross every morning.

HORTENSIO Faith, as you say, there's small choice in rotten apples. But come, since this bar in law makes us friends, it shall be so far forth friendly maintained till by helping Baptista's eldest daughter to a husband we set his youngest free for a husband, and then have to't afresh. Sweet Bianca! Happy man be his dole. He that runs fastest gets the ring. How say you, Signor Gremio?

GREMIO I am agreed, and would I had given him the best
140 horse in Padua to begin his wooing that would thoroughly woo her, wed her, and bed her, and rid the house of her. Come on.   *Exeunt Gremio and Hortensio*

TRANIO

I pray, sir, tell me, is it possible
That love should of a sudden take such hold?

LUCENTIO

    O Tranio, till I found it to be true,
    I never thought it possible or likely.
    But see, while idly I stood looking on,
    I found the effect of love in idleness,
    And now in plainness do confess to thee,
    That art to me as secret and as dear   150
    As Anna to the Queen of Carthage was –
    Tranio, I burn, I pine, I perish, Tranio,
    If I achieve not this young modest girl.
    Counsel me, Tranio, for I know thou canst.
    Assist me, Tranio, for I know thou wilt.

TRANIO

    Master, it is no time to chide you now;
    Affection is not rated from the heart.
    If love have touched you, naught remains but so –
    Redime te captum quam queas minimo.

LUCENTIO

    Gramercies, lad. Go forward, this contents.   160
    The rest will comfort, for thy counsel's sound.

TRANIO

    Master, you looked so longly on the maid,
    Perhaps you marked not what's the pith of all.

LUCENTIO

    O yes, I saw sweet beauty in her face,
    Such as the daughter of Agenor had,
    That made great Jove to humble him to her hand,
    When with his knees he kissed the Cretan strand.

TRANIO

    Saw you no more? Marked you not how her sister
    Began to scold and raise up such a storm
    That mortal ears might hardly endure the din?   170

LUCENTIO

    Tranio, I saw her coral lips to move,
    And with her breath she did perfume the air.

Sacred and sweet was all I saw in her.

TRANIO

    Nay, then 'tis time to stir him from his trance.
    I pray, awake, sir. If you love the maid,
    Bend thoughts and wits to achieve her. Thus it stands:
    Her elder sister is so curst and shrewd
    That till the father rid his hands of her,
    Master, your love must live a maid at home,
180   And therefore has he closely mewed her up,
    Because she will not be annoyed with suitors.

LUCENTIO

    Ah, Tranio, what a cruel father's he!
    But art thou not advised he took some care
    To get her cunning schoolmasters to instruct her?

TRANIO

    Ay, marry, am I, sir – and now 'tis plotted.

LUCENTIO

    I have it, Tranio.

TRANIO   Master, for my hand,
    Both our inventions meet and jump in one.

LUCENTIO

    Tell me thine first.

TRANIO   You will be schoolmaster,
    And undertake the teaching of the maid –
190   That's your device.

LUCENTIO   It is. May it be done?

TRANIO

    Not possible. For who shall bear your part
    And be in Padua here Vincentio's son,
    Keep house and ply his book, welcome his friends,
    Visit his countrymen and banquet them?

LUCENTIO

    Basta, content thee, for I have it full.
    We have not yet been seen in any house,

Nor can we be distinguished by our faces
For man or master. Then it follows thus –
Thou shalt be master, Tranio, in my stead,
Keep house, and port, and servants, as I should.   200
I will some other be – some Florentine,
Some Neapolitan, or meaner man of Pisa.
'Tis hatched, and shall be so. Tranio, at once
Uncase thee, take my coloured hat and cloak.
When Biondello comes, he waits on thee,
But I will charm him first to keep his tongue.

TRANIO
So had you need.
    They exchange garments
In brief, sir, sith it your pleasure is,
And I am tied to be obedient –
For so your father charged me at our parting: 210
'Be serviceable to my son', quoth he,
Although I think 'twas in another sense –
I am content to be Lucentio,
Because so well I love Lucentio.

LUCENTIO
Tranio, be so, because Lucentio loves.
And let me be a slave t'achieve that maid
Whose sudden sight hath thralled my wounded eye.
    Enter Biondello
Here comes the rogue. Sirrah, where have you been?

BIONDELLO Where have I been? Nay, how now, where
are you? Master, has my fellow Tranio stolen your   220
clothes, or you stolen his, or both? Pray, what's the
news?

LUCENTIO
Sirrah, come hither. 'Tis no time to jest,
And therefore frame your manners to the time.
Your fellow Tranio here, to save my life,

Puts my apparel and my countenance on,
And I for my escape have put on his.
For in a quarrel since I came ashore
I killed a man, and fear I was descried.

230 Wait you on him, I charge you, as becomes,
While I make way from hence to save my life.
You understand me?

BIONDELLO   I, sir? Ne'er a whit.

LUCENTIO
And not a jot of Tranio in your mouth.
Tranio is changed into Lucentio.

BIONDELLO
The better for him, would I were so too!

TRANIO
So could I, faith, boy, to have the next wish after,
That Lucentio indeed had Baptista's youngest daughter.
But, sirrah, not for my sake but your master's, I advise
You use your manners discreetly in all kind of com-
          panies.

240 When I am alone, why then I am Tranio,
But in all places else your master Lucentio.

LUCENTIO
Tranio, let's go.
One thing more rests, that thyself execute –
To make one among these wooers. If thou ask me why,
Sufficeth, my reasons are both good and weighty. *Exeunt*
     The Presenters above speak

LORD
My lord, you nod, you do not mind the play.

SLY (*coming to with a start*) Yes, by Saint Anne, do I. A
good matter, surely. Comes there any more of it?

PAGE My lord, 'tis but begun.

250 SLY 'Tis a very excellent piece of work, madam lady.

Would 'twere done!
They sit and mark

PETRUCHIO
Verona, for a while I take my leave,
To see my friends in Padua, but of all
My best belovèd and approvèd friend,
Hortensio; and I trow this is his house.
Here, sirrah Grumio, knock, I say.
GRUMIO Knock, sir? Whom should I knock? Is there any
man has rebused your worship?
PETRUCHIO Villain, I say, knock me here soundly.
GRUMIO Knock you here, sir? Why, sir, what am I, sir,
that I should knock you here, sir?   10
PETRUCHIO
Villain, I say, knock me at this gate,
And rap me well, or I'll knock your knave's pate.
GRUMIO
My master is grown quarrelsome. I should knock you
    first,
And then I know after who comes by the worst.
PETRUCHIO
Will it not be?
Faith, sirrah, an you'll not knock, I'll ring it.
I'll try how you can *sol-fa* and sing it.
    He wrings him by the ears
GRUMIO
Help, masters, help! My master is mad.
PETRUCHIO
Now knock when I bid you, sirrah villain.
    Enter Hortensio

20 HORTENSIO How now, what's the matter? My old friend
      Grumio and my good friend Petruchio! How do you all
      at Verona?

PETRUCHIO
      Signor Hortensio, come you to part the fray?
      Con tutto il cuore ben trovato, may I say.

HORTENSIO
      Alla nostra casa ben venuto,
      Molto honorato signor mio Petruchio.
      Rise, Grumio, rise. We will compound this quarrel.

GRUMIO Nay, 'tis no matter, sir, what he 'leges in Latin. If
      this be not a lawful cause for me to leave his service,
30   look you, sir. He bid me knock him and rap him
      soundly, sir. Well, was it fit for a servant to use his
      master so, being perhaps, for aught I see, two and thirty,
      a pip out?
      Whom would to God I had well knocked at first,
      Then had not Grumio come by the worst.

PETRUCHIO
      A senseless villain. Good Hortensio,
      I bade the rascal knock upon your gate,
      And could not get him for my heart to do it.

GRUMIO Knock at the gate? O heavens! Spake you not
40   these words plain, 'Sirrah, knock me here, rap me here,
      knock me well, and knock me soundly'? And come you
      now with 'knocking at the gate'?

PETRUCHIO
      Sirrah, be gone, or talk not, I advise you.

HORTENSIO
      Petruchio, patience, I am Grumio's pledge.
      Why, this's a heavy chance 'twixt him and you,
      Your ancient, trusty, pleasant servant Grumio.
      And tell me now, sweet friend, what happy gale
      Blows you to Padua here from old Verona?

PETRUCHIO
    Such wind as scatters young men through the world
    To seek their fortunes farther than at home,   50
    Where small experience grows. But in a few,
    Signor Hortensio, thus it stands with me:
    Antonio, my father, is deceased,
    And I have thrust myself into this maze,
    Haply to wive and thrive as best I may.
    Crowns in my purse I have, and goods at home,
    And so am come abroad to see the world.

HORTENSIO
    Petruchio, shall I then come roundly to thee
    And wish thee to a shrewd ill-favoured wife?
    Thou'dst thank me but a little for my counsel,   60
    And yet I'll promise thee she shall be rich,
    And very rich. But th' art too much my friend,
    And I'll not wish thee to her.

PETRUCHIO
    Signor Hortensio, 'twixt such friends as we
    Few words suffice; and therefore, if thou know
    One rich enough to be Petruchio's wife –
    As wealth is burden of my wooing dance –
    Be she as foul as was Florentius' love,
    As old as Sibyl, and as curst and shrewd
    As Socrates' Xanthippe, or a worse,   70
    She moves me not, or not removes at least
    Affection's edge in me, were she as rough
    As are the swelling Adriatic seas.
    I come to wive it wealthily in Padua;
    If wealthily, then happily in Padua.

GRUMIO Nay, look you, sir, he tells you flatly what his
    mind is. Why, give him gold enough and marry him to
    a puppet or an aglet-baby, or an old trot with ne'er a
    tooth in her head, though she have as many diseases

80   as two and fifty horses. Why, nothing comes amiss, so
        money comes withal.

HORTENSIO
        Petruchio, since we are stepped thus far in,
        I will continue that I broached in jest.
        I can, Petruchio, help thee to a wife
        With wealth enough, and young and beauteous,
        Brought up as best becomes a gentlewoman.
        Her only fault – and that is faults enough –
        Is that she is intolerable curst,
        And shrewd and froward so beyond all measure
90   That, were my state far worser than it is,
        I would not wed her for a mine of gold.

PETRUCHIO
        Hortensio, peace. Thou know'st not gold's effect.
        Tell me her father's name and 'tis enough.
        For I will board her though she chide as loud
        As thunder when the clouds in autumn crack.

HORTENSIO
        Her father is Baptista Minola,
        An affable and courteous gentleman.
        Her name is Katherina Minola,
        Renowned in Padua for her scolding tongue.

PETRUCHIO
100   I know her father, though I know not her,
        And he knew my deceasèd father well.
        I will not sleep, Hortensio, till I see her,
        And therefore let me be thus bold with you
        To give you over at this first encounter,
        Unless you will accompany me thither.

GRUMIO I pray you, sir, let him go while the humour lasts.
        O' my word, an she knew him as well as I do, she would
        think scolding would do little good upon him. She may
        perhaps call him half a score knaves or so. Why, that's

nothing; an he begin once, he'll rail in his rope-tricks. 110
I'll tell you what, sir, an she stand him but a little, he
will throw a figure in her face, and so disfigure her with
it that she shall have no more eyes to see withal than a
cat. You know him not, sir.

HORTENSIO
Tarry, Petruchio, I must go with thee,
For in Baptista's keep my treasure is.
He hath the jewel of my life in hold,
His youngest daughter, beautiful Bianca,
And her withholds from me and other more,
Suitors to her and rivals in my love,   120
Supposing it a thing impossible,
For those defects I have before rehearsed,
That ever Katherina will be wooed.
Therefore this order hath Baptista ta'en,
That none shall have access unto Bianca
Till Katherine the curst have got a husband.

GRUMIO
Katherine the curst,
A title for a maid of all titles the worst.

HORTENSIO
Now shall my friend Petruchio do me grace,
And offer me disguised in sober robes   130
To old Baptista as a schoolmaster
Well seen in music, to instruct Bianca,
That so I may by this device at least
Have leave and leisure to make love to her,
And unsuspected court her by herself.

GRUMIO Here's no knavery! See, to beguile the old folks,
how the young folks lay their heads together.

*Enter Gremio, and Lucentio disguised as Cambio, a
schoolmaster*

Master, master, look about you. Who goes there, ha?

HORTENSIO

    Peace, Grumio. It is the rival of my love.

140   Petruchio, stand by a while.

GRUMIO

    A proper stripling and an amorous!

      They stand aside

GREMIO

    O, very well – I have perused the note.

    Hark you, sir, I'll have them very fairly bound –

    All books of love, see that at any hand –

    And see you read no other lectures to her.

    You understand me. Over and beside

    Signor Baptista's liberality,

    I'll mend it with a largess. Take your paper too.

    And let me have them very well perfumed,

150   For she is sweeter than perfume itself

    To whom they go to. What will you read to her?

LUCENTIO

    Whate'er I read to her, I'll plead for you

    As for my patron, stand you so assured,

    As firmly as yourself were still in place,

    Yea, and perhaps with more successful words

    Than you, unless you were a scholar, sir.

GREMIO

    O this learning, what a thing it is!

GRUMIO (*aside*)

    O this woodcock, what an ass it is!

PETRUCHIO (*aside*)

    Peace, sirrah.

HORTENSIO (*aside*)

160   Grumio, mum! (*Coming forward*) God save you, Signor

      Gremio.

GREMIO

    And you are well met, Signor Hortensio.

Trow you whither I am going? To Baptista Minola.
I promised to enquire carefully
About a schoolmaster for the fair Bianca,
And by good fortune I have lighted well
On this young man, for learning and behaviour
Fit for her turn, well read in poetry
And other books – good ones, I warrant ye.

HORTENSIO

'Tis well. And I have met a gentleman
Hath promised me to help me to another,   170
A fine musician to instruct our mistress.
So shall I no whit be behind in duty
To fair Bianca, so beloved of me.

GREMIO

Beloved of me, and that my deeds shall prove.

GRUMIO (*aside*)

And that his bags shall prove.

HORTENSIO

Gremio, 'tis now no time to vent our love.
Listen to me, and if you speak me fair,
I'll tell you news indifferent good for either.
Here is a gentleman whom by chance I met,
Upon agreement from us to his liking,   180
Will undertake to woo curst Katherine,
Yea, and to marry her, if her dowry please.

GREMIO

So said, so done, is well.
Hortensio, have you told him all her faults?

PETRUCHIO

I know she is an irksome brawling scold.
If that be all, masters, I hear no harm.

GREMIO

No, say'st me so, friend? What countryman?

PETRUCHIO

Born in Verona, old Antonio's son.
My father dead, my fortune lives for me,
190 And I do hope good days and long to see.

GREMIO

O sir, such a life with such a wife were strange.
But if you have a stomach, to't a God's name –
You shall have me assisting you in all.
But will you woo this wildcat?

PETRUCHIO   Will I live?

GRUMIO

Will he woo her? Ay, or I'll hang her.

PETRUCHIO

Why came I hither but to that intent?
Think you a little din can daunt mine ears?
Have I not in my time heard lions roar?
Have I not heard the sea, puffed up with winds,
200 Rage like an angry boar chafèd with sweat?
Have I not heard great ordnance in the field,
And heaven's artillery thunder in the skies?
Have I not in a pitchèd battle heard
Loud 'larums, neighing steeds, and trumpets' clang?
And do you tell me of a woman's tongue,
That gives not half so great a blow to hear
As will a chestnut in a farmer's fire?
Tush, tush, fear boys with bugs!

GRUMIO   For he fears none.

GREMIO

Hortensio, hark.
210 This gentleman is happily arrived,
My mind presumes, for his own good and yours.

HORTENSIO

I promised we would be contributors
And bear his charge of wooing, whatsoe'er.

GREMIO

    And so we will – provided that he win her.

GRUMIO

    I would I were as sure of a good dinner.

    Enter Tranio, bravely dressed as Lucentio, and
    Biondello

TRANIO

    Gentlemen, God save you. If I may be bold,

    Tell me, I beseech you, which is the readiest way

    To the house of Signor Baptista Minola?

BIONDELLO He that has the two fair daughters – is't he
    you mean?   220

TRANIO Even he, Biondello.

GREMIO

    Hark you, sir, you mean not her too?

TRANIO

    Perhaps him and her, sir. What have you to do?

PETRUCHIO

    Not her that chides, sir, at any hand, I pray.

TRANIO

    I love no chiders, sir. Biondello, let's away.

LUCENTIO (*aside*)

    Well begun, Tranio.

HORTENSIO   Sir, a word ere you go.

    Are you a suitor to the maid you talk of, yea or no?

TRANIO

    And if I be, sir, is it any offence?

GREMIO

    No, if without more words you will get you hence.

TRANIO

    Why, sir, I pray, are not the streets as free   230

    For me as for you?

GREMIO   But so is not she.

TRANIO

For what reason, I beseech you?

GREMIO   For this reason, if you'll know,

That she's the choice love of Signor Gremio.

HORTENSIO

That she's the chosen of Signor Hortensio.

TRANIO

Softly, my masters! If you be gentlemen,

Do me this right – hear me with patience.

Baptista is a noble gentleman,

To whom my father is not all unknown,

And were his daughter fairer than she is,

240   She may more suitors have and me for one.

Fair Leda's daughter had a thousand wooers,

Then well one more may fair Bianca have.

And so she shall. Lucentio shall make one,

Though Paris came, in hope to speed alone.

GREMIO

What, this gentleman will out-talk us all!

LUCENTIO

Sir, give him head, I know he'll prove a jade.

PETRUCHIO

Hortensio, to what end are all these words?

HORTENSIO

Sir, let me be so bold as ask you,

Did you yet ever see Baptista's daughter?

TRANIO

250   No, sir, but hear I do that he hath two;

The one as famous for a scolding tongue

As is the other for beauteous modesty.

PETRUCHIO

Sir, sir, the first's for me, let her go by.

GREMIO

Yea, leave that labour to great Hercules,

And let it be more than Alcides' twelve.

PETRUCHIO

Sir, understand you this of me in sooth,
The youngest daughter whom you hearken for
Her father keeps from all access of suitors,
And will not promise her to any man
Until the elder sister first be wed.   260
The younger then is free, and not before.

TRANIO

If it be so, sir, that you are the man
Must stead us all – and me amongst the rest –
And if you break the ice and do this feat,
Achieve the elder, set the younger free
For our access – whose hap shall be to have her
Will not so graceless be to be ingrate.

HORTENSIO

Sir, you say well, and well you do conceive.
And since you do profess to be a suitor,
You must, as we do, gratify this gentleman,   270
To whom we all rest generally beholding.

TRANIO

Sir, I shall not be slack. In sign whereof,
Please ye we may contrive this afternoon,
And quaff carouses to our mistress' health,
And do as adversaries do in law,
Strive mightily, but eat and drink as friends.

GRUMIO *and* BIONDELLO

O excellent motion! Fellows, let's be gone.

HORTENSIO

The motion's good indeed, and be it so.
Petruchio, I shall be your *ben venuto*.   *Exeunt*

*

II.I   *Enter Katherina, and Bianca with her hands tied*

BIANCA

Good sister, wrong me not, nor wrong yourself,
To make a bondmaid and a slave of me.
That I disdain. But for these other gauds,
Unbind my hands, I'll pull them off myself,
Yea, all my raiment, to my petticoat,
Or what you will command me will I do,
So well I know my duty to my elders.

KATHERINA

Of all thy suitors here I charge thee tell
Whom thou lov'st best. See thou dissemble not.

BIANCA

10   Believe me, sister, of all men alive
I never yet beheld that special face
Which I could fancy more than any other.

KATHERINA

Minion, thou liest. Is't not Hortensio?

BIANCA

If you affect him, sister, here I swear
I'll plead for you myself but you shall have him.

KATHERINA

O then, belike, you fancy riches more.
You will have Gremio to keep you fair.

BIANCA

Is it for him you do envy me so?
Nay then you jest, and now I well perceive
20   You have but jested with me all this while.
I prithee, sister Kate, untie my hands.

KATHERINA

        Strikes her
If that be jest, then all the rest was so.
        Enter Baptista

BAPTISTA

Why, how now, dame, whence grows this insolence?
Bianca, stand aside. Poor girl, she weeps.

He unties her hands

Go ply thy needle, meddle not with her.
(*To Katherina*) For shame, thou hilding of a devilish
    spirit,
Why dost thou wrong her that did ne'er wrong thee?
When did she cross thee with a bitter word?

KATHERINA

Her silence flouts me, and I'll be revenged.

She flies after Bianca

BAPTISTA

What, in my sight? Bianca, get thee in.   *Exit Bianca*   30

KATHERINA

What, will you not suffer me? Nay, now I see
She is your treasure, she must have a husband.
I must dance bare-foot on her wedding-day,
And for your love to her lead apes in hell.
Talk not to me, I will go sit and weep,
Till I can find occasion of revenge.   *Exit Katherina*

BAPTISTA

Was ever gentleman thus grieved as I?
But who comes here?

*Enter Gremio, with Lucentio, disguised as Cambio, in
the habit of a mean man; Petruchio, with Hortensio,
disguised as Licio; and Tranio, disguised as Lucentio,
with his boy, Biondello, bearing a lute and books*

GREMIO Good morrow, neighbour Baptista.

BAPTISTA Good morrow, neighbour Gremio. God save   40
you, gentlemen.

PETRUCHIO

And you, good sir. Pray have you not a daughter
Called Katherina, fair and virtuous?

BAPTISTA

I have a daughter, sir, called Katherina.

GREMIO

You are too blunt, go to it orderly.

PETRUCHIO

You wrong me, Signor Gremio, give me leave.
I am a gentleman of Verona, sir,
That hearing of her beauty and her wit,
Her affability and bashful modesty,
Her wondrous qualities and mild behaviour,
Am bold to show myself a forward guest
Within your house, to make mine eye the witness
Of that report which I so oft have heard.
And for an entrance to my entertainment
I do present you with a man of mine,
        (*presenting Hortensio*)
Cunning in music and the mathematics,
To instruct her fully in those sciences,
Whereof I know she is not ignorant.
Accept of him, or else you do me wrong.
His name is Licio, born in Mantua.

BAPTISTA

Y'are welcome, sir, and he for your good sake.
But for my daughter Katherine, this I know,
She is not for your turn, the more my grief.

PETRUCHIO

I see you do not mean to part with her,
Or else you like not of my company.

BAPTISTA

Mistake me not, I speak but as I find.
Whence are you, sir? What may I call your name?

PETRUCHIO

Petruchio is my name, Antonio's son,
A man well known throughout all Italy.

BAPTISTA

    I know him well. You are welcome for his sake.   70

GREMIO

    Saving your tale, Petruchio, I pray

    Let us that are poor petitioners speak too.

    Baccare! You are marvellous forward.

PETRUCHIO

    O pardon me, Signor Gremio, I would fain be doing.

GREMIO

    I doubt it not, sir, but you will curse your wooing.

    (*To Baptista*) Neighbour, this is a gift very grateful, I am
    sure of it. To express the like kindness, myself, that have
    been more kindly beholding to you than any, freely give
    unto you this young scholar (*presenting Lucentio*) that
    hath been long studying at Rheims, as cunning in Greek,   80
    Latin, and other languages, as the other in music and
    mathematics. His name is Cambio. Pray accept his
    service.

BAPTISTA A thousand thanks, Signor Gremio. Welcome,
    good Cambio. (*To Tranio*) But, gentle sir, methinks you
    walk like a stranger. May I be so bold to know the cause
    of your coming?

TRANIO

    Pardon me, sir, the boldness is mine own

    That, being a stranger in this city here,

    Do make myself a suitor to your daughter,   90

    Unto Bianca, fair and virtuous.

    Nor is your firm resolve unknown to me

    In the preferment of the eldest sister.

    This liberty is all that I request –

    That, upon knowledge of my parentage,

    I may have welcome 'mongst the rest that woo,

    And free access and favour as the rest.

    And toward the education of your daughters

I here bestow a simple instrument,
And this small packet of Greek and Latin books.
Biondello steps forward with the lute and the books
If you accept them, then their worth is great.

BAPTISTA *(opening one of the books)*
Lucentio is your name? Of whence, I pray?

TRANIO
Of Pisa, sir, son to Vincentio.

BAPTISTA
A mighty man of Pisa. By report
I know him well. You are very welcome, sir.
(To Hortensio) Take you the lute, *(to Lucentio)* and you
    the set of books.
You shall go see your pupils presently.
Holla, within!
    Enter a Servant
                        Sirrah, lead these gentlemen
To my daughters, and tell them both
These are their tutors. Bid them use them well.
                        *Exit Servant, conducting Hortensio
                        and Lucentio, followed by Biondello*
We will go walk a little in the orchard,
And then to dinner. You are passing welcome,
And so I pray you all to think yourselves.

PETRUCHIO
Signor Baptista, my business asketh haste,
And every day I cannot come to woo.
You knew my father well, and in him me,
Left solely heir to all his lands and goods,
Which I have bettered rather than decreased.
Then tell me, if I get your daughter's love,
What dowry shall I have with her to wife?

BAPTISTA
After my death the one half of my lands,

And in possession twenty thousand crowns.

PETRUCHIO

And for that dowry I'll assure her of
Her widowhood – be it that she survive me –
In all my lands and leases whatsoever.
Let specialties be therefore drawn between us,
That covenants may be kept on either hand.

BAPTISTA

Ay, when the special thing is well obtained,
That is, her love; for that is all in all.

PETRUCHIO

Why, that is nothing. For I tell you, father,   130
I am as peremptory as she proud-minded;
And where two raging fires meet together,
They do consume the thing that feeds their fury.
Though little fire grows great with little wind,
Yet extreme gusts will blow out fire and all.
So I to her, and so she yields to me,
For I am rough and woo not like a babe.

BAPTISTA

Well mayst thou woo, and happy be thy speed.
But be thou armed for some unhappy words.

PETRUCHIO

Ay, to the proof, as mountains are for winds,   140
That shakes not though they blow perpetually.

Enter Hortensio with his head broke

BAPTISTA

How now, my friend, why dost thou look so pale?

HORTENSIO

For fear, I promise you, if I look pale.

BAPTISTA

What, will my daughter prove a good musician?

HORTENSIO

I think she'll sooner prove a soldier.

Iron may hold with her, but never lutes.

BAPTISTA

Why then, thou canst not break her to the lute?

HORTENSIO

Why no, for she hath broke the lute to me.
I did but tell her she mistook her frets,
150 And bowed her hand to teach her fingering,
When, with a most impatient devilish spirit,
'Frets, call you these?' quoth she, 'I'll fume with them.'
And with that word she struck me on the head,
And through the instrument my pate made way,
And there I stood amazèd for a while,
As on a pillory, looking through the lute,
While she did call me rascal fiddler
And twangling Jack, with twenty such vile terms,
As had she studied to misuse me so.

PETRUCHIO

160 Now, by the world, it is a lusty wench.
I love her ten times more than e'er I did.
O, how I long to have some chat with her!

BAPTISTA

Well, go with me, and be not so discomfited.
Proceed in practice with my younger daughter,
She's apt to learn and thankful for good turns.
Signor Petruchio, will you go with us,
Or shall I send my daughter Kate to you?

PETRUCHIO

I pray you do.   *Exeunt all but Petruchio*
         I'll attend her here,
And woo her with some spirit when she comes.
170 Say that she rail, why then I'll tell her plain
She sings as sweetly as a nightingale.
Say that she frown, I'll say she looks as clear
As morning roses newly washed with dew.

Say she be mute and will not speak a word,
Then I'll commend her volubility,
And say she uttereth piercing eloquence.
If she do bid me pack, I'll give her thanks,
As though she bid me stay by her a week.
If she deny to wed, I'll crave the day
When I shall ask the banns, and when be married.   180
But here she comes, and now, Petruchio, speak.

      Enter Katherina

Good morrow, Kate – for that's your name, I hear.

KATHERINA

Well have you heard, but something hard of hearing;
They call me Katherine that do talk of me.

PETRUCHIO

You lie, in faith, for you are called plain Kate,
And bonny Kate, and sometimes Kate the curst.
But Kate, the prettiest Kate in Christendom,
Kate of Kate Hall, my super-dainty Kate,
For dainties are all Kates, and therefore, Kate,
Take this of me, Kate of my consolation –   190
Hearing thy mildness praised in every town,
Thy virtues spoke of, and thy beauty sounded,
Yet not so deeply as to thee belongs,
Myself am moved to woo thee for my wife.

KATHERINA

Moved, in good time! Let him that moved you hither
Remove you hence. I knew you at the first
You were a movable.

PETRUCHIO   Why, what's a movable?

KATHERINA

A joint-stool.

PETRUCHIO   Thou hast hit it. Come, sit on me.

KATHERINA

Asses are made to bear, and so are you.

PETRUCHIO

200   Women are made to bear, and so are you.

KATHERINA

No such jade as you, if me you mean.

PETRUCHIO

Alas, good Kate, I will not burden thee!
For knowing thee to be but young and light –

KATHERINA

Too light for such a swain as you to catch,
And yet as heavy as my weight should be.

PETRUCHIO

Should be? Should – buzz!

KATHERINA   Well ta'en, and like a buzzard.

PETRUCHIO

O slow-winged turtle, shall a buzzard take thee?

KATHERINA

Ay, for a turtle, as he takes a buzzard.

PETRUCHIO

Come, come, you wasp, i'faith, you are too angry.

KATHERINA

210   If I be waspish, best beware my sting.

PETRUCHIO

My remedy is then to pluck it out.

KATHERINA

Ay, if the fool could find it where it lies.

PETRUCHIO

Who knows not where a wasp does wear his sting?
In his tail.

KATHERINA In his tongue.

PETRUCHIO   Whose tongue?

KATHERINA

Yours, if you talk of tales, and so farewell.
      She turns to go

PETRUCHIO

What, with my tongue in your tail? Nay, come again.
He takes her in his arms
Good Kate, I am a gentleman –

KATHERINA   That I'll try.
She strikes him

PETRUCHIO

I swear I'll cuff you, if you strike again.

KATHERINA

So may you loose your arms.
If you strike me, you are no gentleman,   220
And if no gentleman, why then no arms.

PETRUCHIO

A herald, Kate? O, put me in thy books!

KATHERINA

What is your crest – a coxcomb?

PETRUCHIO

A combless cock, so Kate will be my hen.

KATHERINA

No cock of mine, you crow too like a craven.

PETRUCHIO

Nay, come, Kate, come, you must not look so sour.

KATHERINA

It is my fashion when I see a crab.

PETRUCHIO

Why, here's no crab, and therefore look not sour.

KATHERINA

There is, there is.

PETRUCHIO

Then show it me.

KATHERINA   Had I a glass, I would.   230

PETRUCHIO

What, you mean my face?

KATHERINA   Well aimed of such a young one.

PETRUCHIO

Now, by Saint George, I am too young for you.

KATHERINA

Yet you are withered.

PETRUCHIO   'Tis with cares.

KATHERINA   I care not.

PETRUCHIO

Nay, hear you, Kate —

She struggles

                              In sooth, you scape not so.

KATHERINA

I chafe you, if I tarry. Let me go.

PETRUCHIO

No, not a whit. I find you passing gentle.
'Twas told me you were rough, and coy, and sullen,
And now I find report a very liar.
For thou art pleasant, gamesome, passing courteous,
240   But slow in speech, yet sweet as spring-time flowers.
Thou canst not frown, thou canst not look askance,
Nor bite the lip, as angry wenches will,
Nor hast thou pleasure to be cross in talk.
But thou with mildness entertain'st thy wooers,
With gentle conference, soft and affable.

He lets her go

Why does the world report that Kate doth limp?
O slanderous world! Kate like the hazel-twig
Is straight and slender, and as brown in hue
As hazel-nuts and sweeter than the kernels.
250   O, let me see thee walk. Thou dost not halt.

KATHERINA

Go, fool, and whom thou keep'st command.

PETRUCHIO

Did ever Dian so become a grove

As Kate this chamber with her princely gait?
O, be thou Dian, and let her be Kate,
And then let Kate be chaste and Dian sportful.

KATHERINA
Where did you study all this goodly speech?

PETRUCHIO
It is extempore, from my mother-wit.

KATHERINA
A witty mother, witless else her son.

PETRUCHIO
Am I not wise?

KATHERINA   Yes, keep you warm.

PETRUCHIO
Marry, so I mean, sweet Katherine, in thy bed.   260
And therefore, setting all this chat aside,
Thus in plain terms – your father hath consented
That you shall be my wife; your dowry 'greed on;
And will you, nill you, I will marry you.
Now, Kate, I am a husband for your turn,
For by this light whereby I see thy beauty,
Thy beauty that doth make me like thee well,
Thou must be married to no man but me.
For I am he am born to tame you, Kate,
And bring you from a wild Kate to a Kate   270
Conformable as other household Kates.
      Enter Baptista, Gremio, and Tranio
Here comes your father. Never make denial;
I must and will have Katherine to my wife.

BAPTISTA
Now, Signor Petruchio, how speed you with my
      daughter?

PETRUCHIO
How but well, sir? How but well?
It were impossible I should speed amiss.

BAPTISTA

    Why, how now, daughter Katherine? In your dumps?

KATHERINA

    Call you me daughter? Now I promise you
    You have showed a tender fatherly regard
280   To wish me wed to one half lunatic,
    A madcap ruffian and a swearing Jack,
    That thinks with oaths to face the matter out.

PETRUCHIO

    Father, 'tis thus – yourself and all the world
    That talked of her have talked amiss of her.
    If she be curst, it is for policy,
    For she's not froward, but modest as the dove.
    She is not hot, but temperate as the morn.
    For patience she will prove a second Grissel,
    And Roman Lucrece for her chastity.
290   And to conclude, we have 'greed so well together
    That upon Sunday is the wedding-day.

KATHERINA

    I'll see thee hanged on Sunday first.

GREMIO

    Hark, Petruchio, she says she'll see thee hanged first.

TRANIO

    Is this your speeding? Nay then, good night our part.

PETRUCHIO

    Be patient, gentlemen, I choose her for myself.
    If she and I be pleased, what's that to you?
    'Tis bargained 'twixt us twain, being alone,
    That she shall still be curst in company.
    I tell you 'tis incredible to believe
300   How much she loves me – O, the kindest Kate!
    She hung about my neck, and kiss on kiss
    She vied so fast, protesting oath on oath,
    That in a twink she won me to her love.

O, you are novices! 'Tis a world to see
How tame, when men and women are alone,
A meacock wretch can make the curstest shrew.
Give me thy hand, Kate, I will unto Venice,
To buy apparel 'gainst the wedding-day.
Provide the feast, father, and bid the guests.
I will be sure my Katherine shall be fine.   310

BAPTISTA

I know not what to say – but give me your hands.
God send you joy! Petruchio, 'tis a match.

GREMIO *and* TRANIO

Amen, say we. We will be witnesses.

PETRUCHIO

Father, and wife, and gentlemen, adieu,
I will to Venice – Sunday comes apace.
We will have rings, and things, and fine array,
And kiss me, Kate, we will be married o' Sunday.

Exeunt Petruchio and Katherina

GREMIO

Was ever match clapped up so suddenly?

BAPTISTA

Faith, gentlemen, now I play a merchant's part,
And venture madly on a desperate mart.   320

TRANIO

'Twas a commodity lay fretting by you,
'Twill bring you gain, or perish on the seas.

BAPTISTA

The gain I seek is quiet in the match.

GREMIO

No doubt but he hath got a quiet catch.
But now, Baptista, to your younger daughter –
Now is the day we long have lookèd for.
I am your neighbour, and was suitor first.

TRANIO
    And I am one that love Bianca more
    Than words can witness or your thoughts can guess.
GREMIO
330   Youngling, thou canst not love so dear as I.
TRANIO
    Greybeard, thy love doth freeze.
GREMIO   But thine doth fry.
    Skipper, stand back, 'tis age that nourisheth.
TRANIO
    But youth in ladies' eyes that flourisheth.
BAPTISTA
    Content you, gentlemen, I will compound this strife.
    'Tis deeds must win the prize, and he of both
    That can assure my daughter greatest dower
    Shall have my Bianca's love.
    Say, Signor Gremio, what can you assure her?
GREMIO
    First, as you know, my house within the city
340   Is richly furnishèd with plate and gold,
    Basins and ewers to lave her dainty hands –
    My hangings all of Tyrian tapestry.
    In ivory coffers I have stuffed my crowns,
    In cypress chests my arras counterpoints,
    Costly apparel, tents, and canopies,
    Fine linen, Turkey cushions bossed with pearl,
    Valance of Venice gold in needlework,
    Pewter and brass, and all things that belongs
    To house or housekeeping. Then at my farm
350   I have a hundred milch-kine to the pail,
    Six score fat oxen standing in my stalls,
    And all things answerable to this portion.
    Myself am struck in years, I must confess,
    And if I die tomorrow this is hers,

If whilst I live she will be only mine.

TRANIO

That 'only' came well in. Sir, list to me.
I am my father's heir and only son.
If I may have your daughter to my wife,
I'll leave her houses three or four as good,
Within rich Pisa walls, as any one   360
Old Signor Gremio has in Padua,
Besides two thousand ducats by the year
Of fruitful land, all which shall be her jointure.
What, have I pinched you, Signor Gremio?

GREMIO

Two thousand ducats by the year of land!
(*Aside*) My land amounts not to so much in all.
(*To them*) That she shall have, besides an argosy
That now is lying in Marseilles road.
What, have I choked you with an argosy?

TRANIO

Gremio, 'tis known my father hath no less   370
Than three great argosies, besides two galliasses
And twelve tight galleys. These I will assure her,
And twice as much whate'er thou off'rest next.

GREMIO

Nay, I have offered all, I have no more,
And she can have no more than all I have.
If you like me, she shall have me and mine.

TRANIO

Why, then the maid is mine from all the world
By your firm promise. Gremio is out-vied.

BAPTISTA

I must confess your offer is the best,
And let your father make her the assurance,   380
She is your own. Else, you must pardon me,
If you should die before him, where's her dower?

TRANIO

That's but a cavil. He is old, I young.

GREMIO

And may not young men die as well as old?

BAPTISTA

Well, gentlemen,
I am thus resolved. On Sunday next you know
My daughter Katherine is to be married.
Now, on the Sunday following shall Bianca
Be bride to you, if you make this assurance;
390   If not, to Signor Gremio.
And so I take my leave, and thank you both.

GREMIO

Adieu, good neighbour.   *Exit Baptista*
                    Now I fear thee not.
Sirrah, young gamester, your father were a fool
To give thee all, and in his waning age
Set foot under thy table. Tut, a toy!
An old Italian fox is not so kind, my boy.   *Exit*

TRANIO

A vengeance on your crafty withered hide!
Yet I have faced it with a card of ten.
'Tis in my head to do my master good.
400   I see no reason but supposed Lucentio
Must get a father, called supposed Vincentio.
And that's a wonder. Fathers commonly
Do get their children; but in this case of wooing
A child shall get a sire, if I fail not of my cunning. *Exit*

*

Enter Lucentio as Cambio, Hortensio as Licio,   III.I
and Bianca

LUCENTIO
Fiddler, forbear, you grow too forward, sir.
Have you so soon forgot the entertainment
Her sister Katherine welcomed you withal?

HORTENSIO
But, wrangling pedant, this is
The patroness of heavenly harmony.
Then give me leave to have prerogative,
And when in music we have spent an hour,
Your lecture shall have leisure for as much.

LUCENTIO
Preposterous ass, that never read so far
To know the cause why music was ordained!   10
Was it not to refresh the mind of man
After his studies or his usual pain?
Then give me leave to read philosophy,
And while I pause serve in your harmony.

HORTENSIO
Sirrah, I will not bear these braves of thine.

BIANCA
Why, gentlemen, you do me double wrong
To strive for that which resteth in my choice.
I am no breeching scholar in the schools,
I'll not be tied to hours nor 'pointed times,
But learn my lessons as I please myself.   20
And, to cut off all strife, here sit we down.
Take you your instrument, play you the whiles –
His lecture will be done ere you have tuned.

HORTENSIO
You'll leave his lecture when I am in tune?

LUCENTIO
That will be never. Tune your instrument.

BIANCA Where left we last?

LUCENTIO Here, madam.
> (*He reads*)
> '*Hic ibat Simois, hic est Sigeia tellus,*
> *Hic steterat Priami regia celsa senis.*'

30 BIANCA Construe them.

LUCENTIO '*Hic ibat*', as I told you before – '*Simois*', I am
Lucentio – '*hic est*', son unto Vincentio of Pisa – '*Sigeia
tellus*', disguised thus to get your love – '*Hic steterat*',
and that Lucentio that comes a-wooing – '*Priami*', is my
man Tranio – '*regia*', bearing my port – '*celsa senis*',
that we might beguile the old pantaloon.

HORTENSIO Madam, my instrument's in tune.

BIANCA Let's hear. (*He plays*) O fie! The treble jars.

LUCENTIO Spit in the hole, man, and tune again.

40 BIANCA Now let me see if I can construe it. '*Hic ibat
Simois*', I know you not – '*hic est Sigeia tellus*', I trust you
not – '*Hic steterat Priami*', take heed he hear us not –
'*regia*', presume not – '*celsa senis*', despair not.

HORTENSIO
    Madam, 'tis now in tune.

LUCENTIO   All but the bass.

HORTENSIO
    The bass is right, 'tis the base knave that jars.
    (*Aside*) How fiery and forward our pedant is.
    Now, for my life, the knave doth court my love.
    Pedascule, I'll watch you better yet.

BIANCA
    In time I may believe, yet I mistrust.

LUCENTIO
50 Mistrust it not – for, sure, Aeacides
    Was Ajax, called so from his grandfather.

BIANCA
    I must believe my master, else, I promise you,

I should be arguing still upon that doubt.
But let it rest. Now, Licio, to you.
Good master, take it not unkindly, pray,
That I have been thus pleasant with you both.

HORTENSIO (*to Lucentio*)
You may go walk, and give me leave awhile.
My lessons make no music in three parts.

LUCENTIO
Are you so formal, sir? Well, I must wait –
(*aside*) And watch withal, for, but I be deceived,   60
Our fine musician groweth amorous.

HORTENSIO
Madam, before you touch the instrument
To learn the order of my fingering,
I must begin with rudiments of art,
To teach you gamut in a briefer sort,
More pleasant, pithy, and effectual,
Than hath been taught by any of my trade.
And there it is in writing fairly drawn.

BIANCA
Why, I am past my gamut long ago.

HORTENSIO
Yet read the gamut of Hortensio.   70

BIANCA (*reads*)
'Gamut *I am, the ground of all accord* –
A re, *to plead Hortensio's passion* –
B mi, *Bianca, take him for thy lord* –
C fa ut, *that loves with all affection* –
D sol re, *one clef, two notes have I* –
E la mi, *show pity or I die.*'
Call you this gamut? Tut, I like it not!
Old fashions please me best. I am not so nice
To change true rules for odd inventions.
    Enter a Servant

SERVANT
80   Mistress, your father prays you leave your books,
      And help to dress your sister's chamber up.
      You know tomorrow is the wedding-day.

BIANCA
      Farewell, sweet masters both, I must be gone.
                              Exeunt Bianca and Servant

LUCENTIO
      Faith, mistress, then I have no cause to stay.   *Exit*

HORTENSIO
      But I have cause to pry into this pedant,
      Methinks he looks as though he were in love.
      Yet if thy thoughts, Bianca, be so humble
      To cast thy wandering eyes on every stale,
      Seize thee that list. If once I find thee ranging,
90   Hortensio will be quit with thee by changing.   *Exit*

III.2   *Enter Baptista, Gremio, Tranio as Lucentio,*
             Katherina, Bianca, Lucentio as Cambio, and
             attendants on Katherina

BAPTISTA (*to Tranio*)
      Signor Lucentio, this is the 'pointed day
      That Katherine and Petruchio should be married,
      And yet we hear not of our son-in-law.
      What will be said? What mockery will it be
      To want the bridegroom when the priest attends
      To speak the ceremonial rites of marriage!
      What says Lucentio to this shame of ours?

KATHERINA
      No shame but mine. I must forsooth be forced
      To give my hand, opposed against my heart,
10   Unto a mad-brain rudesby, full of spleen,
      Who wooed in haste and means to wed at leisure.

I told you, I, he was a frantic fool,
Hiding his bitter jests in blunt behaviour.
And to be noted for a merry man,
He'll woo a thousand, 'point the day of marriage,
Make feast, invite friends, and proclaim the banns,
Yet never means to wed where he hath wooed.
Now must the world point at poor Katherine,
And say 'Lo, there is mad Petruchio's wife,
If it would please him come and marry her.'   20

TRANIO
Patience, good Katherine, and Baptista too.
Upon my life, Petruchio means but well,
Whatever fortune stays him from his word.
Though he be blunt, I know him passing wise,
Though he be merry, yet withal he's honest.

KATHERINA
Would Katherine had never seen him though.
        Exit weeping, followed by Bianca and the other women

BAPTISTA
Go, girl, I cannot blame thee now to weep,
For such an injury would vex a saint,
Much more a shrew of thy impatient humour.
        Enter Biondello

BIONDELLO Master, master, news! And such old news as   30
you never heard of.

BAPTISTA Is it new and old too? How may that be?

BIONDELLO Why, is it not news to hear of Petruchio's
coming?

BAPTISTA Is he come?

BIONDELLO Why, no, sir.

BAPTISTA What then?

BIONDELLO He is coming.

BAPTISTA When will he be here?

40 BIONDELLO When he stands where I am and sees you
there.

TRANIO But say, what to thine old news?

BIONDELLO Why, Petruchio is coming in a new hat and
an old jerkin; a pair of old breeches thrice turned; a
pair of boots that have been candle-cases, one buckled,
another laced; an old rusty sword ta'en out of the town
armoury, with a broken hilt, and chapeless; with two
broken points; his horse hipped – with an old mothy
saddle and stirrups of no kindred – besides, possessed
50 with the glanders and like to mose in the chine, troubled
with the lampass, infected with the fashions, full of
windgalls, sped with spavins, rayed with the yellows,
past cure of the fives, stark spoiled with the staggers,
begnawn with the bots, swayed in the back and shoulder-
shotten, near-legged before, and with a half-cheeked
bit and a headstall of sheep's leather, which, being
restrained to keep him from stumbling, hath been often
burst and new-repaired with knots; one girth six times
pieced, and a woman's crupper of velure, which hath
60 two letters for her name fairly set down in studs, and
here and there pieced with pack-thread.

BAPTISTA Who comes with him?

BIONDELLO O sir, his lackey, for all the world caparisoned
like the horse; with a linen stock on one leg and a kersey
boot-hose on the other, gartered with a red and blue
list; an old hat, and the humour of forty fancies pricked
in't for a feather; a monster, a very monster in apparel,
and not like a Christian footboy or a gentleman's lackey.

TRANIO
'Tis some odd humour pricks him to this fashion.
70 Yet oftentimes he goes but mean-apparelled.

BAPTISTA I am glad he's come, howsoe'er he comes.

BIONDELLO Why, sir, he comes not.

BAPTISTA Didst thou not say he comes?

BIONDELLO Who? That Petruchio came?

BAPTISTA Ay, that Petruchio came.

BIONDELLO No, sir. I say his horse comes with him on his back.

BAPTISTA Why, that's all one.

BIONDELLO

Nay, by Saint Jamy,
I hold you a penny,   80
A horse and a man
Is more than one,
And yet not many.

Enter Petruchio and Grumio

PETRUCHIO Come, where be these gallants? Who's at home?

BAPTISTA You are welcome, sir.

PETRUCHIO And yet I come not well?

BAPTISTA And yet you halt not.

TRANIO Not so well apparelled as I wish you were.

PETRUCHIO

Were it not better I should rush in thus?   90
But where is Kate? Where is my lovely bride?
How does my father? Gentles, methinks you frown.
And wherefore gaze this goodly company
As if they saw some wondrous monument,
Some comet, or unusual prodigy?

BAPTISTA

Why, sir, you know this is your wedding-day.
First were we sad, fearing you would not come,
Now sadder that you come so unprovided.
Fie, doff this habit, shame to your estate,
An eye-sore to our solemn festival.   100

TRANIO

And tell us what occasion of import

Hath all so long detained you from your wife
And sent you hither so unlike yourself?

PETRUCHIO

Tedious it were to tell, and harsh to hear —
Sufficeth I am come to keep my word,
Though in some part enforcèd to digress,
Which at more leisure I will so excuse
As you shall well be satisfied withal.
But where is Kate? I stay too long from her.
110   The morning wears, 'tis time we were at church.

TRANIO

See not your bride in these unreverent robes,
Go to my chamber, put on clothes of mine.

PETRUCHIO

Not I, believe me. Thus I'll visit her.

BAPTISTA

But thus, I trust, you will not marry her.

PETRUCHIO

Good sooth, even thus. Therefore ha' done with words;
To me she's married, not unto my clothes.
Could I repair what she will wear in me
As I can change these poor accoutrements,
'Twere well for Kate and better for myself.
120   But what a fool am I to chat with you,
When I should bid good morrow to my bride,
And seal the title with a lovely kiss.

Exit with Grumio

TRANIO

He hath some meaning in his mad attire.
We will persuade him, be it possible,
To put on better ere he go to church.

BAPTISTA

I'll after him and see the event of this.

Exit followed by Gremio, Biondello, and attendants

TRANIO

But, sir, to love concerneth us to add
Her father's liking, which to bring to pass,
As I before imparted to your worship,
I am to get a man – whate'er he be   130
It skills not much, we'll fit him to our turn –
And he shall be Vincentio of Pisa,
And make assurance here in Padua
Of greater sums than I have promisèd.
So shall you quietly enjoy your hope
And marry sweet Bianca with consent.

LUCENTIO

Were it not that my fellow schoolmaster
Doth watch Bianca's steps so narrowly,
'Twere good methinks to steal our marriage,
Which once performed, let all the world say no,   140
I'll keep mine own despite of all the world.

TRANIO

That by degrees we mean to look into
And watch our vantage in this business.
We'll overreach the greybeard Gremio,
The narrow-prying father Minola,
The quaint musician, amorous Licio –
All for my master's sake, Lucentio.

    Enter Gremio

Signor Gremio, came you from the church?

GREMIO

As willingly as e'er I came from school.

TRANIO

And is the bride and bridegroom coming home?   150

GREMIO

A bridegroom, say you? 'Tis a groom indeed,
A grumbling groom, and that the girl shall find.

TRANIO

    Curster than she? Why, 'tis impossible.

GREMIO

    Why, he's a devil, a devil, a very fiend.

TRANIO

    Why, she's a devil, a devil, the devil's dam.

GREMIO

    Tut, she's a lamb, a dove, a fool to him.

    I'll tell you, Sir Lucentio – when the priest

    Should ask if Katherine should be his wife,

    'Ay, by gogs-wouns', quoth he, and swore so loud

160   That all-amazed the priest let fall the book,

    And as he stooped again to take it up,

    This mad-brained bridegroom took him such a cuff

    That down fell priest and book, and book and priest.

    'Now take them up', quoth he, 'if any list.'

TRANIO

    What said the wench when he rose up again?

GREMIO

    Trembled and shook. For why, he stamped and swore

    As if the vicar meant to cozen him.

    But after many ceremonies done

    He calls for wine. 'A health!' quoth he, as if

170   He had been aboard, carousing to his mates

    After a storm; quaffed off the muscadel,

    And threw the sops all in the sexton's face,

    Having no other reason

    But that his beard grew thin and hungerly

    And seemed to ask him sops as he was drinking.

    This done, he took the bride about the neck,

    And kissed her lips with such a clamorous smack

    That at the parting all the church did echo.

    And I seeing this came thence for very shame,

180   And after me, I know, the rout is coming.

Such a mad marriage never was before.
Hark, hark! I hear the minstrels play.
 Music plays
 Enter Petruchio, Katherina, Bianca, Baptista,
 Hortensio, Grumio, and attendants

PETRUCHIO
Gentlemen and friends, I thank you for your pains.
I know you think to dine with me today,
And have prepared great store of wedding cheer,
But so it is, my haste doth call me hence,
And therefore here I mean to take my leave.

BAPTISTA
Is't possible you will away tonight?

PETRUCHIO
I must away today before night come.
Make it no wonder. If you knew my business,   190
You would entreat me rather go than stay.
And, honest company, I thank you all
That have beheld me give away myself
To this most patient, sweet, and virtuous wife.
Dine with my father, drink a health to me,
For I must hence, and farewell to you all.

TRANIO
Let us entreat you stay till after dinner.

PETRUCHIO
It may not be.

GREMIO   Let me entreat you.

PETRUCHIO
It cannot be.

KATHERINA   Let me entreat you.

PETRUCHIO
I am content.

KATHERINA   Are you content to stay?   200

PETRUCHIO

    I am content you shall entreat me stay –

    But yet not stay, entreat me how you can.

KATHERINA

    Now if you love me stay.

PETRUCHIO   Grumio, my horse.

GRUMIO Ay, sir, they be ready – the oats have eaten the

    horses.

KATHERINA

    Nay then,

    Do what thou canst, I will not go today,

    No, nor tomorrow – not till I please myself.

    The door is open, sir, there lies your way,

210   You may be jogging whiles your boots are green.

    For me, I'll not be gone till I please myself.

    'Tis like you'll prove a jolly surly groom

    That take it on you at the first so roundly.

PETRUCHIO

    O Kate, content thee, prithee be not angry.

KATHERINA

    I will be angry – what hast thou to do?

    Father, be quiet – he shall stay my leisure.

GREMIO

    Ay marry, sir, now it begins to work.

KATHERINA

    Gentlemen, forward to the bridal dinner.

    I see a woman may be made a fool

220   If she had not a spirit to resist.

PETRUCHIO

    They shall go forward, Kate, at thy command.

    Obey the bride, you that attend on her.

    Go to the feast, revel and domineer,

    Carouse full measure to her maidenhead,

    Be mad and merry, or go hang yourselves.

But for my bonny Kate, she must with me.
    He seizes her, as though to protect her from the rest of
    the company, to whom he speaks
Nay, look not big, nor stamp, nor stare, nor fret,
I will be master of what is mine own.
She is my goods, my chattels, she is my house,
My household stuff, my field, my barn,   230
My horse, my ox, my ass, my any thing,
And here she stands. Touch her whoever dare!
I'll bring mine action on the proudest he
That stops my way in Padua. Grumio,
Draw forth thy weapon, we are beset with thieves,
Rescue thy mistress if thou be a man.
Fear not, sweet wench, they shall not touch thee, Kate.
I'll buckler thee against a million.
                Exeunt Petruchio, Katherina, and Grumio

BAPTISTA
Nay, let them go, a couple of quiet ones.

GREMIO
Went they not quickly, I should die with laughing.   240

TRANIO
Of all mad matches never was the like.

LUCENTIO
Mistress, what's your opinion of your sister?

BIANCA
That being mad herself, she's madly mated.

GREMIO
I warrant him, Petruchio is Kated.

BAPTISTA
Neighbours and friends, though bride and bridegroom
        wants
For to supply the places at the table,
You know there wants no junkets at the feast.
Lucentio, you shall supply the bridegroom's place,

And let Bianca take her sister's room.

TRANIO

250 Shall sweet Bianca practise how to bride it?

BAPTISTA

She shall, Lucentio. Come, gentlemen, let's go. *Exeunt*

*

IV.1   *Enter Grumio*

GRUMIO Fie, fie on all tired jades, on all mad masters, and
all foul ways! Was ever man so beaten? Was ever man so
rayed? Was ever man so weary? I am sent before to make
a fire, and they are coming after to warm them. Now
were not I a little pot and soon hot, my very lips might
freeze to my teeth, my tongue to the roof of my mouth, my
heart in my belly, ere I should come by a fire to thaw me.
But I with blowing the fire shall warm myself, for, con-
sidering the weather, a taller man than I will take cold.
10 Holla, ho! Curtis!

          Enter Curtis

CURTIS Who is that calls so coldly?

GRUMIO A piece of ice. If thou doubt it, thou mayst slide
from my shoulder to my heel with no greater a run but
my head and my neck. A fire, good Curtis.

CURTIS Is my master and his wife coming, Grumio?

GRUMIO O ay, Curtis, ay – and therefore fire, fire, cast on
no water.

CURTIS Is she so hot a shrew as she's reported?

GRUMIO She was, good Curtis, before this frost. But thou
20 know'st winter tames man, woman, and beast; for it
hath tamed my old master, and my new mistress, and
myself, fellow Curtis.

CURTIS Away, you three-inch fool! I am no beast.

GRUMIO Am I but three inches? Why, thy horn is a foot, and so long am I at the least. But wilt thou make a fire, or shall I complain on thee to our mistress, whose hand – she being now at hand – thou shalt soon feel, to thy cold comfort, for being slow in thy hot office?

CURTIS I prithee, good Grumio, tell me how goes the world?   30

He kindles a fire

GRUMIO A cold world, Curtis, in every office but thine – and therefore fire. Do thy duty, and have thy duty, for my master and mistress are almost frozen to death.

CURTIS There's fire ready – and therefore, good Grumio, the news.

GRUMIO Why, 'Jack boy, ho boy!' and as much news as wilt thou.

CURTIS Come, you are so full of cony-catching.

GRUMIO Why therefore fire, for I have caught extreme cold. Where's the cook? Is supper ready, the house   40 trimmed, rushes strewed, cobwebs swept, the serving-men in their new fustian, their white stockings, and every officer his wedding-garment on? Be the Jacks fair within, the Jills fair without, the carpets laid, and everything in order?

CURTIS All ready – and therefore, I pray thee, news.

GRUMIO First know my horse is tired, my master and mistress fallen out.

CURTIS How?

GRUMIO Out of their saddles into the dirt, and thereby   50 hangs a tale.

CURTIS Let's ha't, good Grumio.

GRUMIO Lend thine ear.

CURTIS Here.

GRUMIO There.

He boxes Curtis's ear

CURTIS This 'tis to feel a tale, not to hear a tale.

GRUMIO And therefore 'tis called a sensible tale; and this
cuff was but to knock at your ear and beseech listening.
Now I begin. *Imprimis*, we came down a foul hill, my
master riding behind my mistress —

CURTIS Both of one horse?

GRUMIO What's that to thee?

CURTIS Why, a horse.

GRUMIO Tell thou the tale. But hadst thou not crossed
me, thou shouldst have heard how her horse fell, and
she under her horse; thou shouldst have heard in how
miry a place, how she was bemoiled, how he left her
with the horse upon her, how he beat me because her
horse stumbled, how she waded through the dirt to
pluck him off me, how he swore, how she prayed that
never prayed before, how I cried, how the horses ran
away, how her bridle was burst, how I lost my crupper
— with many things of worthy memory, which now shall
die in oblivion, and thou return unexperienced to thy
grave.

CURTIS By this reckoning he is more shrew than she.

GRUMIO Ay, and that thou and the proudest of you all
shall find when he comes home. But what talk I of this?
Call forth Nathaniel, Joseph, Nicholas, Philip, Walter,
Sugarsop, and the rest. Let their heads be slickly
combed, their blue coats brushed, and their garters
of an indifferent knit. Let them curtsy with their left
legs, and not presume to touch a hair of my master's
horse-tail till they kiss their hands. Are they all ready?

CURTIS They are.

GRUMIO Call them forth.

CURTIS Do you hear, ho? You must meet my master to
countenance my mistress.

GRUMIO Why, she hath a face of her own.

CURTIS Who knows not that?   90

GRUMIO Thou, it seems, that calls for company to coun-
     tenance her.

CURTIS I call them forth to credit her.

GRUMIO Why, she comes to borrow nothing of them.

     Enter four or five Servingmen

NATHANIEL Welcome home, Grumio.

PHILIP How now, Grumio.

JOSEPH What, Grumio.

NICHOLAS Fellow Grumio.

NATHANIEL How now, old lad.

GRUMIO Welcome, you. How now, you. What, you.   100
     Fellow, you. And thus much for greeting. Now, my
     spruce companions, is all ready, and all things neat?

NATHANIEL All things is ready. How near is our master?

GRUMIO E'en at hand, alighted by this. And therefore be
     not – Cock's passion, silence! I hear my master.

     Enter Petruchio and Katherina

PETRUCHIO

     Where be these knaves? What, no man at door
     To hold my stirrup nor to take my horse?
     Where is Nathaniel, Gregory, Philip?

ALL SERVINGMEN Here, here sir, here sir.

PETRUCHIO

     Here sir, here sir, here sir, here sir!   110
     You logger-headed and unpolished grooms!
     What, no attendance? No regard? No duty?
     Where is the foolish knave I sent before?

GRUMIO

     Here sir, as foolish as I was before.

PETRUCHIO

     You peasant swain, you whoreson malt-horse drudge!
     Did I not bid thee meet me in the park
     And bring along these rascal knaves with thee?

GRUMIO

    Nathaniel's coat, sir, was not fully made,

    And Gabriel's pumps were all unpinked i'th'heel.

120   There was no link to colour Peter's hat,

    And Walter's dagger was not come from sheathing.

    There were none fine but Adam, Rafe, and Gregory –

    The rest were ragged, old, and beggarly.

    Yet, as they are, here are they come to meet you.

PETRUCHIO

    Go, rascals, go and fetch my supper in.

                            Exeunt Servingmen

    He sings

        Where is the life that late I led?

        Where are those –

    Sit down, Kate, and welcome. Food, food, food, food!

    Enter Servants with supper

    Why, when, I say? Nay, good sweet Kate, be merry.

130   Off with my boots, you rogues! You villains, when?

    He sings

        It was the friar of orders grey,

        As he forth walkèd on his way –

    Out, you rogue! You pluck my foot awry.

    He strikes the Servant

    Take that, and mend the plucking off the other.

    Be merry, Kate. Some water here. What ho!

    Enter one with water

    Where's my spaniel Troilus? Sirrah, get you hence,

    And bid my cousin Ferdinand come hither.

                       Exit another Servingman

    One, Kate, that you must kiss and be acquainted with.

    Where are my slippers? Shall I have some water?

140   Come, Kate, and wash, and welcome heartily.

    He knocks the basin out of the Servant's hands

    You whoreson villain, will you let it fall?

He strikes the Servant

KATHERINA

Patience, I pray you, 'twas a fault unwilling.

PETRUCHIO

A whoreson, beetle-headed, flap-eared knave!
Come, Kate, sit down, I know you have a stomach.
Will you give thanks, sweet Kate, or else shall I?
What's this? Mutton?

FIRST SERVINGMAN   Ay.

PETRUCHIO   Who brought it?

PETER   I.

PETRUCHIO

'Tis burnt, and so is all the meat.
What dogs are these! Where is the rascal cook?
How durst you, villains, bring it from the dresser
And serve it thus to me that love it not?   150
There, take it to you, trenchers, cups, and all.
    He throws the food and dishes at them
You heedless joltheads and unmannered slaves!
What, do you grumble? I'll be with you straight.
                              Exeunt Servants hurriedly

KATHERINA

I pray you, husband, be not so disquiet.
The meat was well, if you were so contented.

PETRUCHIO

I tell thee, Kate, 'twas burnt and dried away,
And I expressly am forbid to touch it,
For it engenders choler, planteth anger;
And better 'twere that both of us did fast,
Since, of ourselves, ourselves are choleric,   160
Than feed it with such over-roasted flesh.
Be patient, tomorrow't shall be mended,
And for this night we'll fast for company.
Come, I will bring thee to thy bridal chamber. *Exeunt*

Enter Servants severally

NATHANIEL Peter, didst ever see the like?

PETER He kills her in her own humour.

Enter Curtis

GRUMIO Where is he?

CURTIS

In her chamber,
Making a sermon of continency to her,
And rails, and swears, and rates, that she, poor soul,
Knows not which way to stand, to look, to speak,
And sits as one new-risen from a dream.
Away, away, for he is coming hither.   *Exeunt*

Enter Petruchio

PETRUCHIO

Thus have I politicly begun my reign,
And 'tis my hope to end successfully.
My falcon now is sharp and passing empty,
And till she stoop she must not be full-gorged,
For then she never looks upon her lure.
Another way I have to man my haggard,
To make her come and know her keeper's call,
That is, to watch her, as we watch these kites
That bate and beat and will not be obedient.
She eat no meat today, nor none shall eat.
Last night she slept not, nor tonight she shall not.
As with the meat, some undeservèd fault
I'll find about the making of the bed,
And here I'll fling the pillow, there the bolster,
This way the coverlet, another way the sheets.
Ay, and amid this hurly I intend
That all is done in reverend care of her.
And, in conclusion, she shall watch all night,
And if she chance to nod I'll rail and brawl,
And with the clamour keep her still awake.

This is a way to kill a wife with kindness,
And thus I'll curb her mad and headstrong humour.
He that knows better how to tame a shrew,
Now let him speak – 'tis charity to show.   *Exit*

Enter Tranio as Lucentio, and Hortensio as Licio   **IV.2**

TRANIO

Is't possible, friend Licio, that Mistress Bianca
Doth fancy any other but Lucentio?
I tell you, sir, she bears me fair in hand.

HORTENSIO

Sir, to satisfy you in what I have said,
Stand by and mark the manner of his teaching.
    They stand aside
    Enter Bianca, and Lucentio as Cambio

LUCENTIO

Now, mistress, profit you in what you read?

BIANCA

What, master, read you? First resolve me that.

LUCENTIO

I read that I profess, *The Art to Love*.

BIANCA

And may you prove, sir, master of your art.

LUCENTIO

While you, sweet dear, prove mistress of my heart.   10
    They court each other

HORTENSIO

Quick proceeders, marry! Now tell me, I pray,
You that durst swear that your mistress Bianca
Loved none in the world so well as Lucentio.

TRANIO

O despiteful love, unconstant womankind!
I tell thee, Licio, this is wonderful.

HORTENSIO

    Mistake no more, I am not Licio,

    Nor a musician as I seem to be,

    But one that scorn to live in this disguise

    For such a one as leaves a gentleman

20   And makes a god of such a cullion.

    Know, sir, that I am called Hortensio.

TRANIO

    Signor Hortensio, I have often heard

    Of your entire affection to Bianca,

    And since mine eyes are witness of her lightness,

    I will with you, if you be so contented,

    Forswear Bianca and her love for ever.

HORTENSIO

    See how they kiss and court! Signor Lucentio,

    Here is my hand, and here I firmly vow

    Never to woo her more, but do forswear her,

30   As one unworthy all the former favours

    That I have fondly flattered her withal.

TRANIO

    And here I take the like unfeignèd oath,

    Never to marry with her though she would entreat.

    Fie on her! See how beastly she doth court him.

HORTENSIO

    Would all the world but he had quite forsworn!

    For me, that I may surely keep mine oath,

    I will be married to a wealthy widow

    Ere three days pass, which hath as long loved me

    As I have loved this proud disdainful haggard.

40   And so farewell, Signor Lucentio.

    Kindness in women, not their beauteous looks,

    Shall win my love – and so I take my leave,

    In resolution as I swore before.   *Exit*

      Tranio joins Lucentio and Bianca

TRANIO
  Mistress Bianca, bless you with such grace
  As 'longeth to a lover's blessèd case!
  Nay, I have ta'en you napping, gentle love,
  And have forsworn you with Hortensio.

BIANCA
  Tranio, you jest – but have you both forsworn me?

TRANIO
  Mistress, we have.

LUCENTIO   Then we are rid of Licio.

TRANIO
  I'faith, he'll have a lusty widow now,   50
  That shall be wooed and wedded in a day.

BIANCA
  God give him joy!

TRANIO
  Ay, and he'll tame her.

BIANCA   He says so, Tranio.

TRANIO
  Faith, he is gone unto the taming-school.

BIANCA
  The taming-school? What, is there such a place?

TRANIO
  Ay, mistress, and Petruchio is the master,
  That teacheth tricks eleven and twenty long,
  To tame a shrew and charm her chattering tongue.
    Enter Biondello

BIONDELLO
  O master, master, I have watched so long
  That I'm dog-weary, but at last I spied   60
  An ancient angel coming down the hill
  Will serve the turn.

TRANIO   What is he, Biondello?

BIONDELLO

  Master, a marcantant or a pedant,
  I know not what – but formal in apparel,
  In gait and countenance surely like a father.

LUCENTIO

  And what of him, Tranio?

TRANIO

  If he be credulous and trust my tale,
  I'll make him glad to seem Vincentio,
  And give assurance to Baptista Minola
70 As if he were the right Vincentio.
  Take in your love, and then let me alone.

                          Exeunt Lucentio and Bianca

  Enter a Pedant

PEDANT

  God save you, sir.

TRANIO   And you, sir. You are welcome.
  Travel you farrer on, or are you at the farthest?

PEDANT

  Sir, at the farthest for a week or two,
  But then up farther, and as far as Rome,
  And so to Tripoli, if God lend me life.

TRANIO

  What countryman, I pray?

PEDANT   Of Mantua.

TRANIO

  Of Mantua? Sir, marry, God forbid!
  And come to Padua, careless of your life?

PEDANT

80 My life, sir? How, I pray? For that goes hard.

TRANIO

  'Tis death for any one in Mantua
  To come to Padua. Know you not the cause?
  Your ships are stayed at Venice, and the Duke,

For private quarrel 'twixt your Duke and him,
Hath published and proclaimed it openly.
'Tis marvel – but that you are newly come,
You might have heard it else proclaimed about.

PEDANT

Alas, sir, it is worse for me than so!
For I have bills for money by exchange
From Florence, and must here deliver them.   90

TRANIO

Well, sir, to do you courtesy,
This will I do, and this I will advise you –
First tell me, have you ever been at Pisa?

PEDANT

Ay, sir, in Pisa have I often been,
Pisa renownèd for grave citizens.

TRANIO

Among them know you one Vincentio?

PEDANT

I know him not, but I have heard of him,
A merchant of incomparable wealth.

TRANIO

He is my father, sir, and sooth to say,
In countenance somewhat doth resemble you.   100

BIONDELLO (*aside*) As much as an apple doth an oyster,
and all one.

TRANIO

To save your life in this extremity,
This favour will I do you for his sake –
And think it not the worst of all your fortunes
That you are like to Sir Vincentio –
His name and credit shall you undertake,
And in my house you shall be friendly lodged.
Look that you take upon you as you should.
You understand me, sir. So shall you stay   110

Till you have done your business in the city.
If this be courtesy, sir, accept of it.

PEDANT

O, sir, I do, and will repute you ever
The patron of my life and liberty.

TRANIO

Then go with me to make the matter good.
This, by the way, I let you understand –
My father is here looked for every day
To pass assurance of a dower in marriage
'Twixt me and one Baptista's daughter here.
120   In all these circumstances I'll instruct you.
Go with me, sir, to clothe you as becomes you.

Exeunt

IV.3   *Enter Katherina and Grumio*

GRUMIO

No, no, forsooth, I dare not for my life.

KATHERINA

The more my wrong, the more his spite appears.
What, did he marry me to famish me?
Beggars that come unto my father's door
Upon entreaty have a present alms,
If not, elsewhere they meet with charity.
But I, who never knew how to entreat,
Nor never needed that I should entreat,
Am starved for meat, giddy for lack of sleep,
10   With oaths kept waking, and with brawling fed.
And that which spites me more than all these wants,
He does it under name of perfect love,
As who should say, if I should sleep or eat,
'Twere deadly sickness or else present death.
I prithee go and get me some repast,

I care not what, so it be wholesome food.

GRUMIO

What say you to a neat's foot?

KATHERINA

'Tis passing good, I prithee let me have it.

GRUMIO

I fear it is too choleric a meat.

How say you to a fat tripe finely broiled?   20

KATHERINA

I like it well. Good Grumio, fetch it me.

GRUMIO

I cannot tell, I fear 'tis choleric.

What say you to a piece of beef and mustard?

KATHERINA

A dish that I do love to feed upon.

GRUMIO

Ay, but the mustard is too hot a little.

KATHERINA

Why then, the beef, and let the mustard rest.

GRUMIO

Nay then, I will not. You shall have the mustard,

Or else you get no beef of Grumio.

KATHERINA

Then both, or one, or anything thou wilt.

GRUMIO

Why then, the mustard without the beef.   30

KATHERINA

Go, get thee gone, thou false deluding slave,
  She beats him
That feed'st me with the very name of meat.
Sorrow on thee and all the pack of you
That triumph thus upon my misery!
Go, get thee gone, I say.
  Enter Petruchio and Hortensio with meat

PETRUCHIO
How fares my Kate? What, sweeting, all amort?
HORTENSIO
Mistress, what cheer?
KATHERINA   Faith, as cold as can be.
PETRUCHIO
Pluck up thy spirits, look cheerfully upon me.
Here, love, thou seest how diligent I am,
40 To dress thy meat myself, and bring it thee.
        He sets the dish down
I am sure, sweet Kate, this kindness merits thanks.
What, not a word? Nay then, thou lov'st it not,
And all my pains is sorted to no proof.
Here, take away this dish.
KATHERINA   I pray you, let it stand.
PETRUCHIO
The poorest service is repaid with thanks,
And so shall mine before you touch the meat.
KATHERINA
I thank you, sir.
HORTENSIO
Signor Petruchio, fie, you are to blame.
Come, Mistress Kate, I'll bear you company.
PETRUCHIO (*aside to Hortensio*)
50 Eat it up all, Hortensio, if thou lovest me.
(*To Katherina*) Much good do it unto thy gentle heart!
Kate, eat apace. And now, my honey love,
Will we return unto thy father's house
And revel it as bravely as the best,
With silken coats and caps, and golden rings,
With ruffs and cuffs and farthingales and things,
With scarfs and fans and double change of bravery,
With amber bracelets, beads, and all this knavery.
What, hast thou dined? The tailor stays thy leisure,

To deck thy body with his ruffling treasure.   60
   Enter Tailor
Come, tailor, let us see these ornaments.
Lay forth the gown.
   Enter Haberdasher
                  What news with you, sir?

HABERDASHER
Here is the cap your worship did bespeak.

PETRUCHIO
Why, this was moulded on a porringer –
A velvet dish. Fie, fie, 'tis lewd and filthy!
Why, 'tis a cockle or a walnut-shell,
A knack, a toy, a trick, a baby's cap.
Away with it! Come, let me have a bigger.

KATHERINA
I'll have no bigger. This doth fit the time,
And gentlewomen wear such caps as these.   70

PETRUCHIO
When you are gentle, you shall have one too,
And not till then.

HORTENSIO (*aside*) That will not be in haste.

KATHERINA
Why sir, I trust I may have leave to speak,
And speak I will. I am no child, no babe.
Your betters have endured me say my mind,
And if you cannot, best you stop your ears.
My tongue will tell the anger of my heart,
Or else my heart concealing it will break,
And rather than it shall, I will be free
Even to the uttermost, as I please, in words.   80

PETRUCHIO
Why, thou say'st true – it is a paltry cap,
A custard-coffin, a bauble, a silken pie.
I love thee well in that thou lik'st it not.

KATHERINA

    Love me or love me not, I like the cap,
    And it I will have, or I will have none.

PETRUCHIO

    Thy gown? Why, ay. Come, tailor, let us see't.

                        Exit Haberdasher

    O mercy, God! What masquing stuff is here?
    What's this? A sleeve? 'Tis like a demi-cannon.
    What, up and down carved like an apple-tart?
90   Here's snip and nip and cut and slish and slash,
    Like to a censer in a barber's shop.
    Why, what a devil's name, tailor, call'st thou this?

HORTENSIO (*aside*)

    I see she's like to have neither cap nor gown.

TAILOR

    You bid me make it orderly and well,
    According to the fashion and the time.

PETRUCHIO

    Marry, and did. But if you be remembered,
    I did not bid you mar it to the time.
    Go, hop me over every kennel home,
    For you shall hop without my custom, sir.
100   I'll none of it. Hence, make your best of it.

KATHERINA

    I never saw a better-fashioned gown,
    More quaint, more pleasing, nor more commendable.
    Belike you mean to make a puppet of me.

PETRUCHIO

    Why, true, he means to make a puppet of thee.

TAILOR

    She says your worship means to make a puppet of her.

PETRUCHIO

    O monstrous arrogance! Thou liest, thou thread, thou
       thimble,

Thou yard, three-quarters, half-yard, quarter, nail,
Thou flea, thou nit, thou winter-cricket thou!
Braved in mine own house with a skein of thread?
Away, thou rag, thou quantity, thou remnant,   110
Or I shall so bemete thee with thy yard
As thou shalt think on prating whilst thou liv'st.
I tell thee, I, that thou hast marred her gown.

TAILOR
Your worship is deceived – the gown is made
Just as my master had direction.
Grumio gave order how it should be done.

GRUMIO I gave him no order, I gave him the stuff.

TAILOR
But how did you desire it should be made?

GRUMIO Marry, sir, with needle and thread.

TAILOR
But did you not request to have it cut?   120

GRUMIO Thou hast faced many things.

TAILOR I have.

GRUMIO Face not me. Thou hast braved many men, brave
not me. I will neither be faced nor braved. I say unto
thee, I bid thy master cut out the gown, but I did not
bid him cut it to pieces. Ergo, thou liest.

TAILOR Why, here is the note of the fashion to testify.

PETRUCHIO Read it.

GRUMIO The note lies in's throat, if he say I said so.

TAILOR (reads) 'Imprimis, a loose-bodied gown.'   130

GRUMIO Master, if ever I said loose-bodied gown, sew me
in the skirts of it and beat me to death with a bottom of
brown thread. I said a gown.

PETRUCHIO Proceed.

TAILOR 'With a small compassed cape.'

GRUMIO I confess the cape.

TAILOR 'With a trunk sleeve.'

GRUMIO I confess two sleeves.

TAILOR 'The sleeves curiously cut.'

140 PETRUCHIO Ay, there's the villainy.

GRUMIO Error i'th'bill, sir, error i'th'bill! I commanded
   the sleeves should be cut out, and sewed up again; and
   that I'll prove upon thee, though thy little finger be
   armed in a thimble.

TAILOR This is true that I say; an I had thee in place
   where, thou shouldst know it.

GRUMIO I am for thee straight. Take thou the bill, give
   me thy mete-yard, and spare not me.

HORTENSIO God-a-mercy, Grumio, then he shall have no
150   odds.

PETRUCHIO Well sir, in brief, the gown is not for me.

GRUMIO You are i'th'right, sir, 'tis for my mistress.

PETRUCHIO Go, take it up unto thy master's use.

GRUMIO Villain, not for thy life! Take up my mistress'
   gown for thy master's use!

PETRUCHIO Why sir, what's your conceit in that?

GRUMIO
   O sir, the conceit is deeper than you think for.
   Take up my mistress' gown to his master's use!
   O fie, fie, fie!

PETRUCHIO (aside)
160   Hortensio, say thou wilt see the tailor paid.
   (To the Tailor) Go take it hence, be gone, and say no more.

HORTENSIO (aside)
   Tailor, I'll pay thee for thy gown tomorrow.
   Take no unkindness of his hasty words.
   Away, I say, commend me to thy master.   Exit Tailor

PETRUCHIO
   Well, come my Kate, we will unto your father's
   Even in these honest mean habiliments.
   Our purses shall be proud, our garments poor,

For 'tis the mind that makes the body rich,
And as the sun breaks through the darkest clouds,
So honour peereth in the meanest habit.   170
What, is the jay more precious than the lark
Because his feathers are more beautiful?
Or is the adder better than the eel
Because his painted skin contents the eye?
O no, good Kate, neither art thou the worse
For this poor furniture and mean array.
If thou account'st it shame, lay it on me.
And therefore frolic. We will hence forthwith
To feast and sport us at thy father's house.
(*To Grumio*) Go call my men, and let us straight to him,   180
And bring our horses unto Long-lane end,
There will we mount, and thither walk on foot.
Let's see, I think 'tis now some seven o'clock,
And well we may come there by dinner-time.

KATHERINA

I dare assure you, sir, 'tis almost two,
And 'twill be supper-time ere you come there.

PETRUCHIO

It shall be seven ere I go to horse.
Look what I speak, or do, or think to do,
You are still crossing it. Sirs, let't alone,
I will not go today, and ere I do,   190
It shall be what o'clock I say it is.

HORTENSIO

Why, so this gallant will command the sun.   *Exeunt*

Enter Tranio as Lucentio, and the Pedant, booted,   **IV.4**
and dressed like Vincentio

TRANIO

Sir, this is the house – please it you that I call?

PEDANT

Ay, what else? And but I be deceived
Signor Baptista may remember me
Near twenty years ago in Genoa,
Where we were lodgers at the Pegasus.

TRANIO

'Tis well, and hold your own, in any case,
With such austerity as 'longeth to a father.
    Enter Biondello

PEDANT

I warrant you. But sir, here comes your boy.
'Twere good he were schooled.

TRANIO

10   Fear you not him. Sirrah Biondello,
Now do your duty throughly, I advise you.
Imagine 'twere the right Vincentio.

BIONDELLO

Tut, fear not me.

TRANIO

But hast thou done thy errand to Baptista?

BIONDELLO

I told him that your father was at Venice,
And that you looked for him this day in Padua.

TRANIO

Th'art a tall fellow, hold thee that to drink.
    Enter Baptista, and Lucentio as Cambio
Here comes Baptista. Set your countenance, sir.
Signor Baptista, you are happily met.
20   (*To the Pedant*) Sir, this is the gentleman I told you of.
I pray you stand good father to me now,
Give me Bianca for my patrimony.

PEDANT

Soft, son!
Sir, by your leave, having come to Padua

To gather in some debts, my son Lucentio
Made me acquainted with a weighty cause
Of love between your daughter and himself.
And – for the good report I hear of you,
And for the love he beareth to your daughter,
And she to him – to stay him not too long,   30
I am content, in a good father's care,
To have him matched; and, if you please to like
No worse than I, upon some agreement
Me shall you find ready and willing
With one consent to have her so bestowed.
For curious I cannot be with you,
Signor Baptista, of whom I hear so well.

BAPTISTA

Sir, pardon me in what I have to say.
Your plainness and your shortness please me well.
Right true it is your son Lucentio here   40
Doth love my daughter, and she loveth him,
Or both dissemble deeply their affections.
And therefore if you say no more than this,
That like a father you will deal with him,
And pass my daughter a sufficient dower,
The match is made, and all is done –
Your son shall have my daughter with consent.

TRANIO

I thank you, sir. Where then do you know best
We be affied and such assurance ta'en
As shall with either part's agreement stand?   50

BAPTISTA

Not in my house, Lucentio, for you know
Pitchers have ears, and I have many servants.
Besides, old Gremio is hearkening still,
And happily we might be interrupted.

TRANIO
    Then at my lodging, an it like you.
    There doth my father lie; and there this night
    We'll pass the business privately and well.
    Send for your daughter by your servant here.
       He winks at Lucentio
    My boy shall fetch the scrivener presently.
60   The worst is this, that at so slender warning
    You are like to have a thin and slender pittance.
BAPTISTA
    It likes me well. Cambio, hie you home,
    And bid Bianca make her ready straight.
    And, if you will, tell what hath happenèd –
    Lucentio's father is arrived in Padua,
    And how she's like to be Lucentio's wife. *Exit Lucentio*
BIONDELLO
    I pray the gods she may, with all my heart.
TRANIO
    Dally not with the gods, but get thee gone.
                             Exit Biondello

    Enter Peter, a Servingman
    Signor Baptista, shall I lead the way?
70   Welcome! One mess is like to be your cheer.
    Come sir, we will better it in Pisa.
BAPTISTA
    I follow you.   *Exeunt*
    Enter Lucentio and Biondello
BIONDELLO
    Cambio.
LUCENTIO What say'st thou, Biondello?
BIONDELLO
    You saw my master wink and laugh upon you?
LUCENTIO Biondello, what of that?
BIONDELLO Faith, nothing – but 'has left me here behind
    to expound the meaning or moral of his signs and tokens.

LUCENTIO I pray thee moralize them.

BIONDELLO Then thus – Baptista is safe, talking with the
deceiving father of a deceitful son.   80

LUCENTIO And what of him?

BIONDELLO His daughter is to be brought by you to the
supper.

LUCENTIO And then?

BIONDELLO The old priest at Saint Luke's church is at
your command at all hours.

LUCENTIO And what of all this?

BIONDELLO I cannot tell, except they are busied about a
counterfeit assurance. Take you assurance of her, *cum
privilegio ad imprimendum solum*. To th'church! Take   90
the priest, clerk, and some sufficient honest witnesses.
If this be not that you look for, I have no more to say,
But bid Bianca farewell for ever and a day.

He turns to go

LUCENTIO Hear'st thou, Biondello?

BIONDELLO I cannot tarry. I knew a wench married in an
afternoon as she went to the garden for parsley to stuff a
rabbit. And so may you, sir; and so adieu, sir. My master
hath appointed me to go to Saint Luke's to bid the
priest be ready to come against you come with your
appendix.   *Exit*   100

LUCENTIO

I may and will, if she be so contented.
She will be pleased, then wherefore should I doubt?
Hap what hap may, I'll roundly go about her.
It shall go hard if Cambio go without her.   *Exit*

Enter Petruchio, Katherina, Hortensio and Servants   IV.5

PETRUCHIO

Come on, a God's name, once more toward our father's.
Good Lord, how bright and goodly shines the moon!

KATHERINA

The moon? The sun! It is not moonlight now.

PETRUCHIO

I say it is the moon that shines so bright.

KATHERINA

I know it is the sun that shines so bright.

PETRUCHIO

Now by my mother's son, and that's myself,
It shall be moon, or star, or what I list,
Or e'er I journey to your father's house.
(*To the Servants*) Go on and fetch our horses back again.
10   Evermore crossed and crossed, nothing but crossed!

HORTENSIO

Say as he says, or we shall never go.

KATHERINA

Forward, I pray, since we have come so far,
And be it moon, or sun, or what you please.
And if you please to call it a rush-candle,
Henceforth I vow it shall be so for me.

PETRUCHIO

I say it is the moon.

KATHERINA   I know it is the moon.

PETRUCHIO

Nay, then you lie. It is the blessèd sun.

KATHERINA

Then, God be blessed, it is the blessèd sun.
But sun it is not, when you say it is not,
20   And the moon changes even as your mind.
What you will have it named, even that it is,
And so it shall be so for Katherine.

HORTENSIO (*aside*)

Petruchio, go thy ways, the field is won.

PETRUCHIO

Well, forward, forward! Thus the bowl should run,

And not unluckily against the bias.
But soft, company is coming here.
    Enter Vincentio
(*To Vincentio*) Good morrow, gentle mistress, where
        away?
Tell me, sweet Kate, and tell me truly too,
Hast thou beheld a fresher gentlewoman?
Such war of white and red within her cheeks!   30
What stars do spangle heaven with such beauty
As those two eyes become that heavenly face?
Fair lovely maid, once more good day to thee.
Sweet Kate, embrace her for her beauty's sake.

HORTENSIO (*aside*) 'A will make the man mad, to make the
    woman of him.

KATHERINA
Young budding virgin, fair and fresh and sweet,
Whither away, or where is thy abode?
Happy the parents of so fair a child,
Happier the man whom favourable stars   40
Allots thee for his lovely bedfellow.

PETRUCHIO
Why, how now, Kate, I hope thou art not mad!
This is a man, old, wrinkled, faded, withered,
And not a maiden, as thou say'st he is.

KATHERINA
Pardon, old father, my mistaking eyes,
That have been so bedazzled with the sun
That everything I look on seemeth green.
Now I perceive thou art a reverend father.
Pardon, I pray thee, for my mad mistaking.

PETRUCHIO
Do, good old grandsire, and withal make known   50
Which way thou travellest – if along with us,
We shall be joyful of thy company.

VINCENTIO

    Fair sir, and you my merry mistress,

    That with your strange encounter much amazed me,

    My name is called Vincentio, my dwelling Pisa,

    And bound I am to Padua, there to visit

    A son of mine, which long I have not seen.

PETRUCHIO

    What is his name?

VINCENTIO   Lucentio, gentle sir.

PETRUCHIO

    Happily met – the happier for thy son.

60   And now by law, as well as reverend age,

    I may entitle thee my loving father.

    The sister to my wife, this gentlewoman,

    Thy son by this hath married. Wonder not,

    Nor be not grieved – she is of good esteem,

    Her dowry wealthy, and of worthy birth,

    Beside, so qualified as may beseem

    The spouse of any noble gentleman.

    Let me embrace with old Vincentio,

    And wander we to see thy honest son,

70   Who will of thy arrival be full joyous.

VINCENTIO

    But is this true, or is it else your pleasure,

    Like pleasant travellers, to break a jest

    Upon the company you overtake?

HORTENSIO

    I do assure thee, father, so it is.

PETRUCHIO

    Come, go along and see the truth hereof,

    For our first merriment hath made thee jealous.

                         Exeunt all but Hortensio

HORTENSIO

    Well, Petruchio, this has put me in heart.

Have to my widow! And if she be froward,
Then hast thou taught Hortensio to be untoward. *Exit*

*

Enter Biondello, Lucentio as himself, and Bianca.   V.I
Gremio is out before

BIONDELLO Softly and swiftly, sir, for the priest is ready.
LUCENTIO I fly, Biondello. But they may chance to need
thee at home, therefore leave us.
                                        Exeunt Lucentio and Bianca
BIONDELLO Nay, faith, I'll see the church a your back,
and then come back to my master's as soon as I can.
                                                                Exit

GREMIO
I marvel Cambio comes not all this while.
    Enter Petruchio, Katherina, Vincentio and Grumio,
    with attendants

PETRUCHIO
Sir, here's the door, this is Lucentio's house.
My father's bears more toward the market-place.
Thither must I, and here I leave you, sir.

VINCENTIO
You shall not choose but drink before you go.   10
I think I shall command your welcome here,
And by all likelihood some cheer is toward.
    He knocks

GREMIO They're busy within. You were best knock louder.
    More knocking
    Pedant looks out of the window

PEDANT What's he that knocks as he would beat down the
gate?

VINCENTIO Is Signor Lucentio within, sir?

PEDANT He's within, sir, but not to be spoken withal.

VINCENTIO What if a man bring him a hundred pound or
two to make merry withal?

20 PEDANT Keep your hundred pounds to yourself. He shall
need none so long as I live.

PETRUCHIO Nay, I told you your son was well beloved in
Padua. Do you hear, sir? To leave frivolous circumstances, I pray you tell Signor Lucentio that his father is
come from Pisa, and is here at the door to speak with
him.

PEDANT Thou liest. His father is come from Mantua, and
here looking out at the window.

VINCENTIO Art thou his father?

30 PEDANT Ay sir, so his mother says, if I may believe her.

PETRUCHIO (*to Vincentio*) Why how now, gentleman!
Why, this is flat knavery, to take upon you another man's
name.

PEDANT Lay hands on the villain. I believe 'a means to
cozen somebody in this city under my countenance.

Enter Biondello

BIONDELLO (*aside*) I have seen them in the church together. God send 'em good shipping! But who is here?
Mine old master Vincentio! Now we are undone and
brought to nothing.

40 VINCENTIO (*seeing Biondello*) Come hither, crack-hemp.

BIONDELLO I hope I may choose, sir.

VINCENTIO Come hither, you rogue. What, have you forgot me?

BIONDELLO Forgot you? No, sir. I could not forget you,
for I never saw you before in all my life.

VINCENTIO What, you notorious villain, didst thou never
see thy master's father, Vincentio?

BIONDELLO What, my old worshipful old master? Yes,

marry, sir – see where he looks out of the window.

VINCENTIO Is't so, indeed?   50

He beats Biondello

BIONDELLO Help, help, help! Here's a madman will
murder me.   *Exit*

PEDANT Help, son! Help, Signor Baptista!

Exit from the window

PETRUCHIO Prithee, Kate, let's stand aside and see the
end of this controversy.

They stand aside
*Enter Pedant below, with Servants, Baptista, and
Tranio*

TRANIO Sir, what are you that offer to beat my servant?

VINCENTIO What am I, sir? Nay, what are you, sir? O
immortal gods! O fine villain! A silken doublet, a velvet
hose, a scarlet cloak, and a copatain hat! O, I am undone,
I am undone! While I play the good husband at home,   60
my son and my servant spend all at the university.

TRANIO How now, what's the matter?

BAPTISTA What, is the man lunatic?

TRANIO Sir, you seem a sober ancient gentleman by your
habit, but your words show you a madman. Why, sir,
what 'cerns it you if I wear pearl and gold? I thank my
good father, I am able to maintain it.

VINCENTIO Thy father? O villain, he is a sail-maker in
Bergamo.

BAPTISTA You mistake, sir, you mistake, sir. Pray, what   70
do you think is his name?

VINCENTIO His name? As if I knew not his name! I have
brought him up ever since he was three years old, and
his name is Tranio.

PEDANT Away, away, mad ass! His name is Lucentio, and
he is mine only son, and heir to the lands of me, Signor
Vincentio.

VINCENTIO Lucentio? O, he hath murdered his master!
Lay hold on him, I charge you, in the Duke's name. O,
my son, my son! Tell me, thou villain, where is my son
Lucentio?

TRANIO Call forth an officer.

Enter an Officer

Carry this mad knave to the gaol. Father Baptista, I
charge you see that he be forthcoming.

VINCENTIO Carry me to the gaol?

GREMIO Stay, officer. He shall not go to prison.

BAPTISTA Talk not, Signor Gremio. I say he shall go to
prison.

GREMIO Take heed, Signor Baptista, lest you be cony-
catched in this business. I dare swear this is the right
Vincentio.

PEDANT Swear if thou dar'st.

GREMIO Nay, I dare not swear it.

TRANIO Then thou wert best say that I am not Lucentio.

GREMIO Yes, I know thee to be Signor Lucentio.

BAPTISTA Away with the dotard, to the gaol with him!

VINCENTIO Thus strangers may be haled and abused. O
monstrous villain!

Enter Biondello, with Lucentio and Bianca

BIONDELLO O, we are spoiled, and yonder he is! Deny
him, forswear him, or else we are all undone.

LUCENTIO (*kneeling*)
Pardon, sweet father.

VINCENTIO   Lives my sweet son?

Exeunt Biondello, Tranio and Pedant, as fast as may be

BIANCA
Pardon, dear father.

BAPTISTA   How hast thou offended?
Where is Lucentio?

LUCENTIO   Here's Lucentio,

Right son to the right Vincentio,
That have by marriage made thy daughter mine,
While counterfeit supposes bleared thine eyne.

GREMIO
Here's packing, with a witness, to deceive us all.

VINCENTIO
Where is that damnèd villain, Tranio,
That faced and braved me in this matter so?

BAPTISTA
Why, tell me, is not this my Cambio?   110

BIANCA
Cambio is changed into Lucentio.

LUCENTIO
Love wrought these miracles. Bianca's love
Made me exchange my state with Tranio,
While he did bear my countenance in the town,
And happily I have arrived at last
Unto the wishèd haven of my bliss.
What Tranio did, myself enforced him to;
Then pardon him, sweet father, for my sake.

VINCENTIO I'll slit the villain's nose that would have sent
me to the gaol.   120

BAPTISTA (*to Lucentio*) But do you hear, sir? Have you
married my daughter without asking my good will?

VINCENTIO Fear not, Baptista, we will content you, go to.
But I will in to be revenged for this villainy.   *Exit*

BAPTISTA And I to sound the depth of this knavery.
Exit

LUCENTIO Look not pale, Bianca – thy father will not
frown.   *Exeunt Lucentio and Bianca*

GREMIO
My cake is dough, but I'll in among the rest,
Out of hope of all but my share of the feast.   *Exit*

130 KATHERINA Husband, let's follow to see the end of this
ado.

PETRUCHIO First kiss me, Kate, and we will.

KATHERINA What, in the midst of the street?

PETRUCHIO What, art thou ashamed of me?

KATHERINA No, sir, God forbid – but ashamed to kiss.

PETRUCHIO

Why then, let's home again.

(*To Grumio*) Come, sirrah, let's away.

KATHERINA

Nay, I will give thee a kiss.

She kisses him

Now pray thee, love, stay.

PETRUCHIO

140 Is not this well? Come, my sweet Kate.

Better once than never, for never too late.

Exeunt

V.2   *Enter Baptista with Vincentio, Gremio with the*
Pedant, Lucentio with Bianca, Petruchio with
Katherina, Hortensio with the Widow; followed by
Tranio, Biondello, and Grumio, with the Servingmen
bringing in a banquet

LUCENTIO

At last, though long, our jarring notes agree,

And time it is when raging war is done

To smile at scapes and perils overblown.

My fair Bianca, bid my father welcome,

While I with self-same kindness welcome thine.

Brother Petruchio, sister Katherina,

And thou, Hortensio, with thy loving widow,

Feast with the best, and welcome to my house.

My banquet is to close our stomachs up

After our great good cheer. Pray you, sit down,   10
For now we sit to chat as well as eat.

They sit

PETRUCHIO
Nothing but sit and sit, and eat and eat!

BAPTISTA
Padua affords this kindness, son Petruchio.

PETRUCHIO
Padua affords nothing but what is kind.

HORTENSIO
For both our sakes I would that word were true.

PETRUCHIO
Now, for my life, Hortensio fears his widow.

WIDOW
Then never trust me if I be afeard.

PETRUCHIO
You are very sensible, and yet you miss my sense:
I mean Hortensio is afeard of you.

WIDOW
He that is giddy thinks the world turns round.   20

PETRUCHIO
Roundly replied.

KATHERINA   Mistress, how mean you that?

WIDOW
Thus I conceive by him.

PETRUCHIO
Conceives by me! How likes Hortensio that?

HORTENSIO
My widow says thus she conceives her tale.

PETRUCHIO
Very well mended. Kiss him for that, good widow.

KATHERINA
'He that is giddy thinks the world turns round' –
I pray you tell me what you meant by that.

WIDOW
    Your husband, being troubled with a shrew,
    Measures my husband's sorrow by his woe.
30 And now you know my meaning.
KATHERINA
    A very mean meaning.
WIDOW   Right, I mean you.
KATHERINA
    And I am mean, indeed, respecting you.
PETRUCHIO
    To her, Kate!
HORTENSIO
    To her, widow!
PETRUCHIO
    A hundred marks, my Kate does put her down.
HORTENSIO
    That's my office.
PETRUCHIO
    Spoke like an officer – ha' to thee, lad.
        He drinks to Hortensio
BAPTISTA
    How likes Gremio these quick-witted folks?
GREMIO
    Believe me, sir, they butt together well.
BIANCA
40 Head and butt! An hasty-witted body
    Would say your head and butt were head and horn.
VINCENTIO
    Ay, mistress bride, hath that awakened you?
BIANCA
    Ay, but not frighted me, therefore I'll sleep again.
PETRUCHIO
    Nay, that you shall not. Since you have begun,
    Have at you for a bitter jest or two.

BIANCA

Am I your bird? I mean to shift my bush,
And then pursue me as you draw your bow.
You are welcome all.

Exeunt Bianca, Katherina, and Widow

PETRUCHIO

She hath prevented me. Here, Signor Tranio,
This bird you aimed at, though you hit her not —   50
Therefore a health to all that shot and missed.

TRANIO

O sir, Lucentio slipped me like his greyhound,
Which runs himself, and catches for his master.

PETRUCHIO

A good swift simile, but something currish.

TRANIO

'Tis well, sir, that you hunted for yourself.
'Tis thought your deer does hold you at a bay.

BAPTISTA

O, O, Petruchio! Tranio hits you now.

LUCENTIO

I thank thee for that gird, good Tranio.

HORTENSIO

Confess, confess, hath he not hit you here?

PETRUCHIO

'A has a little galled me, I confess;   60
And as the jest did glance away from me,
'Tis ten to one it maimed you two outright.

BAPTISTA

Now, in good sadness, son Petruchio,
I think thou hast the veriest shrew of all.

PETRUCHIO

Well, I say no. And therefore for assurance
Let's each one send unto his wife,
And he whose wife is most obedient,

To come at first when he doth send for her,
Shall win the wager which we will propose.

HORTENSIO

70   Content. What's the wager?

LUCENTIO   Twenty crowns.

PETRUCHIO

Twenty crowns?
I'll venture so much of my hawk or hound,
But twenty times so much upon my wife.

LUCENTIO

A hundred then.

HORTENSIO   Content.

PETRUCHIO   A match! 'Tis done.

HORTENSIO

Who shall begin?

LUCENTIO   That will I. Biondello,
Go bid your mistress come to me.

BIONDELLO   I go.   *Exit*

BAPTISTA

Son, I'll be your half Bianca comes.

LUCENTIO

I'll have no halves. I'll bear it all myself.
    Enter Biondello
How now, what news?

BIONDELLO   Sir, my mistress sends you word

80   That she is busy and she cannot come.

PETRUCHIO

How? She's busy, and she cannot come!
Is that an answer?

GREMIO   Ay, and a kind one too.
Pray God, sir, your wife send you not a worse.

PETRUCHIO

I hope better.

HORTENSIO
Sirrah Biondello, go and entreat my wife
To come to me forthwith.   *Exit Biondello*

PETRUCHIO   O ho, entreat her!
Nay, then she must needs come.

HORTENSIO   I am afraid, sir,
Do what you can, yours will not be entreated.
      Enter Biondello
Now, where's my wife?

BIONDELLO
She says you have some goodly jest in hand.   90
She will not come. She bids you come to her.

PETRUCHIO
Worse and worse, she will not come! O vile,
Intolerable, not to be endured!
Sirrah Grumio, go to your mistress,
Say I command her come to me.   *Exit Grumio*

HORTENSIO
I know her answer.

PETRUCHIO   What?

HORTENSIO   She will not.

PETRUCHIO
The fouler fortune mine, and there an end.
      Enter Katherina

BAPTISTA
Now, by my holidame, here comes Katherina.

KATHERINA
What is your will, sir, that you send for me?

PETRUCHIO
Where is your sister, and Hortensio's wife?   100

KATHERINA
They sit conferring by the parlour fire.

PETRUCHIO
Go fetch them hither. If they deny to come,

Swinge me them soundly forth unto their husbands.
Away, I say, and bring them hither straight.

Exit Katherina

LUCENTIO
Here is a wonder, if you talk of a wonder.

HORTENSIO
And so it is. I wonder what it bodes.

PETRUCHIO
Marry, peace it bodes, and love, and quiet life,
An awful rule, and right supremacy,
And, to be short, what not that's sweet and happy.

BAPTISTA
110   Now fair befall thee, good Petruchio!
The wager thou hast won, and I will add
Unto their losses twenty thousand crowns –
Another dowry to another daughter,
For she is changed, as she had never been.

PETRUCHIO
Nay, I will win my wager better yet,
And show more sign of her obedience,
Her new-built virtue and obedience.

Enter Katherina with Bianca and Widow

See where she comes, and brings your froward wives
As prisoners to her womanly persuasion.
120   Katherine, that cap of yours becomes you not.
Off with that bauble, throw it under foot.

She obeys

WIDOW
Lord, let me never have a cause to sigh
Till I be brought to such a silly pass!

BIANCA
Fie, what a foolish duty call you this?

LUCENTIO
I would your duty were as foolish too!

The wisdom of your duty, fair Bianca,
Hath cost me a hundred crowns since supper-time.

BIANCA
The more fool you for laying on my duty.

PETRUCHIO
Katherine, I charge thee, tell these headstrong women
What duty they do owe their lords and husbands.   130

WIDOW
Come, come, you're mocking. We will have no telling.

PETRUCHIO
Come on, I say, and first begin with her.

WIDOW
She shall not.

PETRUCHIO
I say she shall. And first begin with her.

KATHERINA
Fie, fie, unknit that threatening unkind brow,
And dart not scornful glances from those eyes
To wound thy lord, thy king, thy governor.
It blots thy beauty as frosts do bite the meads,
Confounds thy fame as whirlwinds shake fair buds,
And in no sense is meet or amiable.   140
A woman moved is like a fountain troubled,
Muddy, ill-seeming, thick, bereft of beauty,
And while it is so, none so dry or thirsty
Will deign to sip or touch one drop of it.
Thy husband is thy lord, thy life, thy keeper,
Thy head, thy sovereign; one that cares for thee,
And for thy maintenance; commits his body
To painful labour both by sea and land,
To watch the night in storms, the day in cold,
Whilst thou liest warm at home, secure and safe;   150
And craves no other tribute at thy hands
But love, fair looks, and true obedience –

Too little payment for so great a debt.
Such duty as the subject owes the prince,
Even such a woman oweth to her husband.
And when she is froward, peevish, sullen, sour,
And not obedient to his honest will,
What is she but a foul contending rebel
And graceless traitor to her loving lord?
160   I am ashamed that women are so simple
To offer war where they should kneel for peace,
Or seek for rule, supremacy, and sway,
When they are bound to serve, love, and obey.
Why are our bodies soft, and weak, and smooth,
Unapt to toil and trouble in the world,
But that our soft conditions and our hearts
Should well agree with our external parts?
Come, come, you froward and unable worms,
My mind hath been as big as one of yours,
170   My heart as great, my reason haply more,
To bandy word for word and frown for frown.
But now I see our lances are but straws,
Our strength as weak, our weakness past compare,
That seeming to be most which we indeed least are.
Then vail your stomachs, for it is no boot,
And place your hands below your husband's foot.
In token of which duty, if he please,
My hand is ready, may it do him ease.

PETRUCHIO
Why, there's a wench! Come on, and kiss me, Kate.

LUCENTIO
180   Well, go thy ways, old lad, for thou shalt ha't.

VINCENTIO
'Tis a good hearing when children are toward.

LUCENTIO
But a harsh hearing when women are froward.

PETRUCHIO

  Come, Kate, we'll to bed.

  We three are married, but you two are sped.

  (*To Lucentio*) 'Twas I won the wager, though you hit
     the white,

  And being a winner, God give you good night!

                    Exeunt Petruchio and Katherina

HORTENSIO

  Now go thy ways, thou hast tamed a curst shrew.

LUCENTIO

  'Tis a wonder, by your leave, she will be tamed so.

                                Exeunt

The Sly Scenes in
The Taming of A Shrew

In *The Taming of A Shrew* Christopher Sly is involved in the action, after the Induction is over, on five subsequent occasions. Pope inserted these passages into his edition of Shakespeare's play, and many producers have found them irresistible. They are, therefore, given here.

(i) Occurring at a point for which there is no precise equivalent in *The Taming of the Shrew*, this intervention by Sly would, if used in a modern production of Shakespeare's play, best come at the end of II.1.

SLY Sim, when will the fool [Sander, the equivalent of Grumio] come again?
LORD He'll come again, my lord, anon.
SLY Gi's some more drink here. Zounds, where's the tapster? Here, Sim, eat some of these things.
LORD So I do, my lord.
SLY Here, Sim, I drink to thee.
LORD My lord, here comes the players again.
SLY O brave! Here's two fine gentlewomen.

(ii) Sly's next intervention comes between the end of IV.4 and the beginning of IV.5, the scene in which Petruchio and Katherina dispute about the sun and the moon. Polidor

and Aurelius have just gone off to marry Emelia and
Phylema.

SLY Sim, must they be married now?
LORD Ay, my lord.
    Enter Ferando and Kate and Sander
SLY Look, Sim, the fool is come again now.

(iii) Sly is at his most lordly on the final occasion that he
intrudes on the play that is being performed for his benefit.
This happens at V.1.101 of Shakespeare's play, the stage
direction with which the passage opens coinciding exactly
with his direction *Exeunt Biondello, Tranio and Pedant,
as fast as may be*. The Duke of Cestus has just given orders
that the impostors, Phylotus and Valeria, should be sent
to prison.

                    Phylotus and Valeria run away
    Then Sly speaks
SLY I say we'll have no sending to prison.
LORD My lord, this is but the play, they're but in jest.
SLY I tell thee, Sim, we'll have no sending to prison, that's
    flat. Why, Sim, am I not Don Christo Vary? Therefore
    I say they shall not go to prison.
LORD No more they shall not, my lord. They be run away.
SLY Are they run away, Sim? That's well. Then gi's some
    more drink, and let them play again.
LORD Here, my lord.
    Sly drinks and then falls asleep

(iv) Between the end of V.1 and the beginning of V.2 Sly
is removed.

                                                Exeunt omnes

    Sly sleeps

LORD

    Who's within there? Come hither, sirs.
    Enter Servants

                          My lord's
    Asleep again. Go take him easily up,
    And put him in his own apparel again,
    And lay him in the place where we did find him,
    Just underneath the alehouse side below,
    But see you wake him not in any case.

BOY It shall be done, my lord. Come help to bear him
    hence.

(v) When the play proper is over, and all the characters
have left the stage, this follows:

    Then enter two bearing of Sly in his own apparel again,
    and leave him where they found him, and then go out.
    Then enter the Tapster

TAPSTER

    Now that the darksome night is overpast,
    And dawning day appears in crystal sky,
    Now must I haste abroad. But soft, who's this?
    What, Sly? O wondrous! Hath he lain here all night?
    I'll wake him. I think he's starved by this,
    But that his belly was so stuffed with ale.
    What ho, Sly! Awake for shame.

SLY Sim, gi's some more wine. What's all the players gone?
    Am not I a lord?

TAPSTER A lord, with a murrain. Come, art thou drunken still?

SLY Who's this? Tapster! O Lord, sirrah, I have had the bravest dream tonight that ever thou heardest in all thy life.

TAPSTER Ay, marry, but you had best get you home, for your wife will course [thrash] you for dreaming here tonight.

SLY Will she? I know now how to tame a shrew. I dreamt upon it all this night till now, and thou hast waked me out of the best dream that ever I had in my life. But I'll to my wife presently, and tame her too an if she anger me.

TAPSTER

Nay tarry, Sly, for I'll go home with thee,
And hear the rest that thou hast dreamt tonight.

Exeunt omnes

An Account of the Text

In 1594 a quarto was published entitled *A Pleasant Conceited Historie, called The taming of a Shrew. As it was sundry times acted by the Right honorable the Earle of Pembrook his seruants.* This volume, however, though it was regarded by the publishing trade throughout the rest of Shakespeare's life and, indeed, even as late as 1631, as being commercially identical with *The Taming of the Shrew*, has, it is generally agreed, no authority whatever. The exact nature of its relationship to Shakespeare's play is still a matter of dispute – in the view of the present editor it is essentially a 'bad quarto', a very garbled version of the original, put together, probably by an actor or actors, from memory, eked out by extensive patches of verse culled from *Dr Faustus* and *Tamburlaine* – but the crucial point is that, no matter what its origin, it does not go back for its text to a Shakespeare manuscript, or to any copy of such a manuscript. In these circumstances, the sole primary text of the play is that given in the Folio of 1623 (F), where it was printed for the first time.

It is very difficult to determine the kind of copy that the printers of F had at their disposal when they came to set up this particular play. It cannot have been the prompt book used in the playhouse, because neither entrances nor exits are properly or adequately marked. To take a glaring example, the stage direction at the opening of V.2 reads as follows: *Enter Baptista, Vincentio, Gremio, the Pedant, Lucentio, and Bianca. Tranio, Biondello Grumio, and Widdow: The Seruingmen with Tranio bringing in a Banquet.* Tranio, who has only four lines to speak, is mentioned twice, while Petruchio and Katherina, much the most important characters in the scene, are not mentioned at all, nor is Hortensio. As a direction to the actors, this is quite useless. Other instances of entrances and exits that have been omitted will be found in the Commentary. Furthermore, the causes that have led to the muddles about who says what, which occur at III.1.46–56 and at IV.2.4–8, would, of necessity, have been cleared up in a prompt book.

It seems equally impossible that the text can have been set entirely from the author's manuscript. The stage direction at IV.2.5, *Enter Bianca.*, instead of *Enter Bianca and Lucentio*, which is what is required, must be the work of someone who has been misled by the wrong assigning of lines 4 and 5 to *Luc.* into thinking that Lucentio is already on stage. The curious stage direction at the beginning of V.1, *Enter Biondello, Lucentio and Bianca, Gremio is out before.*, is also suspect. The last four words in it, meaning that Gremio comes on before the other three characters, look distinctly like an afterthought by someone, evidently not the author, who has discovered, on reaching line 6, that Gremio has been on stage all the time, though hitherto he has said nothing. Yet there are other features that do point to the author's manuscript. Some of the stage directions are, from a purely theatrical point of view, unnecessarily elaborate and descriptive, rather as though Shakespeare is reminding himself of who is who; which is what he seems to be doing at I.1.45, where we find *Enter Baptista with his two daughters, Katerina & Bianca, Gremio a Pantelowne, Hortentio sister* [for *suitor*] *to Bianca. Lucen. Tranio, stand by*. Other directions are of the vague and indefinite sort normal in a manuscript draft, such as *Enter foure or fiue seruingmen.* at IV.1.94. It is the Servingmen's first entrance and Shakespeare has not yet made up his mind how many of them he will need.

The most attractive theory to account for, and even to reconcile, these contradictory kinds of evidence (the one pointing to some sort of outside interference with Shakespeare's manuscript and the other to that manuscript itself) is the view that what the printers of F were using was not the manuscript itself, but a transcript of it, made by someone other than Shakespeare. Further support for this theory is to be found in the state of the text itself. The most obvious and troublesome feature of it is the large number of lines of verse that have been made unmetrical by the omission of a small word, or even part of a word. At Induction

2.2, for example, F reads *Wilt please your Lord drink a cup of sacke?*, which is neither good metre nor idiomatic English. As early as 1632 it was recognized that something was wrong here, and those who were responsible for the preparation of the Second Folio (F2), which came out in that year, put the matter right – much as they did in a number of similar cases – by substituting 'Lordship' for 'Lord'. In prose, errors of this kind are much more difficult to detect, but when Baptista asks Biondello, at III.2.32, *Is it new and olde too? how may that be?* it is clear that the word 'olde' must have appeared somewhere – it is impossible to be sure exactly where – in Biondello's previous speech, though there is no sign of it in the F text. As the compositors who set F were not, to judge from the evidence of other verse plays in it, very prone to this kind of mistake, it follows that the copy they were using was probably at fault. One only has to imagine that they were working from a transcript of Shakespeare's manuscript, made rather hurriedly and carelessly, to see how it could all have come about.

The Taming of the Shrew is closely connected with a period of great turmoil and change in the history of the Elizabethan acting companies. The worst plague of the reign broke out in 1592, and continued, with a short break, right on into 1594. For the greater part of this time the theatres in London were closed, and the companies tried to make ends meet by touring the provinces. Some of them split up, others lost their identity altogether. Among these latter were the Earl of Pembroke's men, for whom this play seems to have been written. A company that was breaking up into two different groups might well need hurried transcripts of the most popular plays in its repertory, so that each group could act them; and, in the final stages of the company's disintegration, its more indigent members, cut off from all access to its 'books', could easily have been driven to the expedient of vamping up a text from memory for some such occasion as that which Shakespeare depicts in his Induction. The copy used for the F text of *The Taming of the Shrew* is probably a result of the first process, and that used for *The Taming of A Shrew*, published in 1594, perhaps a result of the second.

G. R. Hibbard

COLLATIONS

ɩ

The following list contains the substantial additions and alterations that have been made in the present edition to the stage directions, and Act divisions and speech headings, of F. The reading of the present text is to the left of the bracket, and that of F to the right of it.

(a) Stage Directions

INDUCTION *ɩ*

  o *Enter Christopher Sly and the Hostess*] *Enter Begger and Hostes, Christophero Sly.*

  8 *He lies on the ground*] not in F

  10 *Exit*] not in F

  71 *Sly is carried away*] not in F
    A trumpet sounds] *Sound trumpets.*

  72 *Exit Servingman*] not in F

  136 *Exeunt*] not in F

INDUCTION 2

  o *Enter aloft Sly*] *Enter aloft the drunkard*

  23 *A Servingman brings him a pot of ale*] not in F

  24 *He drinks*] not in F

  97 *Enter Page as a lady, with attendants. One gives Sly a pot of ale*] *Enter Lady with Attendants.*

  100 *He drinks*] not in F

  115 *Exeunt Lord and Servingmen*] not in F

  126 *Enter the Lord as a Messenger*] this editor; *Enter a Messenger.*

  141 *They sit*] not in F

I.1

  45 *suitor*] *sister*

  91 *Exit Bianca*] not in F

  142 *Exeunt Gremio and Hortensio*] *Exeunt ambo. Manet Tranio and Lucentio*

  207 *They exchange garments*] not in F

  247 *(coming to with a start)*] not in F

I.2

137   *disguised as Cambio, a schoolmaster*] disgused.
141   *They stand aside*] not in F
215   *Tranio, bravely dressed as Lucentio*] Tranio braue

II.1

   0   *Bianca with her hands tied*] Bianca.
  24   *He unties her hands*] not in F
  36   *Exit Katherina*] not in F
  38   *Petruchio, with Hortensio, disguised as Licio; and
          Tranio*] Petruchio with Tranio
 100   *Biondello steps forward with the lute and the books*] not
          in F
 102   *(opening one of the books)*] not in F
 110   *Exit Servant, conducting Hortensio and Lucentio,
          followed by Biondello*] not in F
 168   *Exeunt all but Petruchio*] Exit. Manet Petruchio.
 215   *She turns to go*] not in F
 216   *He takes her in his arms*] not in F
 234   *She struggles*] not in F
 245   *He lets her go*] not in F

III.1

  83   *Exeunt Bianca and Servant*] not in F
  84   *Exit*] not in F

III.2

   0   *Lucentio as Cambio*] not in F
  26   *followed by Bianca and the other women*] not in F
 122   *with Grumio*] not in F
 126   *followed by Gremio, Biondello, and attendants*] not
          in F
 182   *Grumio, and attendants*] not in F
 226   *He seizes her, as though to protect her from the rest of
          the company, to whom he speaks*] not in F
 238   *and Grumio*] not in F

IV.1

  30   *He kindles a fire*] not in F
  55   *He boxes Curtis's ear*] not in F
 133   *He strikes the Servant*] not in F
 137   *Exit another Servingman*] not in F
 140   *He knocks the basin out of the Servant's hands*] not in F

IV.1
    141 *He strikes the Servant*] not in F
    151 *He throws the food and dishes at them*] not in F
    153 *Exeunt Servants hurriedly*] not in F
    173 *Exeunt*] not in F

IV.2
     5 *and Lucentio as Cambio*] not in F
    10 *They court each other*] not in F
    43 *Exit*] not in F
    71 *Exeunt Lucentio and Bianca*] not in F

IV.3
    40 *He sets the dish down*] not in F
    86 *Exit Haberdasher*] not in F
   180 *(To Grumio)*] not in F
   192 *Exeunt*] not in F

IV.4
     0 *Pedant, booted, and dressed*] Pedant drest
    17 *Lucentio as Cambio*] Lucentio: Pedant booted and bare
        headed.
    58 *He winks at Lucentio*] not in F
    66 *Exit Lucentio*] not in F
    93 *He turns to go*] not in F

V.1
     3 *Exeunt Lucentio and Bianca*] Exit.
     5 *Exit*] not in F
    52 *Exit*] not in F
    53 *Exit from the window*] not in F
    82 *Enter an Officer*] not in F
   129 *Exit*] not in F

V.2
     0 *Petruchio with Katherina, Hortensio*] not in F
    48 *Exeunt Bianca, Katherina, and Widow*] Exit Bianca.
   104 *Exit Katherina*] not in F
   121 *She obeys*] not in F
   186 *Exeunt Petruchio and Katherina*] Exit Petruchio
   188 *Exeunt*] not in F

(b) Act divisions and speech headings

INDUCTION] *Actus primus. Scœna Prima.*

INDUCTION 1

1 SLY] *Begger.*

3 (and before all subsequent speeches) SLY] *Beg.*

80 FIRST PLAYER] 2. *Player.*

86 FIRST PLAYER] *Sincklo.*

INDUCTION 2

99 (and in all subsequent speeches) PAGE] *Lady.*

127 LORD] this editor; *Mes.*

I.1

0 I.1] not marked in F

246 LORD] this editor; 1. *Man.*

II.1

0 II.1] not marked in F

III.1

46–9 How fiery and forward our pedant is . . . mistrust]
assigned to *Luc.* in F

50 LUCENTIO] *Bian.*

52 BIANCA] *Hort.*

80 SERVANT] *Nicke.*

IV.1

0 IV.1] No Act division here in F

23 CURTIS] *Gru.*

IV.2

4 HORTENSIO] *Luc.*

6 LUCENTIO] *Hor.*

8 LUCENTIO] *Hor.*

71 Take in your love, and then let me alone] F heads
this line *Par.*

IV.3

0 IV.3] *Actus Quartus. Scena Prima.*

63 HABERDASHER] *Fel.*

IV.4

5 Where we were lodgers at the Pegasus] assigned to
Tra. in F

V.1

      o V.1] no division here in F

V.2

      o V.2] *Actus Quintus.*

2

The following list is of words that have been added to, or, more rarely, omitted from, the text of F, in order to regularize the metre or improve the sense. Most of these changes were first made in the seventeenth and eighteenth centuries – many of them in one or the other of the three seventeenth-century reprints of the Folio (F2, F3 and F4); these are noted. The reading to the left of the bracket is that of this edition; that to the right, of F.

INDUCTION *1*

      62 he is Sly, say] he is, say

INDUCTION *2*

      2 lordship] F2; Lord

I.2

      45 this's a] this a
      72 she as] F2; she is as
    119 me and other] me. Other

II.1

      8 charge thee tell] F2; charge tel
    79 unto you this] vnto this

III.2

      16 Make feast, invite friends] Make friends, inuite
      28 a saint] F2; a very saint
      29 of thy impatient] F2; of impatient
      30 such old news] such newes
      90 Were it not better] Were it better
    127 But, sir, to love] But sir, Loue
    129 As I before] As before
    165 rose up again] F2; rose againe

IV.2

      60 I'm] I am
      86 are newly] are but newly
    121 Go with me, sir, to] F2; Go with me to

IV.3

    81 it is a paltry] F2; it is paltrie
    88 like a demi-cannon] F2; like demi cannon

IV.5

    78 she be froward] F2; she froward

V.1

    115 arrived at last] F2; arriued at the last

3

Below are listed other departures in the present text from that of
F. Obvious minor misprints are not noted, nor are changes in
lineation and punctuation unless they are of special significance,
nor cases in which F prints verse as prose, or prose as verse. Most
of these emendations were made by editors in the eighteenth
century. Those suggested by modern editors are gratefully
acknowledged. The F reading is to the right of the bracket.

The Characters in the Play] not in F
INDUCTION *1*

    9–10 thirdborough] Headborough
      15 Breathe] (C. J. Sisson, 1954); Brach F

INDUCTION *2*

      52 wi'th'] with
      72 Christophero] F2; Christopher
    135 I will. Let them play it. Is not] I will let them play, it
         is not

I.1

      13 Vincentio come] *Vincentio's* come
  17–18 study | Virtue] studie, | Vertue
      25 *Mi perdonato*] *Me Pardonato*
    106 There! Love] Their loue
    204 coloured] F3; Conlord
    241 your] F2; you

I.2

      18 masters] mistris
      24 *Con tutto il cuore ben trovato*] *Contutti le core bene
         trobatto*
  25–6 *ben venuto,* | *Molto honorato*] *bene venuto multo honorata*

        51 grows. But] growes but
       170 help me] helpe one
       188 Antonio's] *Butonios*
       222 her too?] her to –
       264 feat] seeke
       279 *ben*] F2; *Been*

II.1

         3 gauds] goods
      75–6 wooing. | Neighbour] wooing neighbors
        90 a suitor] as utor
    104–5 Pisa. By report | I] *Pisa* by report, | I
       186 bonny] F4; bony
       241 askance] a sconce
       323 quiet in] quiet me
       368 Marseilles] Marcellus; Marsellis F2

III.1

28 and 41 *Sigeia*] F2; *sigeria*
        32 *Sigeia*] F2; *Sigeria*
        79 change true rules for odd] charge true rules for old

III.2

        33 hear] F2; heard
        54 swayed] Waid
        58 new-repaired] now repaired
       152 grumbling] F2; grumlling

IV.1

        42 their white] F3; the white
       128 Food, food, food, food!] J. Dover Wilson, 1928;
            Soud, soud, soud, soud.

IV.2

        13 none] me
        31 her] F3; them
        71 Take in] Take me
        73 farrer] this editor; farre
        78 Of Mantua? Sir,] Of *Mantua* Sir

IV.3

       177 account'st] accountedst

IV.4

         1 Sir] Sirs
        88 except] expect

90 *imprimendum solum*] F2; *Impremendum solem*

IV.5
  18 it is] F2; it in
  38 Whither away, or where] F2; Whether away, or
      whether
  41 Allots] F2; A lots

V.1
   5 master's] mistris
  27 Mantua] *Padua*
  47 master's] F2; Mistris
 135 No, sir] Mo sir

V.2
   2 done] come
  37 ha' to thee] F2; ha to the
  39 butt] But
  45 bitter jest or two] better iest or too
  62 two] too
  65 therefore for] F2; therefore sir
75–6 That will I. Biondello | Go] this editor; That will
      I. | Goe *Biondello*
 127 a hundred] fiue hundred
 131 you're] your
 147 maintenance; commits] maintenance. Commits

4

The following list contains emendations of the F text which have
some measure of plausibility, but which have not been adopted
in this edition. The reading to the left of the bracket is that
of this edition; the reading to the right of it is the unadopted
emendation.

INDUCTION *1*
  15 Breathe] Brach F; Broach (J. Dover Wilson, 1928)
INDUCTION *2*
 135 comonty] commodity (J. Dover Wilson, 1928)
I.1
 181 she] he
 202 meaner man] mean man

I.2

151 go to] go
191 O sir] Sir
206 to hear] to th'ear
211 yours] ours

II.1

109 To my daughters, and tell them both] In to my
   daughters; tell them both from me
141 shakes] shake F2
168 I'll] I will
201 such jade] such a jade
337 have my Bianca's] have Bianca's F2

III.2

16 Make feast, invite friends] (Make friends, inuite F);
   Make friends invited
127 But, sir, to love] (But sir, Loue F); But to her love
165 rose up again] (rose againe F); arose again
208 tomorrow – not till] (to morrow, not till F);
   tomorrow, till

IV.1

37 wilt thou] thou wilt F2
56 This 'tis] This is
106 at door] at the door

IV.5

26 soft, company] soft, what company
36 the woman] a woman F2

V.1

27–8 and here] and is here

V.2

105 of a wonder] of wonder
147 maintenance; commits] maintenance commits

Commentary

F here refers to the first Folio edition of the play (1623), F2 to the second Folio (1632). All references to other plays by Shakespeare are to the Penguin Shakespeare series.

The Characters in the Play: No list of the Characters is given in F. An alternative way of arranging the characters in the play proper, so as to bring out the extent to which they fall into groups, would be to put the three old men (Baptista, Gremio and Vincentio) together; then the three young men (Petruchio, Lucentio and Hortensio); then the three young women (Katherina, Bianca and the Widow); and finally the rest, who are all servants and tradesmen, or, in the case of the Pedant, a sort of employee.

Induction

The opening of this play is of peculiar interest, because in no other of his works does Shakespeare make use of an Induction (see Introduction, pp. xxi–xxiii). The setting, it soon becomes plain, is outside an alehouse in the playwright's native Warwickshire, and then, for the second scene, in a large country house. Shakespeare is clearly drawing on direct personal experience in his depiction of country people and their activities. The tang and raciness of the altercation between Sly and the Hostess has the stamp of observed reality about it, making their brief but lively dialogue a fitting prelude to the fuller evocation of life in Elizabethan England that is to follow.

Although it is obviously a separate part of the play, the Induction is not distinguished from the rest of it in F, where the text, like many others, is simply headed *Actus primus. Scœna Prima*.

I.

0 *Enter Christopher Sly and the Hostess*: F reads *Enter Begger and Hostes, Christophero Sly*. Sly's speeches are consistently headed *Beg.*, and the Lord refers to him as *the beggar* at 39, though according to Sly himself he is in fact a tinker. The distinction between beggars and tinkers was not a very sharp one, and both were proverbially noted for their fondness for ale. The name Christophero Sly in this initial direction is evidently an afterthought, derived from the text (Ind.2.5), and may well be an addition made by the prompter. The implications of the neutral word *Enter* are well brought out by the corresponding stage direction in *The Taming of A Shrew*, which reads: 'Enter a Tapster, beating out of his doores *Slie Droonken*.'

1 *pheeʒe you*: Settle your hash, fix you. Given in the *Oxford English Dictionary* under the commoner spelling 'feeze', this word originally meant 'to drive away or frighten off', but by Shakespeare's time it seems to have taken on an abusive connotation and to have become part of the language of the tavern. It occurs again in *Troilus and Cressida* (II.3.199), where Ajax says of Achilles: 'An he be proud with me, I'll pheese his pride', and, with a punning reference to 'vizier', in *The Merry Wives of Windsor* (I.3.9), where the Host calls Falstaff his 'Pheazar'.

3 *Y'are*: You are (colloquial).
baggage: Good-for-nothing woman, strumpet.

4 *Richard Conqueror*: Sly's knowledge of history, like his knowledge of hagiology, is rather shaky – he has confused Richard Coeur-de-Lion with William the Conqueror. But his pretensions to aristocratic descent, though intended primarily to impress the Hostess, also prepare the way for his assumption of a lordly role in Ind.2.

5 *paucas pallabris*: This phrase, which was something of a cant term in Shakespeare's England, is a corruption of the Spanish *pocas palabras* (few words). Its use here may well be a reminiscence of, or a jesting allusion to,

Thomas Kyd's *The Spanish Tragedy* (III.14.118), where
Hieronimo, the hero of the play, cautions himself
against revealing too much of what he knows by saying
'*Pocas Palabras*, mild as the Lamb'.

let the world slide: Let the world go by, don't worry.
The phrase, a proverbial one, was recorded by John
Heywood in 1546 in the following form: 'To let the
world wag, and take mine ease in mine inn.' It sums
up Sly's general attitude to life very well and is substantially repeated by him at Ind.2.141 when he tells his
wife to *let the world slip*.

Sessa: The precise meaning of this exclamation, vari-
ants of which are also used by Edgar in *King Lear*
(III.4.97 and III.6.73), is uncertain. In all three cases
it appears to be an incitement to haste, roughly equivalent to 'Off you go!' or 'Be off with you!'

6 *burst*: Broken, smashed.

7 *denier*: Pronounced to rhyme with 'many a'. It was a
very small French coin worth one twelfth of a sou.

Go by, Saint Jeronimy: Sly is misquoting from *The
Spanish Tragedy* (III.12.31), where Hieronimo warns
himself against over-hasty action by saying, '*Hieronimo*
beware; go by, go by.' The words became a popular
catch-phrase. Kyd's editor comments: 'Perhaps no
single passage in Elizabethan drama became so notorious as this. It is quoted over and over again as the stock
phrase to imply impatience of anything disagreeable,
inconvenient, or old-fashioned' (*The Works of Thomas
Kyd*, ed. F. S. Boas (1901), p. 406). Sly characteristic-
ally mixes Hieronimo up with St Jerome, as well he
might, since *The Spanish Tragedy* seems to be his Bible.

7–8 *go to thy cold bed and warm thee*: Almost exactly these
words, which may have had some proverbial associa-
tion with beggars whose cold bed frequently was the
ground, are used by Edgar, disguised as Poor Tom, in
King Lear (III.4.46).

9–10 *thirdborough*: Petty constable of a township or manor.
F reads *Headborough* (another name for the same
officer), but Sly's rejoinder demands the emendation.

11–12 *by law*: With judicial proceedings, in court. Sly is still
       trying to give the impression that he is a man of impor-
       tance.

   12 *budge an inch*: Sly is quibbling on the literal sense of
       the phrase and on its metaphorical sense of giving way
       on a matter of principle.
       boy: Servant, inferior (used here as a term of abuse).
       Cf. *Coriolanus*, V.6.101–17.

12–13 *and kindly*: Naturally, of course, by all means. Sly is
       being ironical.

   13 *Wind horns*: This command is intended for those in
       charge of the effects in Shakespeare's theatre.
       train: Retinue, followers.

   14 *tender well*: Take good care of.

   15 *Breathe Merriman*: Give Merriman a breathing space.
       Breathe is C. J. Sisson's emendation of the F reading
       Brach which does not make very good sense. A 'brach'
       is a bitch-hound, whereas Merriman looks like the name
       of a dog-hound; the sentence requires a verb at this
       point to go with 'couple' in the next line; and the repe-
       tition of 'brach' at the end of the sentence is ugly and
       unconvincing. 'Breathing' would be the right treatment
       for a hound that was dead beat. Dover Wilson reads
       'Broach', meaning 'bleed'.
       embossed: Foaming at the mouth (with exhaustion).

   16 *couple*: Leash together. The Elizabethans took their
       hounds to and from the hunt in couples.

   17 *made it good*: Put matters right (by picking up the scent).

   18 *in the coldest fault*: At the point where the scent was
       most completely lost. A 'fault' is a break in the scent.

   21 *cried upon it at the merest loss*: Yelped out on the right
       scent when it was totally lost.

   26 *sup them well*: Give them a good supper.
       look unto: Take care of.

   31 *a bed but cold*: But a cold bed in which.

   33 *image*: Likeness. Sly, in his drunken stupor, looks like
       a dead man.

   34 *practise*: Play a trick.

   38 *brave*: Fine, handsomely dressed.

39 *forget himself*: Lose consciousness of his own identity.

40 *he cannot choose*: He must, he is bound to.

41 *strange*: Incredible, wonderful.

46 *Balm*: Anoint, bathe.

distillèd waters: Fragrant liquids, such as rose-water (54), made from flowers and herbs.

47 *burn sweet wood to make the lodging sweet*: It was a common Elizabethan practice to burn sweet-scented wood, such as juniper, in a musty room. Cf. *Much Ado About Nothing*, I.3.54–5, where Borachio says, 'as I was smoking a musty room'.

48 *Procure me music*: Here, *me* is the dative, meaning 'for me'.

49 *dulcet*: Melodious.

51 *reverence*: Bow, obeisance.

55 *ewer*: A pitcher with a wide spout to bring water for washing the hands.

diaper: Towel.

60 *disease*: Disorder of the mind.

62 *And when he says he is Sly, say that he dreams*: F reads *And when he sayes he is, say that he dreames*, which does not make very good sense, since there is no point in getting Sly to admit that he is mad and then telling him that he is merely dreaming. Dr Johnson's suggestion, that the word 'Sly' was omitted by the printer because of its similarity to the word 'say', has been adopted in this edition. It receives strong support from Sly's reaction in the next scene (16–19) to the statement that he is deranged: *What, would you make me mad? Am not I Christopher Sly . . . ?*

64 *kindly*: Naturally, convincingly.

gentle: Kind.

65 *passing*: Surpassingly, extremely.

66 *husbanded with modesty*: Managed with moderation, not carried too far.

68 *As*: So that.

by: As a result of.

true: Fitting, proper.

70 *to bed with him*: Put him to bed.

71 *to his office*: Go about his duty.

Sly is carried away: There is no direction for the removal of Sly in F, but *The Taming of A Shrew* reads '*Exeunt* two with *Slie*'.

A trumpet sounds: F reads *Sound trumpets*, but the following line shows that only one is required.

75 *An't*: If it.

77–102 *Now, fellows, you are welcome . . . nothing that my house affords*: This little episode shows the kind of reception that an acting company, on tour in the provinces, would hope for at a great house, even if they did not always receive it. It has the further interest of anticipating the similar but more extended scene (*Hamlet*, II.2.420–542), in which Hamlet welcomes the actors to Elsinore. Moreover, there are parallels between the Prince's views on acting (III.2.1–53) and the Lord's praise of a part that was *naturally performed* (85).

80 *So please*: If it so please. F allots this speech to *2. Player*, though there has been no mention of a First Player.

86 *I think 'twas Soto that your honour means*: F assigns this speech to *Sincklo*, and so provides the name of the actor for whom the part was written. John Sincklo or Sincler was a performer of minor roles in Shakespeare's company and his name turns up on several other occasions. He is first mentioned as a member of the cast that played *The Second Part of the Seven Deadly Sins*, which was probably staged about 1591 and of which only the 'plot' or outline survives. His name appears again in the F text of *Henry VI, Part III* (III.1.1), where he plays a forester; then in the Quarto version of *Henry IV, Part II* (V.4.0), where he takes the part of the Beadle; and, finally, in the Induction to John Marston's play *The Malcontent*, which was published in 1604. The remarks made about him by Doll Tearsheet and the Hostess in *Henry IV, Part II* suggest that he was abnormally thin. Doll calls him 'you thin man in a censer', 'Goodman death, goodman bones', and 'you thin thing'; while the Hostess addresses him as 'you starved bloodhound' and as 'Thou Atomy [she

means 'anatomy'], thou' (V.4.18–30). Other parts
which may well have been written with Sincklo's peculiar appearance in mind are those of the Apothecary
in *Romeo and Juliet*, Robert Faulconbridge in *King
John* and Starveling in *A Midsummer Night's Dream*.
Since Shakespeare thought of the pantaloon as 'lean'
(*As You Like It*, II.7.159), it seems likely that Sincklo
took the part of Gremio in the main action of *The
Taming of the Shrew*.

A character called Soto, who is a farmer's son, appears
in John Fletcher's play *Women Pleased*. It is unlikely,
however, that Shakespeare is alluding to this particular
play here, since it dates from somewhere between 1619
and 1623 – almost thirty years after the composition of
The Taming of the Shrew, and nearly twenty after the
last recorded reference to Sincklo – and since his
description of Soto's role does not tally with what
happens in *Women Pleased*. Most modern critics are of
the opinion that Fletcher's play, which is, for him, rather
old-fashioned and not at all well constructed, is probably a revision of a much older play that is no longer
extant, and that it is to the part of Soto in this lost play
that Shakespeare is referring here. (See G. E. Bentley,
The Jacobean and Caroline Stage, vol. 3, (1956), pp.
431–2.)

88 *in happy time*: Just at the right time.

89 *The rather for*: The more so because.

90 *cunning*: Art, professional skill.

92 *doubtful of your modesties*: Unsure about your ability to
control yourselves.

93 *over-eyeing of*: Observing.

95 *merry passion*: Irresistible burst of merriment. Cf. 'idle
merriment, | A passion hateful to my purposes' (*King
John*, III.3.46–7).

97 *impatient*: Angry, annoyed.

98 *contain*: Restrain.

99 *the veriest antic*: The most complete buffoon, the oddest
and most fantastical fellow.

102 *affords*: Has to offer.

103–4 *Sirrah, go you to Barthol'mew my page . . . a lady*: The Lord is cleverly adapting the Elizabethan stage convention that all female parts were played by boys to the purposes of a practical joke in everyday life. The same trick becomes the central motif of an entire play in Ben Jonson's *The Silent Woman* (1609).

104 *in all suits*: In all respects (with a pun on 'suits' in the sense of dress).

106 *do him obeisance*: Show him the respect due to a superior.

108 *honourable action*: Decent behaviour befitting one of high rank.

110 *accomplishèd*: Performed.

112 *lowly courtesy*: Humble curtsy.

117 *with declining head into his bosom*: With his head drooping on his chest.

120 *esteemèd him*: Thought himself.

123 *commanded*: Forced, feigned.

124 *for such a shift*: As an expedient, to serve the turn.

125 *close*: Secretly, covertly.

126 *in despite*: Notwithstanding.

128 *Anon*: Soon, immediately afterwards.

129 *usurp*: Counterfeit, assume.

130 *action*: Bodily movements.

133 *simple*: Mere.

134 *I'll in*: I'll go in. In Elizabethan English the verb of motion was frequently omitted after words implying purpose, such as 'will', 'shall' and 'must'.
Haply: Perhaps.

135 *spleen*: Impulse to uncontrollable laughter. In Shakespeare's day the spleen was regarded as the seat of any sudden outburst of feeling, whether of mirth or of anger. Laughter and melancholy both came under its control.

136 *grow into extremes*: Become quite excessive, get out of hand.
Exeunt: This direction, though it does not appear in F, is clearly implied by the Lord's remark *I'll in* (134) and by the massed entry, in which he takes part, that follows.

The Taming of A Shrew, at the corresponding point in its action, has '*Exeunt omnes*'.

2

This scene, in which Sly's attitude changes from one of complete incredulity to an assured assumption of the lordly role that has been thrust upon him, is not only one of the richest and subtlest pieces of comedy that Shakespeare ever wrote, but is also one of the most important documents about the Elizabethan stage that we have. The stage direction with which it opens reads as follows in F: *Enter aloft the drunkard with attendants, some with apparel, Bason and Ewer, & other appurtenances, & Lord*. The word *aloft* clearly indicates that the entire scene was played on some kind of upper stage. Where and how was it done? There are 141 lines of dialogue; at least six characters – and probably more, since the Page is accompanied by attendants when he enters as Sly's wife – must be on the stage at the same time; and somewhere, either on the stage or just off it, there must be a bed or some indication of one. It seems improbable that a scene of this length and complexity could have been properly or satisfactorily portrayed on the kind of upper stage that is usually thought of as a balustraded gallery, forming part of the façade of the tiring-house. An audience would surely have found difficulty in sustaining its interest in a scene of this length when separated from the actors by railings and by the large expanse of unoccupied main stage. An attractive solution to the problem is suggested by C. Walter Hodges, who thinks that for extended scenes 'aloft', such as this, a temporary structure was employed, jutting out from the façade of the tiring-house and in front of the stage gallery. Consisting essentially of a platform, raised about seven feet above the floor of the main stage, this acting area would have needed nothing more than a single rail around it, so that there would have been no real obstacle to vision, and it would have served to bring the action well forward from the rear wall of the theatre. Attempting to visualize how this particular scene might have been produced effectively, yet with a minimum of properties and without taking up too much space, Hodges writes:

I will allow myself to imagine the porch-like booth [the temporary structure] hung with its arras, standing between the two tiring-house doors [the two large doors, one on either side of the main stage at the rear of it, that provided the chief means of access to it]. It backs up to the gallery floor, where, behind closed curtains, Sly lies snoring. A light stairway leads up one side, and up this from below come the servants with apparel, basin and ewer. They are now standing on top of the porch-booth in front of the curtain which represents the bed. They draw the curtain. Sly emerges. 'For God's sake,' he groans, 'a pot of small ale.' And so it begins. (C. Walter Hodges, *The Globe Restored* (1953), pp. 64–5; see also pp. 56–64)

  1 *small ale*: The weakest and therefore the cheapest form of the beverage.
  2 *lordship*: This reading, essential both for sense and metre, comes from F2. F reads *Lord*.
    sack: A general name for a class of white wines formerly imported from Spain and the Canaries.
  3 *conserves*: Candied fruits.
  7 *conserves of beef*: Salt beef.
  8 *doublets*: Close-fitting body-garments, with or without sleeves, worn by men in Shakespeare's day.
 11 *as*: That.
 12 *idle humour*: Empty fancy, foolish aberration of mind.
 15 *infusèd with so foul a spirit*: Inspired by such mad ideas, filled with such diseased notions.
16–23 *Am not I . . . in Christendom*: This passage is full of references to Warwickshire, and gives the impression that Shakespeare is drawing on direct personal experience.
 17 *old Sly's son of Burton-heath*: Old Sly of Burton-heath's

son. Burton-heath has been identified with Barton-on-
the-Heath, a village about sixteen miles from Stratford,
where Shakespeare's aunt Joan Lambert lived.

18 *cardmaker*: One who made cards – instruments with
iron teeth, used for combing out the fibres of wool by
hand. This occupation might well be taken up by a
boy living at Barton-on-the-Heath on the edge of the
Cotswolds, which was one of the chief wool- and
cloth-producing areas of the country in Shakespeare's
time.

19 *bear-herd*: A man who led a performing bear about the
country.

20 *Marian Hacket, the fat ale-wife of Wincot*: The woman
referred to here may well have been a real person, since
Sara, the daughter of Robert Hacket, was baptized in
Quinton church on 21 November 1591. The hamlet of
Wincot, four miles south of Stratford, lay partly in the
parish of Quinton and partly in that of Clifford
Chambers.

21 *on the score*: In debt. The score was originally an account
kept by making notches in a piece of wood; later chalk
marks were used for the purpose.

22 *sheer ale*: Ale taken alone without solid food to accom-
pany it. Cf. Hal's remark about the bill found in
Falstaff's pocket: 'O monstrous! But one halfpenny-
worth of bread to this intolerable deal of sack?' (*Henry
IV, Part I*, II.4.525–6).
score me up: Chalk me up.

22–3 *the lyingest knave in Christendom*: Humphrey, Duke of
Gloucester, addresses the impostor Saunder Simpcox
with precisely these words (*Henry VI, Part II*,
II.1.124–5).

23 *A Servingman brings him a pot of ale*: This direction,
like the *He drinks* that follows it, is not to be found in
F. It seems to be called for, however, for three reasons:
first, Sly has asked for a pot of ale (line 1); secondly,
he is going to demand a pot of ale *once again* (74); and,
thirdly, nothing is more likely to convince him that he
is *not bestraught* than the appearance of what is to him

the most important thing in life.

24 *bestraught*: Distracted, out of my mind.

Here's –: This sentence, had Sly ever finished it, might possibly have run 'Here's proof.'

26 *droop*: Feel despondent.

28 *As beaten*: As if driven, feeling themselves driven.

29 *bethink thee of*: Remember, recollect.

30 *ancient thoughts*: Former manner of thinking.

33 *office*: Place of duty.

beck: Nod, or other mute signal, indicating a command.

34 *Apollo*: God of music and song in classical mythology.

37 *lustful*: Provocative of lust.

38 *trimmed up*: Luxuriously prepared.

Semiramis: Legendary queen of Assyria, proverbial for her voluptuousness and promiscuity.

39 *bestrew*: Scatter or cover (presumably with rushes).

40 *trapped*: Caparisoned, decked with an ornamented covering.

41 *studded all with*: Adorned all over with studs of.

44–5 *Thy hounds . . . hollow earth*: The Elizabethans took much pleasure in the noise their hounds made and went to some pains to ensure that the cry of the pack was a tunable one. Cf. the dialogue between Theseus and Hippolyta (*A Midsummer Night's Dream*, IV.1.104–26).

44 *welkin*: Sky.

46 *course*: The technical word for hunting the hare with greyhounds.

47 *breathèd*: Long-winded, strong of wind.

48–59 *Dost thou love pictures . . . are drawn*: The paintings described here are examples of the *wanton pictures* referred to by the Lord in the previous scene (Ind.1.45). It is not easy to decide whether Shakespeare had actual paintings in mind when he wrote this passage. The subjects, all of them mythological, were frequently handled by the Italian masters of the late Renaissance, such as Correggio and Giulio Romano, the only Italian artist Shakespeare ever mentions by name (*The Winter's Tale*, V.2.95). But there seem to have been very few Italian pictures in this country in the sixteenth century;

and there is no reliable evidence that Shakespeare ever visited Italy. He may, of course, have heard something about Italian art from men who had been to that country; but the most likely explanation for the similarity between these descriptions and actual paintings is that the Italian painters, like Shakespeare himself, especially in his early work, were deeply influenced by Ovid. (For fuller discussion of the whole topic than is possible here, see A. Lytton Sells, *The Italian Influence in English Poetry* (1955), pp. 188–209; and Mario Praz, *The Flaming Heart* (1958), pp. 162–4.)

49–50 *Adonis . . . Cytherea*: According to Ovid (*Metamorphoses*, 10.520–739) Cytherea, more commonly known as Venus the goddess of love, became enamoured of Adonis, a youth who returned her love. Ultimately, however, Adonis, who was even fonder of hunting than he was of Venus, was killed by a boar. Finding his body, Venus changed his blood into a flower – the anemone. Both in this passage and in his elaborate poem on the subject, *Venus and Adonis*, published in 1593, Shakespeare depicts a reluctant and uncooperative Adonis, pursued by a demanding and exigent Venus. His version of the story here was probably influenced by Spenser, who, in *The Faerie Queene* (III.1.34–8), describes a tapestry portraying it in which Venus watches Adonis bathing,

> And whilst he bath'd, with her two crafty spies,
> She secretly would search each dainty limb.

Indeed, Spenser's imagined tapestry may well be the 'picture' Shakespeare was thinking of.

51 *wanton*: Behave in an amorous fashion.

52 *wi'th'*: With the (abbreviated colloquial form).

53 *Io*: Ovid relates (*Metamorphoses*, 1.588–600) how Jupiter saw Io, the daughter of the river-god Inachus, and fell in love with her. Io fled from him, but Jupiter pursued her and raped her under cover of a dense mist, which he created in order to hide his activities from

the eyes of Juno.

55 *As lively painted as the deed was done*: Whenever Shakespeare describes a work of art it is verisimilitude that he looks for and praises. Cf. 49–52 and 56–9. Similar views, all stemming probably from the Renaissance commonplace that poetry was a speaking picture and painting a dumb poem, are to be found in *The Rape of Lucrece* (1371–1442), *Timon of Athens* (I.1.30–39), *Cymbeline* (II.4.68–85) and *The Winter's Tale* (V.2.92–9).

56 *Daphne*: As Ovid tells the story (*Metamorphoses*, 1.452–567), Daphne was the daughter of the river-god Peneus. Cupid, in order to demonstrate his power to the scornful Apollo, caused the god to fall in love with her, but filled her with an aversion for him. As a result, when Apollo wooed her she fled from him, and, as he was about to overtake her, she prayed to her father for help. Thereupon she was changed into a laurel.

57 *that one shall swear*: So that one must swear, so that one is forced to swear.

59 *So workmanly*: With such art, so skilfully.

62 *this waning age*: The belief that the whole history of man had been a steady degeneration from the state of physical and intellectual perfection that had existed in the Garden of Eden was widely held in the sixteenth and seventeenth centuries. See Spenser, *The Faerie Queene*, V.Proem.1–9.

64 *o'errun*: Ran over, flowed over. 'Run' as the form of the past tense is fairly common in Shakespeare's work. Cf. *Macbeth*, II.3.107–8:

> The expedition of my violent love
> Outrun the pauser reason.

66 *yet*: Nevertheless, still, even so.

72 *Christophero*: This is the reading of F2. F has *Christopher*, which is unmetrical.

76 *wit*: Understanding, mental faculties.

77 *knew but*: Only knew.

80 *By my fay*: By my faith.
    goodly: Considerable.

81 *of all that time*: In all that time.

82 *idle*: Meaningless, empty, silly.

83 *goodly*: Fine, well-proportioned.

84 *beaten out of door*: Driven out of the house.

86 *present her at the leet*: Bring her up for trial before the manorial court. The *leet* was the equivalent of the modern police court.

87 *sealed quarts*: Quart measures officially stamped to show that they held the correct quantity. Sly is suggesting, of course, that the *stone jugs* are a swindle because they hold less than they are supposed to.

88 *Cicely Hacket*: Cf. note to Ind.2.20.

89 *the woman's maid of the house*: The mistress of the house's maid, the landlady's maid.
    house: Inn, tavern.

91 *reckoned up*: Mentioned, enumerated.

92–3 *Stephen Sly . . . John Naps . . . Peter Turph . . . Henry Pimpernell*: These could well be the names of real people. A Stephen Sly was living at Stratford in January 1615. (See E. K. Chambers, *William Shakespeare* (1930), vol. 2, p. 144.)

92 *Greece*: It has been suggested that this is a misreading of Greet, a hamlet not far from Stratford, but there were Greeks in England in the sixteenth century, and *John Naps* might be the English version of a Greek name.

95 *nor no man*: Nor any man. Shakespeare frequently uses the double negative for the sake of emphasis.

96 *amends*: Recovery, improvement in health.

97 *One gives Sly a pot of ale*: This direction, which does not appear in F, is called for because Sly has asked for *a pot o'th'smallest ale* some twenty lines earlier and he now thanks one of the servants.

99–100 *How fares . . . I fare well*: There is a quibble here. The Page enquires about Sly's state of health and Sly replies that he is well supplied with *fare* in the sense of drink.

100 *Marry*: Derived originally from the name of the Virgin
Mary, used as an oath or asseveration, this exclamation
meant no more in Shakespeare's day than 'why, to be
sure'.

104 *goodman*: Husband.

114 *abandoned*: Banished.

115 *Exeunt Lord and Servingmen*: F provides no direction
here, but, as Dover Wilson points out, one is required
because Sly has just expressed his desire to be left alone
with his *wife*, and because the upper stage must be
cleared of all except the three *Presenters* (I.1.245) before
the play proper can begin.

121 *In peril to incur*: On peril of your incurring.

123 *stands for*: Is valid as, can be accepted as.

124 *it stands*: A bawdy quibble alluding to the erection of
the male organ.

tarry: Wait, stay.

126 *the flesh and the blood*: Sexual desire.

Enter the Lord as a Messenger: F reads *Enter a Messenger*.
In this edition the role of the Messenger has been
assigned to the Lord for the following reasons: (1) the
Lord has had the play put on in order to enjoy Sly's
reactions to it, and must, therefore, be in a position
where he can best observe them; (2) in *The Taming of
A Shrew* it is the Lord who announces the play to Sly
in the following words, which are very close to the
Messenger's first two lines:

May it please you, your honour's players be come
To offer your honour a play,

and he remains on the upper stage until the play is
almost done; (3) if the Lord is with Sly and the Page,
the reference to *The Presenters above*, in the stage direction at I.1.245 makes much better sense than it does if
he is not; and (4), who but the Lord could appear on
the upper stage, and, in his role as servant to Sly, give
the necessary parallel to the Lucentio–Tranio relationship?

128 *pleasant*: Merry.
129 *For so*: Because.
      meet: Suitable, fitting, right.
130–31 *Seeing too much sadness . . . frenzy*: For the general atti-
      tude to the relationship between physical and psycho-
      logical states, cf. *King John*, III.3.42–4:

      Or if that surly spirit, melancholy,
      Had baked thy blood, and made it heavy, thick,
      Which else runs tickling up and down the veins . . .

131 *nurse*: Nourisher.
134 *bars*: Prevents.
135 *Marry, I will. Let them play it. Is not a comonty*: F reads
      Marrie I will let them play, it is not a Comontie, which
      does not make satisfactory sense, since *comonty* must
      be Sly's blunder for 'comedy'.
136 *gambold*: Frolic, caper.
137 *stuff*: Matter, material (in its literary sense).
138 *household stuff*: Furnishings. Sly, in his drunken state,
      has taken the word *stuff* in its most literal sense.
139 *history*: Story, narrative.
141 *They sit*: This does not appear in F though clearly
      demanded by the dialogue.
      A flourish of trumpets to announce the play: F reads simply
      Flourish, and places this direction at the head of what
      is, in modern editions, I.1.

The Play
I.1

      The opening of this scene is a rather primitive piece
      of exposition, of the kind that Sheridan guyed so well
      in *The Critic*. Lucentio tells Tranio many things that
      Tranio should know already, for the benefit of the
      audience, who need to know where the scene is and
      what the two characters are doing there. The scene
      comes to full dramatic life only with the entrance of
      Baptista, his daughters and their suitors. At this point
      the purveying of information is replaced by action.

o *Tranio*: This name appears in Plautus's *Mostellaria*, the character who bears it being a wily townsman. It is quite possible that it was associated in Shakespeare's mind with the word 'train', meaning 'deceit' or 'trickery'.

1 *for*: Because of, owing to.

2 *fair Padua, nursery of arts*: Shakespeare knew what he was writing about. The University of Padua, founded in 1228, was one of the oldest in Europe, and was still in the sixteenth century the main centre for the diffusion of Aristotelian teaching.

3 *I am arrived for*: I have arrived in. In Shakespeare's time 'be' as well as 'have' was commonly used to form the past tense of verbs of motion.

8 *breathe*: Live, settle down.
   haply institute: Auspiciously begin.

9 *ingenious studies*: Intellectual studies, liberal studies.

11 *Gave me . . . first*: First gave me.

12 *of great traffic through*: With much business throughout.

13 *come of*: Descended from.

14–16 *Vincentio's son, brought up in Florence . . . his virtuous deeds*: The sense of this rather stilted and Latinate sentence is: 'It is right that Vincentio's son, brought up in Florence, should fulfil the hopes men have of him by adorning his prosperity with virtuous deeds.'

17 *for the time*: At present.

17–18 *study | Virtue,*: F reads *studie, | Vertue*. The change in the position of the comma makes the statement much more pointed.

19 *apply*: Pursue, devote myself to.
   treats of: Deals with.

19–20 *happiness . . . be achieved*: The idea of achieving happiness through virtuous action is central to Aristotle's *Ethics*.

23 *plash*: Pool, puddle.

25 *Mi perdonato*: Excuse me (Italian).

26 *in all affected as*: In entire agreement with.

29 *admire*: Regard with reverence.

31 *stoics*: Rigorists, people who despise pleasure.

stocks: Senseless unfeeling people.
There is a quibble on the two words.
32 *devote*: Devoted, addicted.
checks: Restraints, counsels of moderation.
33 *As*: That.
Ovid: Latin poet who lived from 43 BC to about AD 17.
In his *Ars Amatoria* Ovid calls himself *praeceptor amoris*,
the Professor of Love, and it is in this capacity that
Tranio cites him here.
34 *Balk logic*: Chop logic.
acquaintance: Acquaintances, friends.
35 *common talk*: Ordinary conversation.
36 *to quicken you*: To refresh yourself, as recreation.
38 *Fall to them as you find your stomach serves you*: Take
them up when you feel so inclined. *Fall to* means literally 'begin eating', and [*when*] *your stomach serves you*
'when you have an appetite'. The metaphors indicate
the practical bent of Tranio's mind.
39 *No profit grows where is no pleasure ta'en*: These words
are an adaptation of Horace's celebrated comment,
which was the foundation of Renaissance aesthetics:
Omne tulit punctum qui miscuit utile dulci – the most
successful artist is the man who has contrived to mix
the pleasurable with the instructive (*Ars Poetica*, 343).
ta'en: Taken (colloquial).
40 *affect*: Love, enjoy.
41 *Gramercies*: Many thanks (Old French *grant merci*).
45 *Katherina*: This name appears under the forms
Katerina, *Katherina*, *Katherine* and, of course, *Kate*
in F.
a pantaloon: The pantaloon (*pantalone* in Italian) was
a stock figure, and indeed the central figure, in the
Italian *Commedia dell'arte* (Comedy of skill). He was
always portrayed as an old man, a Venetian by origin
and dialect, and invariably appeared clad in tights, a
red jacket, a long black-sleeved gown and black slip-
pers. His main role was to serve as an obstacle to the
lovers. (For a full discussion of the character and the
part see Allardyce Nicoll, *The World of Harlequin*

(1963), pp. 44–55.) Gremio is explicitly referred to as *the old pantaloon* by Lucentio at III.1.36.

47 *show*: Play, spectacle, pageant.

50 *bestow*: Give in marriage.

55 *To cart her*: 'Carting' – undergoing a whipping while being drawn through the streets either in, or at the tail of, an open cart – was the punishment inflicted on bawds and whores. There is, of course, a quibble (in the sense of 'punning') on *court* in the previous line.
rough: Bad-tempered.

56 *will you*: Do you want.

58 *a stale of me amongst these mates*: A laughing-stock of me among these contemptible fellows (with a quibble on *stale* meaning 'harlot').

59 *Mates . . . No mates*: (1) Contemptible fellows; (2) husbands.

60 *mould*: Frame, nature.

62 *Iwis it is not halfway to her heart*: Certainly marriage (with you) is not a matter that she takes even half seriously.

63 *doubt not her care should be*: Be sure she would take care.

64 *comb your noddle*: Give you a dressing, beat you about the head.

65 *paint your face*: Scratch your face till it bleeds. In *The Taming of A Shrew* (scene 5, line 24) Katherina threatens to set her 'ten commandments' (finger-nails) in Ferando's face.
use: Treat.

68 *Husht*: Be quiet, not a word.
toward: On hand, about to begin.

69 *wonderful froward*: Incredibly disobedient, perverse.

73 *Mum*: Keep quiet.

74 *make good*: Perform, carry out.

78 *peat*: Pet, spoilt darling.

78–9 *It is best . . . an she knew why*: The best thing she can do is to make herself weep, if she knew of some excuse. 'To put finger in the eye and weep' was a proverbial expression. Shakespeare uses it again in *The Comedy of Errors*, where Adriana says:

> Come, come, no longer will I be a fool,
> To put the finger in the eye and weep. II.2.213–14

80 *content you in my discontent*: Take pleasure in my sorrow.
81 *pleasure*: Will, command.
    subscribe: Submit.
82 *instruments*: Musical instruments.
84 *Minerva*: The goddess of wisdom.
85 *strange*: Distant, unfriendly.
86 *effects*: Causes.
87 *mew her up*: Shut her up, confine her.
88 *for*: On account of.
90 *content ye*: Compose yourselves, be satisfied.
92 *for*: Because.
97 *Prefer*: Direct, recommend.
    cunning: Well-qualified, skilful.
103 *be appointed hours*: Be given a timetable.
105 *the devil's dam*: The devil's mother (proverbially thought of as worse than the devil himself and as the archetype of shrews).
    gifts: Endowments, natural qualities.
106 *hold*: Retain, keep.
    There! Love: F reads *Their loue*, which could mean 'the love of women', but confusion of 'their' and 'there' is common in early texts of the plays, and Gremio is fond of *There* as an exclamation (cf. 56).
106–8 *Love is not so great . . . but we may blow our nails together, and fast it fairly out*: The general sense of this passage is: 'Our rivalry over Bianca is not so important that we can't remain on friendly terms while we wait for things to improve.'
107 *but*: But that.
    blow our nails: Wait patiently.
108 *fast it fairly out*: Pass our period of abstention from love in a friendly manner.
    Our cake's dough on both sides: Our efforts have ended in failure for both of us. 'My cake is dough' was a proverbial way of announcing failure. Gremio uses the

phrase again at V.1.128.

110 *light on*: Find, come across.

111 *wish him*: Commend him, invite him to offer service.

113–14 *yet never brooked parle*: Never yet allowed for negotiations between us.

114 *upon advice*: On careful reflection.

it toucheth: It concerns, it is a matter of importance to.

117 *labour and effect*: Strive to carry out.

123 *so very a fool to*: Such an absolute fool as to.

125 *pass*: Exceed, go beyond.

127 *good fellows*: Rogues, needy adventurers.

an: If, provided that.

129 *I cannot tell*: I don't know what to say.

as lief: As soon, as readily.

130 *high-cross*: Market-cross in the centre of a town.

133 *bar in law*: Legal impediment (Baptista's refusal to allow them to court Bianca).

134 *it shall be so far forth friendly maintained till*: Our agreement shall be kept up in a friendly manner until.

136–7 *have to't afresh*: Let us renew our rivalry, to battle again.

137 *Happy man be his dole*: May the best man win. This proverbial expression for wishing someone good luck means, literally, 'may his lot be that of a happy man'.

137–8 *He that runs fastest gets the ring*: This proverb is given by John Heywood in 1546 under the following form:

> Where wooers hop in and out, long time may bring
> Him that hoppeth best, at last to have the ring [wedding-ring].

Shakespeare seems to have given the old saying an original twist here by relating it to the jousting-game in which each of a number of riders attempted to carry off on the point of his lance a circlet of metal suspended from a post.

139 *would I*: I wish that I. Gremio is continuing with the metaphor of 'running at the ring'.

141 *woo her, wed her, and bed her*: This is another proverb, very common in the sixteenth century, describing the progress

of a love affair from the wooing to the consummation.
rid: Free. Gremio has added a bit of his own to the original proverb.

144 *take such hold*: Take such firm root, gain such a hold of a man.

148 *love in idleness*: Lucentio is playing with two ideas: (1) the proverb 'Idleness begets lust'; (2) 'Love-in-idleness' as another name for the pansy, or Heartsease, as it was called. Cf. Oberon's description of it as 'a little western flower' (*A Midsummer Night's Dream*, II.1.166–8).

149 *plainness*: Frankness.

150 *as secret*: As intimate, as much in my confidence.

151 *As Anna to the Queen of Carthage was*: In Virgil's *Aeneid* (IV.8–30) Dido, queen of Carthage, confides to her sister Anna that she has fallen in love with her guest, Aeneas. The scene between the two sisters had been dramatized by Christopher Marlowe in his play *The Tragedy of Dido, Queen of Carthage* (III.1.55–78), published in 1594.

153 *achieve*: Win.

157 *Affection is not rated from the heart*: It's no use trying to expel love from the heart by scolding it.

158 *naught remains but so*: There's nothing left to be done but this.

159 *Redime te captum quam queas minimo*: Free yourself from captivity at the lowest ransom you can. Shakespeare took this line from Lily's *Latin Grammar* and not from the original source, Terence's *Eunuchus* (I.1.30), where it appears in a slightly different form.

160 *Go forward, this contents*: Carry on, this is the right sort of advice.

162 *longly*: Persistently.

163 *marked*: Noticed.
the pith of all: The central issue, the main point of it all.

165 *the daughter of Agenor*: Europa. According to Ovid (*Metamorphoses*, 2.846–75), Jupiter fell in love with her, and, in order to win her, appeared to her as a snow-white bull. He knelt before her and behaved so gently

that eventually she mounted on his back. He promptly rose, rushed into the sea and carried her off from Tyre, where her father was king, to Crete.

167 *Cretan strand*: Shore of Crete. It looks as though Shakespeare thought Europa had been carried off *from* Crete, instead of to it.

176 *Bend*: Apply, strain (as in bending a bow).
Thus it stands: This is the situation.

177 *curst and shrewd*: Waspish and difficult.

180 *closely mewed her up*: Confined her strictly to the house.

181 *Because she will not*: In order that she shall not.
annoyed with: Molested by.

183 *art thou not advised*: Didn't you notice.

185 *marry*: Indeed, to be sure.

186 *for my hand*: By my hand.

187 *Both our inventions meet and jump in one*: Our two plans concur and operate as one.

190 *device*: Scheme, plot.

193 *Keep house*: Entertain in the appropriate style.
ply his book: Study.

194 *countrymen*: Fellow-countrymen (natives of Pisa).

195 *Basta*: Enough (Italian).
I have it full: I've hit on the answer.

200 *port*: State, manner of life suiting my station.

202 *meaner*: Poorer (than I really am).

204 *Uncase thee*: Take off your outer garments.
coloured hat and cloak: The dress of an Elizabethan gentleman, as distinct from the *blue coats* (IV.1.81) worn by servants.

206 *charm him first to keep his tongue*: First give him strict orders not to blab.

207 *So had you need*: You need to. The broken line here gives the impression that there has been a cut, especially as Tranio does not explain why it is so necessary to keep Biondello quiet but continues his speech with the inconsequential words *In brief*.

208 *sith it your pleasure is*: Since it is your will.

209 *tied*: Obliged, bound.

211 *serviceable*: Diligent to serve.

212 *in another sense*: It did not occur to Lucentio's father that his son would require Tranio to change places with him.

216–17 *And let me be a slave t'achieve that maid | Whose sudden sight hath thralled my wounded eye*: The paradoxes here are the conventional ones of Elizabethan love-poetry.

217 *Whose sudden sight*: The sudden sight of whom.
thralled: Enslaved.

224 *frame your manners to the time*: Suit your behaviour to the occasion.

226 *countenance*: Manner.

229 *descried*: Seen, observed.

230 *as becomes*: As is fitting, in the proper manner.

231 *make way*: Go.

232 *Ne'er a whit*: Not in the least.

236–41 *So could I ... Lucentio*: Printed as prose in F, these lines are, in fact, doggerel verse of a kind that is also to be found in *The Comedy of Errors* (III.1.11–83) and in *Love's Labour's Lost* (IV.2.23–33)

236–7 *after ... daughter*: These two words, probably pronounced as 'arter' and 'darter', rhymed in Shakespeare's day. Cf. the Fool's lines in *King Lear* (I.4.314–18):

> A fox, when one has caught her,
> And such a daughter
> Should sure to the slaughter,
> If my cap would buy a halter –
> So the fool follows after.

243 *rests, that thyself execute*: Remains for you to carry out.

244–5 *To make ... weighty*: Another patch of doggerel verse.

244 *make one*: Become one.

245 *Sufficeth*: It is enough to say, I need only say.
The Presenters above speak: The presenter, who was a fairly common figure in Elizabethan drama (see, for example, Kyd's *The Spanish Tragedy*, Robert Greene's *James IV* and Ben Jonson's *Every Man Out of His Humour*), was the character, either human or

allegorical, who was responsible for the presentation or putting-on of a play. He normally sat *above*, and often commented on the progress of the action. In this play the Lord, whose idea it is that the show should be put on before Sly and his 'wife', has the best title to the role, while they can also be considered as 'Presenters' by virtue of their remarks on the play.

246 *LORD*: F reads 1. *Man.*, but no provision has been made for anyone other than a Messenger to be present with Sly and the Page, and neither a Messenger nor a Servant can really be called a 'Presenter'. See note to Ind. 2.126.

mind: Attend to, take notice of.

247 *coming to with a start*: Though not in F, this piece of business is obviously demanded by the context.

248 *matter*: Subject, story.

surely: No doubt.

249 *but*: Only just.

251 *Would*: I would that, I wish.

They sit and mark: These words clearly imply that the three *Presenters* were to remain in their places. The problem of why they say nothing further, especially after Sly has made his views on it all so plain, is a difficult one. See The Play in Performance, pp. lx–lxii.

I.2

0 *Petruchio*: The spelling of this name, with the 'ch' pronounced as in 'Charles', represents Shakespeare's attempt to find an English equivalent for the Italian name *Petruccio*. There is a servant called *Petrucio* in George Gascoigne's *Supposes*.

Grumio: Shakespeare may have got this name from Plautus's *Mostellaria*, where one of the characters, a downright countryman, is so called, but it could also be the result of an effort to give the English word 'groom' an Italian appearance.

1–4 *Verona . . . house*: Like Lucentio at the opening of the previous scene, Petruchio begins with a bit of self-explanation, but on this occasion it is kept down to a bare minimum and gives way almost at once to dramatic

action. The relationship between Petruchio and Grumio
here forms a nice contrast to that between Lucentio
and Tranio in I.1.

2 *but of all*: But especially, but above all.

4 *trow*: Believe, know.

his house: Having come on to the stage by one of the
main doors, Petruchio and Grumio cross to the other
main door, which now becomes the entrance to
Hortensio's house.

5 *knock*: Rap for admittance. Grumio takes the word in
its other sense of 'beat' or 'strike'.

7 *rebused*: Grumio's mistake for 'abused'.

8 *Villain*: Slave, wretch.

knock me here soundly: The *me* here is a relic of the old
dative meaning 'for me' – Grumio, of course, takes it
as the accusative – but by Shakespeare's time it had
become a device for lending life and colour to a statement and amounted to 'mark me' or 'I tell you'.

13–14 *I should knock you first . . . worst*: You are asking me to
strike you, so that you can then have an excuse for
giving me a drubbing.

16 *an*: If.

I'll ring it: I'll ring. The *it* is superfluous, as it is also
in *sing it*, and there is a quibble on 'ring' and 'wring'.

17 *sol-fa*: Sing.

He wrings him by the ears: He twists Grumio's ears.

21 *How do you*: How are you.

23 *part the fray*: Separate the combatants, stop the brawl.

24 *Con tutto il cuore ben trovato*: With all my heart well met
(Italian).

25–6 *Alla nostra casa ben venuto, | Molto honorato signor mio
Petruchio*: (Italian) Welcome to our house, most
worshipful Petruchio.

27 *compound*: Amicably settle.

28 *'leges*: Alleges.

in Latin: Grumio, despite his name, is a good solid
English character who does not know the difference
between Latin and Italian.

31 *use*: Treat.

32–3 *two and thirty, a pip out*: This is a jesting allusion to the
card game of 'one-and-thirty', the 'pips' being the
marks on the cards. According to John Ray in his
Collection of English Proverbs (1678), to be 'one-and-
thirty' meant to be drunk. It seems more likely to the
present editor, however, that Grumio is saying that his
master, like a gamester who has overshot the mark by
scoring thirty-two instead of thirty-one, is 'not quite
right – in the head'.

36 *A senseless*: An unreasonable.

38 *for my heart*: For my life.

41–2 *come you now with*: Do you now come along with.

44 *pledge*: Surety.

45 *this's*: This is (colloquial). F reads *this*.
heavy chance: Sad misunderstanding.

46 *ancient*: Of long standing.
pleasant: Merry, entertaining.

51 *in a few*: In short, to be brief.

54 *maze*: Chancy business (of looking for a wife).

55 *Haply*: With luck, fortunately.
to wive and thrive: Two proverbs, both of which help
to explain why Petruchio thinks of his enterprise as a
maze, are relevant here: 'It is hard to wive [get married]
and thrive both in a year' and 'In wiving and thriving
a man should take counsel of all the world, lest he light
upon a curse while he seeks for a blessing'. Petruchio
takes counsel, but then wisely disregards it.

58 *come roundly*: Speak plainly.

59 *And wish thee to a shrewd ill-favoured wife*: And
commend you to a sharp-tongued ill-conditioned wife
(*ill-favoured* must mean 'endowed with bad qualities',
rather than 'ugly', because at 85 Hortensio describes
Katherina as *beauteous*).

60 *Thou'dst*: Thou wouldst.

62 *th' art*: Thou art (abbreviated colloquial form).

67 *burden*: Musical accompaniment.

68 *foul*: Ugly, plain.
Florentius' love: Florentius is a knight in Gower's
Confessio Amantis. His life depends on his answering

the riddle 'what do women most desire', and he agrees
to marry a loathsome old hag on condition that she
tells him the answer. The same story is told by Chaucer
in *The Wife of Bath's Tale*.

69 *Sibyl*: In the *Metamorphoses* (14.130–51) Ovid has the
Sibyl of Cumae tell Aeneas how Apollo granted her as
many years of life as the number of grains of sand that
she could pick up in a handful.

   curst and shrewd: Waspish and shrewish.

70 *Xanthippe*: Wife of Socrates, notorious for her bad temper.

71 *moves me not*: Can't make any impression on me, can't
alter my plans.

71–2 *or not removes at least* | *Affection's edge in me*: Or at
least she can't destroy the keenness of my desire.

76 *flatly*: Plainly, downright.

77 *mind*: Intention.

78 *aglet-baby*: Small figure, often in the shape of a death's-
head, forming the tag of a lace.

78 *old trot*: Decrepit old woman, hag.

80–81 *so money comes withal*: Provided money comes with it.

82 *are stepped thus far in*: Have gone so far.

83 *that I broached*: That which I began.

88 *intolerable*: Intolerably.

90 *state*: Fortune.

94 *board*: Woo. Cf. Sir Toby Belch's similarly figurative
use of the naval word 'board' when he tells Sir Andrew,
'"Accost" is front her, board her, woo her, assail her'
(*Twelfth Night*, I.3.53–4).

   chide: Scold.

95 *crack*: Go off with a bang (like a gun).

97 *An affable*: A polite, kind.

103–4 *let me be thus bold with you* | *To give you over at this
first encounter*: Let me take the liberty of leaving you
at this our first meeting.

107 *O' my word*: On my word.

108 *do little good upon*: Have little effect on.

110 *an he begin once, he'll rail in his rope-tricks*: This is one
of the most obscure passages in the whole play. The
present editor thinks it means 'if he once begins, he'll

scold in his outrageous rhetoric'. The nonce-word *rope-tricks* is probably Grumio's version of 'rope-rhetorics', a term used by Thomas Nashe in his pamphlet *Have with You to Saffron-Walden*, published in 1596. There Nashe writes of Gabriel Harvey's 'Paracelsian rope-rethorique', apparently meaning 'bombastic rhetoric for which the author deserved to be hanged' (*The Works of Thomas Nashe*, ed. R. B. McKerrow (1904–10), vol. 3, p. 15). In view of the interest the Elizabethans had in 'the tropes of rhetoric', it is quite possible that the word 'trope-tricks', meaning 'subtleties of rhetoric', may well have existed as a slang term, though there is no record of it. If it did, the transition to *rope-tricks* would have been an easy one.

111   *stand*: Face, resist, withstand.

111–14 *he will throw a figure in her face . . . a cat*: The general sense of this passage is that Petruchio will use figures of rhetoric to such effect that Katherina will be quite overcome.

112   *throw a figure in her face*: Grumio is probably quibbling on two senses: (1) hurl a figure of speech at her; (2) subject her to the influence of the kind of spell-binding figure used by conjurers and magicians.
      disfigure: Deform, mar. But perhaps the word is used metaphorically to mean 'change her attitude'.

113–14 *than a cat*: Shakespeare may be ridiculing the casual and unthinking use of terms such as this.

116   *keep*: Keeping, custody.

117   *hold*: Safe-keeping.

119   *other more*: Others besides; *other* was a common form of the plural.

122   *For those defects*: On account of those faults.
      rehearsed: Recited.

124   *this order*: These measures.

129   *do me grace*: Do me a favour.

132   *Well seen*: Well served, well qualified.

139   *the rival of my love*: My rival in love (Gremio).

141   *A proper stripling and an amorous*: Grumio is being ironical at Gremio's expense.

     proper: Fine, handsome.

142 *note*: List of the books.

143 *them*: The books.
     fairly: Handsomely.

144 *see that at any hand*: See to that in any case.

145 *read no other lectures*: Give no other lessons.

148 *mend it with a largess*: Improve it with a donation.
     paper: The *note* or list of 142.

149 *them*: The books.

154 *as yourself were still in place*: As if you yourself were present all the time.

158 *woodcock*: Dupe, simpleton. The Elizabethans thought of the woodcock as a stupid bird.

161 *you are well met*: I'm glad to meet you.

162 *Trow you*: Do you know, can you guess?

167 *turn*: Needs.

170 *help me to*: Assist me in obtaining.

175 *bags*: Money-bags, wealth.

176 *vent*: Give vent to, utter.

178 *news indifferent good for either*: News that is equally good for each of us.

180 *Upon agreement from us to his liking*: On our agreement to conditions that suit him. The conditions, that Gremio and Hortensio bear the cost of Petruchio's wooing, are mentioned later (212–14).

183 *So said, so done, is well*: It's fine when actions come up to promises.

187 *What countryman*: Where do you come from, where's your home?

191 *were strange*: Would be surprising.

192 *if you have a stomach, to't a God's name*: If you have an inclination to try, get on with it in God's name.

194 *Will I live*: Certainly!

195 *Will he woo her . . . or I'll hang her*: Cf. Feste's remark: 'Many a good hanging prevents a bad marriage' (*Twelfth Night*, I.5.18).

196 *but to that intent*: Except for that purpose.

200 *chafèd*: Annoyed, enraged (the sweat of the hunted boar being compared with the foam of a stormy sea).

201 *field*: Battlefield.

204 *'larums*: Alarums, calls to arms made with drum and trumpet.

206 *to hear*: So F; but the emendation 'to th'ear', first suggested in the eighteenth century, makes good sense.

208 *fear boys with bugs*: Frighten boys with bugbears (bogies or hobgoblins).

   fears none: Is afraid of none.

211 *yours*: So F. The reading has been emended to 'ours' by some editors, so obscuring the dramatic point that Gremio is eager to shift any expense involved on to Hortensio.

213 *charge*: Expense.

215 *bravely dressed*: F reads *braue*, that is, 'richly attired'.

216 *be bold*: Take the liberty.

217 *readiest*: Easiest, quickest.

219–20 *He that has the two fair daughters – is't he you mean*: Biondello's remark has been prearranged as part of Tranio's opening gambit.

222 *her too*: F reads *her to –*, denoting either that a word is missing or that the compositor could not make out the sense of what he had printed. If a word is missing, it must be 'woo', but this does not fit Tranio's answer. 'Too' on the other hand, which is interchangeable in Shakespeare texts with 'to', follows naturally on Biondello's *you mean* (220) and fits in perfectly with Tranio's reply.

223 *What have you to do*: What is that to you?

224 *at any hand*: In any case.

233 *choice*: Chosen, appointed.

235 *Softly*: Gently, just a moment.

236 *Do me this right*: Do me this justice.

238 *not all*: Not altogether.

239 *And were his daughter fairer*: And even if his daughter were more beautiful.

241 *Fair Leda's daughter*: The lovely daughter of Leda (Helen of Troy). The *thousand wooers* was probably suggested by Marlowe's famous line, 'Was this the face that launched a thousand ships?' (*Dr Faustus*, 13.91).

242 *one more*: One more than she has already.

244 *Though Paris came*: Though Paris (the son of Priam, king of Troy, who stole Helen away from her husband Menelaus) were to come.

in hope to speed alone: Hoping to be the winner.

246 *give him head, I know he'll prove a jade*: Give him free scope, I know he'll soon tire. The language here is that of horsemanship – to give a horse its head is to cease checking it, and a jade is a poor worthless horse that soon grows tired.

248 *as ask*: As to ask.

253 *let her go by*: Leave her alone.

254–5 *Hercules . . . Alcides' twelve*: Hercules, otherwise known as Alcides, was the legendary hero of classical mythology who carried out twelve stupendous tasks, or labours as they were called. Gremio calls Petruchio Hercules and implies that he has taken on an even greater task.

255 *let it be more than*: Admit that it surpasses.

256 *understand you this of me in sooth*: Take this from me for certain.

257 *hearken for*: Lie in wait for, seek to win.

263 *Must stead*: Who must help, who must be of use to.

266 *whose hap shall be*: He whose good fortune it shall be.

267 *so graceless be to be ingrate*: Be so lacking in all decency as to be ungrateful.

268 *conceive*: Understand the situation.

270 *gratify*: Reward, requite.

271 *rest generally beholding*: Remain without exception under an obligation.

272 *slack*: Remiss, backward.

273 *contrive*: Spend, while away.

274 *quaff carouses*: Drink toasts.

277 *motion*: Proposal.

279 *ben venuto*: Literally, 'welcome' (Italian). Hortensio means that he will pay for Petruchio's entertainment.

II.1

0 *Enter Katherina, and Bianca with her hands tied*: F, which has neither Act nor scene heading here, reads *Enter*

Katherina and Bianca, but Bianca's first speech clearly
indicates the state in which she appears.

1 *wrong*: (1) Harm; (2) disgrace.

3 *gauds*: Pieces of finery, gewgaws. F reads *goods*.

12 *fancy*: Like, love.

13 *Minion*: Spoilt brat.

14 *affect*: Love.

17 *fair*: Fine, well dressed.

18 *envy*: Hate, feel jealous of (pronounced with the stress
   on the second syllable).

23 *dame*: Mistress, madam (implying a rebuke).
   whence grows this insolence: What is the reason for this
   disgraceful behaviour?

25 *meddle not*: Have nothing to do with.

26 *hilding*: Base wretch, baggage.

28 *cross*: Contradict, annoy.

29 *flouts*: Mocks, shows contempt of.

31 *suffer me*: Let me have my own way.

33 *I must dance bare-foot on her wedding-day*: An elder
   sister who remained unmarried was supposed to dance
   bare-foot at her younger sister's wedding. The phrase
   thus became proverbial for being unmarried.

34 *lead apes in hell*: This is another proverbial occupation
   of old maids – they led apes in hell because they had
   no children to lead into heaven. Cf. Beatrice's remarks
   on the same subject in *Much Ado About Nothing*,
   II.1.34–41.

36 *occasion of*: Opportunity for.

37 *grieved*: Afflicted.

38 *Enter Gremio . . . with Hortensio . . . books*: F's
   direction, omitting all mention of Hortensio, reads
   *Enter Gremio, Lucentio, in the habit of a meane man,
   Petruchio with Tranio, with his boy bearing a Lute and
   Bookes*.
   habit of a mean man: Dress of a poor man. Cf. Lucentio's
   description of the disguise he intends to assume, given
   at I.1.201–2.
   Cambio: A significant name, since it is the Italian for
   'exchange'.

45 *go to it orderly*: Go about the business in a proper orderly manner.

46 *give me leave*: Excuse me.

49 *affability*: Kindness, gentle behaviour.

54 *for an entrance to my entertainment*: As an entrance-fee for my reception, to show that I am in earnest.

57 *sciences*: Branches of knowledge.

59 *Accept of*: Accept.

61 *Y'are*: You are (colloquial).

62 *for*: As for.

63 *She is not for your turn*: She will not come up to your requirements, she's not the girl for you.

65 *like not of my company*: Don't approve of me.

67 *What may I call your name*: What is your name?

71 *Saving*: With all respect for, no offence meant to.

73 *Baccare*: Stand back! give place! A sixteenth-century proverb ran: 'Backare, quoth Mortimer to his sow.' The word, always used in a jocular sense, seems to have been made up from the adverb *back* with the addition of *-are*, the ending of the Latin infinitive.

74 *I would fain be doing*: I am eager for action (probably with a quibble on 'doing' in the sense of having sex).

76 *grateful*: Agreeable, welcome.

80 *Rheims*: The seat of a university founded in 1547.

86 *walk like a stranger*: Seem to be on your own, not one of the party.

93 *In the preferment of*: In giving precedence to.

95 *upon knowledge of*: When you know about.

98 *toward*: As a contribution to.

102 *opening one of the books*: This direction, which is not in F, seems necessary in order that Baptista may see Lucentio's name, which has not yet been mentioned, on the fly-leaf.

104 *mighty*: Illustrious, important, leading.

109 *To my daughters, and tell them both*: The line is unmetrical and something has probably been omitted from it; but it is impossible to say what the missing word was. F2 reads *To my two daughters*.

112 *dinner*: The main meal of the day in Shakespeare's

England, served between eleven o'clock and noon.

passing: Very, most.

114 *asketh*: Requires, demands.

122 *in possession*: In immediate possession.

123-4 *for that dowry I'll assure her of | Her widowhood*: In
exchange for that dowry I'll guarantee her her widow's
rights.

widowhood: The word here means 'the estate settled
upon a widow' in the marriage contract.

126 *Let specialties be therefore drawn between us*: Let explicit
detailed contracts between us therefore be drawn up.

130 *father*: Father-in-law. Petruchio's self-assurance is
splendidly brought out here.

131 *peremptory*: Always accented on the first syllable in
Shakespeare.

133 *the thing that feeds their fury*: The fuel Petruchio is
referring to is Katherina's shrewishness.

134-5 *Though little fire grows great . . . blow out fire and all*:
Petruchio makes it plain, through his use of this
analogy, that he thinks Katherina's headstrong temper
has been encouraged by the feeble opposition (*little
wind*) that it has encountered hitherto. His own opposition (*extreme gusts*) will be of a sterner kind, and so
more effective.

138 *happy be thy speed*: May the outcome be fortunate for
you.

139 *unhappy*: Harsh, inauspicious.

140 *to the proof*: So as to be invulnerable.

141 *shakes*: Shake (the old plural).

broke: Bruised and bleeding.

143 *I promise you*: Let me tell you, I assure you.

145 *prove a soldier*: A quibble on (1) become a soldier, and
(2) put a soldier to the test.

146 *hold with her*: Stand up to her handling, not break in
her hands.

147 *break her to the lute*: Train her to play the lute (as a horse
is broken to the bit). This is the first of a number of
analogies in which the taming of Katherina is compared
to the taming of a high-spirited animal or bird.

148 *broke the lute to me*: The comic effect of these lines is much increased if Hortensio appears with the broken lute draped round his neck like a horse-collar.

149 *frets*: Rings of gut or bars of wood upon the lute to regulate the fingering.

152 *Frets*: Vexations (quibbling).
     fume: Be in a rage (as in 'fret and fume').

156 *pillory*: An instrument of punishment, consisting of a pair of movable boards raised on a post, with holes through which the culprit's head and hands were thrust so that he appeared to be framed in wood.

157 *rascal*: Base, good-for-nothing.

158 *Jack*: A term of contempt used of a base or silly fellow.

159 *As had she studied to misuse me so*: As though she had given a lot of careful thought to how she might abuse me so.

160 *lusty*: Merry, high-spirited.

164 *Proceed in practice*: Carry on your lessons.

168 *attend*: Await.

170–80 *Say that she rail . . . be married*: Petruchio, to enable the audience to enjoy the ensuing scene to the full, announces his plan of campaign.

172 *clear*: Serenely beautiful.

176 *piercing*: Moving.

177 *pack*: Be gone.

179 *deny*: Refuse.

183 *heard . . . hard*: The two words were both pronounced 'hard', giving a pun.

186 *bonny*: Fine, strapping.

189 *dainties are all Kates*: Quibbling on 'cates' meaning 'delicacies'.

190 *consolation*: Comfort.

192 *sounded*: Proclaimed, praised aloud.

193 *deeply as to thee belongs*: Loudly as you deserve.

194 *moved*: Impelled.

195 *in good time*: Indeed, forsooth! Katherina is taking *moved* in its literal sense.

196–7 *I knew you at the first | You were a movable*: I recognized you from the start for (1) the piece of movable furniture that you are; (2) a person given to change.

198 *A joint-stool*: A wooden stool made by a joiner. The proverbial remark used by the Fool in *King Lear*, III.6.51, 'Cry you mercy, I took you for a joint-stool,' was a taunting apology for overlooking a person, as Katherina affects to do here.

199 *to bear*: To carry burdens. Petruchio gives the words a bawdy turn in the next line.

201 *jade*: A horse (of either sex) that soon tires. Katherina is impugning Petruchio's virility.

202 *burden*: (1) Lie heavy on; (2) make accusations against. For the second sense, which is the more important here, cf. *The Comedy of Errors*, V.1.209, 'this is false he burdens me withal'.

203 *light*: (1) Slight, slender; (2) wanton.

204 *Too light for such a swain as you to catch*: Too quick-witted to be caught by a country bumpkin like you.

205 *as heavy as my weight should be*: The right weight for one of my standing. Katherina has switched the allusion to money. Clipped and counterfeit coins were *Too light*. She is saying that she is good sound currency; her reputation as a woman is untarnished, and therefore no charge of lightness can touch her.

206 *Should be? Should – buzz*: Petruchio is quibbling here, first on 'be' and 'bee', and then on 'buzz' as (1) the noise made by bees, and (2) rumour or scandal. In effect he tells Katherina, 'You should just hear what is said about you.'

   ta'en: Taken, caught.

   buzzard: (1) Useless kind of hawk; (2) according to the *Oxford English Dictionary*, 'a worthless, stupid, or ignorant person'. In the opinion of the present editor, however, 'scandal-monger' or 'tale-bearer' fit this context much better. A similar use of the word will be found at *Richard III*, I.1.133, 'kites and buzzards prey at liberty'.

207 *turtle*: Turtle-dove (the symbol of faithful love).

208 *Ay, for a turtle, as he takes a buzzard*: The best explanation of this difficult passage is given by Dover Wilson,

who paraphrases it thus: 'the fool will take me for a
faithful wife, as the turtle-dove swallows the cock-
chafer [yet another meaning of 'buzzard']'.

215 *tales*: Rumours, discreditable gossip (with, of course,
a pun on 'tails' meaning 'backsides').

216 *What, with my tongue in your tail*: Apart from its obvious
lewdness, this means, 'What, are you going to turn tail
on my repartee?'
come again: (1) Come back; (2) let's renew the combat.
Cf. *Hamlet*, V.2.297, 'Nay, come again.'
He takes her in his arms: Not in F, but clearly indicated
by Katherina's remark at 219.

217 *try*: Test, make trial of.

219 *loose your arms*: (1) Relax your hold; (2) lose your coat
of arms (the mark of a gentleman).

222 *in thy books*: To be in the herald's books was to be registered as a gentleman, but there is also a pun on being
in someone's good books.

223 *crest*: (1) Figure or device borne above the shield and
helmet in a coat of arms; (2) a tuft of feathers or the
like on an animal's head.
coxcomb: A fool's cap, like a cock's comb in shape and
colour.

224 *so*: Provided that.

225 *craven*: A fighting-cock that is not game.

227 *crab*: (1) Crab-apple; (2) sour-tempered person with a
sour-looking face.

231 *Well aimed of such a young one*: A good guess for one
so raw.

232 *too young*: Too strong.

234 *scape*: Escape.

235 *chafe*: (1) Vex, annoy; (2) excite, heat.

236 *passing*: Very, extremely.

238 *a very liar*: An absolute liar.

239 *pleasant*: Merry.
gamesome: Sportive, gay.

240 *But slow in speech*: Not a bit sharp-tongued.

241 *askance*: Scornfully, with disdain.

243 *cross*: Given to contradiction, perverse.

244 *entertain'st*: Receivest.

245 *conference*: Conversation.

251 *whom thou keep'st command*: Order your own servants about, not me.

252 *Dian*: Diana, the goddess of chastity and hunting.
become: Adorn, grace.

255 *sportful*: Amorous, wanton.

256 *study*: Learn off by heart.

257 *mother-wit*: Natural intelligence.

258 *A witty mother, witless else her son*: A wise mother she must be, for without her help her son has no wits of his own.

259 *Am I not wise . . . keep you warm*: The retort is an allusion to the proverb 'He is wise enough that can keep himself warm'. Katherina means that Petruchio has the bare minimum of intelligence necessary for existence, and no more.

263 *'greed*: Agreed.

264 *will you, nill you*: Whether you will or whether you won't.

265 *for your turn*: To fit your needs, exactly right for you.

267 *like*: Love.

270 *wild Kate*: With a pun on 'wild-cat'.

271 *Conformable*: Tractable, compliant.
household: Domestic.

274 *how speed you*: How are you getting on, what progress are you making?

276 *speed amiss*: Not make good progress.

277 *In your dumps*: Are you feeling down-hearted?

278 *I promise you*: I can tell you.

282 *to face the matter out*: To get his own way by sheer effrontery.

285 *for policy*: As a deliberate policy, for her own purposes.

286 *froward*: Difficult, refractory.

287 *hot*: Violent, passionate.

288 *a second Grissel*: The famous story of Patient Griselda, the model of wifely obedience, is the subject of Chaucer's *The Clerk's Tale*. Borrowed by Chaucer from Boccaccio's *Decameron*, it was subsequently treated in

numerous tales and ballads in English. Two plays on
the theme had been written by the time Shakespeare
was two years old, and another, entitled *Patient Grissell*,
by Dekker, Chettle and Haughton was first acted in
1600.

289 *Roman Lucrece*: The tale of Lucrece, the legendary
Roman heroine who committed suicide after having
been raped by Tarquin, is told by Shakespeare himself
in his elaborate narrative poem *The Rape of Lucrece*,
first published in 1594.

294 *speeding*: Success.
good night our part: Farewell to our share in the business.

302 *vied*: Redoubled. To 'vie' was a technical term in card-
playing meaning 'to raise the stakes'.

303 *twink*: Twinkling, instant.

304 *'Tis a world to see*: It's a treat to see.

306 *meacock*: Spiritless.
shrew: The sixteenth-century pronunciation of this
word is indicated by F's spelling *shrow* at V.2.187, and
confirmed by the rhymes at IV.1.196–7 and V.2.28–9.

308 *'gainst*: In readiness for (colloquial form of 'against').

310 *fine*: Handsomely dressed, in her finery.

311–13 *give me your hands . . . witnesses*: This brief ceremony
before witnesses was the essential part of an Elizabethan
marriage. Once this pre-contract, as it was called, had
been made, neither party could marry another person.
Cf. the Duke's words to Mariana in *Measure for Measure*,
IV.1.71–2:

> He [Angelo] is your husband on a pre-contract.
> To bring you thus together, 'tis no sin.

315 *apace*: Quickly, soon.

318 *clapped up*: Fixed up in a hurry, arranged in an impro-
vised manner.

320 *desperate mart*: Reckless and chancy business arrangement – one that is probably doomed to failure.

321 *'Twas a commodity lay fretting by you*: It (referring to

Katherina) was a piece of goods that was deteriorating
in value while it remained on your hands. There is a
quibble on *fretting*: (1) decaying through moth and
rust; (2) chafing with vexation.

323 *quiet in*: F reads *quiet me*, the compositor having taken
'inne' for 'me'. The same mistake occurs again at IV.2.71.

330 *Youngling*: Stripling, novice.

332 *Skipper*: Light-brained skipping fellow. Cf. *Henry IV,
Part I*, III.2.60, where the King contemptuously
describes Richard II as 'The skipping King'.
nourisheth: Provides the good things of life.

333 *flourisheth*: Prospers, thrives.

334 *compound*: Compose, make an amicable settlement of.

335 *deeds*: (1) Actions; (2) legal deeds, title-deeds.
he of both: The one of you two.

336 *dower*: The land and goods which the husband settled
on his wife at marriage in order to provide for her
widowhood in case she survived him.

340 *plate*: Utensils of silver.

341 *lave*: Wash.

342 *hangings*: Draperies with which beds and walls were
hung.

343 *crowns*: Coins worth five shillings (25p) each.

344 *arras counterpoints*: Counterpanes of Arras tapestry.

345 *tents*: Bed-testers or canopies.

346 *bossed*: Embossed, studded.

347 *Valance of Venice gold in needlework*: Valances (fringes
on the canopy of a bed) adorned with Venetian embroidery in gold thread.

348 *belongs*: The old plural.

350 *milch-kine to the pail*: Cows whose milk goes to the
dairy (not to feed calves).

352 *answerable to this portion*: Corresponding to an estate
on this scale.

353 *struck in years*: Advanced in age, old.

356 *came well in*: Was mentioned at the right time, was very
apropos – since Tranio now makes great play with the
fact that he is an only son.
list: Listen.

360 *rich Pisa walls*: The walls of rich Pisa.

362–3 *two thousand ducats ... fruitful land*: Fertile land bringing in an income of two thousand ducats a year. A ducat was a Venetian gold coin worth about nine shillings (45p).

363 *her jointure*: The estate settled on her to provide for her widowhood.

364 *pinched you*: Put you in a tight corner, gained an advantage in the argument.

366 *My land amounts not to so much in all*: The capital value of my land does not come to that.

367 *argosy*: Merchant-vessel of the largest size, especially one from Ragusa – whence the name – or Venice.

368 *Marseilles road*: The roadstead (sheltered anchorage) at Marseilles. F reads *Marcellus roade*, and thus indicates the sixteenth-century pronunciation of 'Marseilles'.

371 *galliasses*: Heavy, low-built vessels, larger than galleys.

372 *tight*: Sound, watertight.

378 *out-vied*: Out-bidden. A card-player was *out-vied* when he refused to stake any more on his hand.

383 *but a cavil*: Merely a captious objection.

393 *gamester*: Adventurer, gambler. Gremio has picked up the allusion implicit in Tranio's use of the word *out-vied* at 378.

395 *Set foot under thy table*: Live on your charity.
     a toy: Sheer nonsense.

398 *faced it with a card of ten*: Brazened the matter out by playing a card with ten pips. To 'outface with a card of ten' was a proverbial phrase for bluffing.

399 *'Tis in my head*: I have a scheme.

400 *I see no reason but*: I see it is necessary that.
     supposed: The pretended, the substitute.

402 *wonder*: Miracle.

403 *get*: Beget.

404 *I fail not of my cunning*: I don't lose my ingenuity.

III.1

This scene is headed *Actus Tertia.* in F, though there is no indication there of where the second Act begins. It shows a side of Bianca's character that has not been apparent up to this point.

1–3 *Fiddler, forbear, you grow too forward, sir . . . withal*:
From these lines it looks as though Hortensio, when
the scene opens, is holding Bianca's hand to *teach her
fingering*, as he sought to do with Katherina at II.1.150.

2 *entertainment*: Reception.

3 *withal*: With.

4 *But, wrangling pedant, this is*: The line is metrically
defective but it is impossible to say what has been
omitted from it.

6 *prerogative*: Precedence.

8 *lecture*: Lesson.

9 *Preposterous*: The word is used here in its literal sense,
meaning 'one who inverts the natural order of things',
'one who puts the cart before the horse'.

10 *ordained*: Created, instituted.

12 *usual pain*: Customary toil, normal work.

14 *serve in*: Serve up – Lucentio's way of voicing his
contempt for Hortensio and his music.

15 *braves*: Bravadoes, ostentatious displays of defiance.

18 *no breeching scholar in the schools*: No schoolboy liable
to be flogged.

19 *'pointed*: Appointed.

22 *the whiles*: The while.

25 *That will be never*: Lucentio is deliberately taking *in
tune* in the sense of 'being in a good temper'.

28–9 *Hic ibat Simois, hic est Sigeia tellus . . . senis*: These
lines from Ovid (*Heroides*, 1.33–4) mean 'Here ran the
[river] Simois; here is the Sigeian land [Troy]; here
stood the lofty palace of old Priam.'

35 *port*: State, style.

36 *the old pantaloon*: Gremio. See second note to I.1.45.

38 *fie*: An exclamation of disgust.

39 *Spit in the hole, man, and tune again*: This is a perver-
sion of the proverb that was used to encourage someone
to make a second attempt, 'Spit in your hands and take
better hold.' Lucentio is showing his ignorance of
music, because to spit in the sound-hole of a lute would
not help to tune it.

46–56 *How fiery and forward our pedant is . . . you both*: In F the speeches in this section of the dialogue are wrongly assigned as follows:

Luc. How fiery . . .
                              . . . I mistrust.
Bian. Mistrust it . . .
                              . . . grandfather.
Hort. I must . . .
                              . . . you both.

The prime cause of the confusion was probably the use of *Lic.*, the shortened form of Hortensio's assumed name Licio, in the speech-prefixes, since *Lic.* would be very difficult to distinguish from *Luc.* Similar confusion occurs at IV.2.4–8 (see note).

48 *Pedascule*: A nonce-word coined as a contemptuous diminutive of 'pedant' on the analogy of *didaskalos* – the Greek for 'master'.

50–51 *Aeacides | Was Ajax . . . grandfather*: Ajax Telamonius, one of the Greek heroes in the Trojan War, was also known as Aeacides from the name of his grandfather Aeacus. Lucentio, in an attempt to blind Hortensio with Ovid, has moved on to the next line of *Heroides*, 1, which begins 'Illic Aeacides'.

55–6 *Good master, take it not unkindly . . . you both*: Bianca is addressing Hortensio, who alone has reason to be displeased; and *pleasant with you both* stretches her apology to cover Lucentio's chaff, and her laughter at it.

57 *give me leave*: A polite way of saying 'Please go'.

59 *formal*: Punctilious, concerned for your professional rights.

60 *withal*: At the same time.
   but: Unless.

63 *order*: Method.

65 *gamut*: The musical scale.
   briefer sort: Quicker fashion.

66 *pithy*: Condensed.
   effectual: Effective.

71   *ground of all accord*: Basis of all harmony.

74   *ut*: Corresponds to the 'doh' of modern usage.

75   *one clef, two notes*: It has been suggested that the *one clef* is love and the *two notes* Hortensio's real and his assumed personality.

78–9 *so nice | To change*: So capricious as to exchange.

79   *odd inventions*: Fantastical new ideas.

80   *SERVANT*: F heads this speech *Nicke.*, which some editors have taken as the name of the actor who first played the part. However, it seems most improbable that Shakespeare would have had a particular actor in mind for a part that only amounts to three lines.

87–8 *if thy thoughts, Bianca, be so humble | To cast*: If your inclinations, Bianca, are so low that you cast.

88   *stale*: Decoy, lure. The metaphor, from falconry, is carried on in the next line. Hortensio is beginning to see Bianca as a hawk that will stoop to anything.

89   *Seize thee that list*: Let anyone who wishes have you.
     ranging: (1) Straying (of a hawk); (2) being inconstant (of a lover or wife).

90   *will be quit with thee by changing*: Will get even with you by loving another.

III.2

0   *Enter Baptista . . . Lucentio as Cambio . . . Katherina*: F's direction reads *Enter Baptista, Gremio, Tranio, Katherine, Bianca, and others, attendants*. The omission of Lucentio from it is probably due to the fact that he says nothing until 137.

5   *To want*: To be without.

10   *rudesby, full of spleen*: Rough unmannerly fellow full of whims and caprices.

14   *to be noted for*: In order to be known as, to get a reputation as.

16   *Make feast, invite friends, and*: F reads *Make friends, inuite, and*, which is neither good sense nor good metre. The reading adopted in this edition is based on Petruchio's line at II.1.309: 'Provide the feast, father, and bid the guests.'

22–5 *Upon my life, Petruchio means but well . . . honest*: At

some stage in the evolution of *The Taming of the Shrew*
these lines must have belonged to Hortensio, who is
Petruchio's friend and therefore knows a good deal
about him. They are out of place in the mouth of
Tranio, who, from this point onwards, appears to have
taken over much that must originally have been written
for Hortensio.

23 *Whatever fortune stays him from his word*: Whatever
accident prevents him from keeping his promise.

25 *merry*: Facetious, a bit of a joker.

honest: One who keeps his word.

26 *Exit weeping, followed by Bianca and the other women*:
F's direction *Exit weeping* is simpler and more dramatic,
but it has been expanded in order to get the bridal train
off the stage.

27 *now to weep*: For weeping now.

29 *of thy impatient*: F reads *of impatient*, but the necessary
thy appears in F2.

30 *such old news*: F reads *such newes*, but Baptista's comment
in the next speech shows that *old*, meaning 'good old'
or 'rare old', has been omitted.

42 *what to*: What of.

44 *jerkin*: Short outer coat or jacket.

45 *boots that have been candle-cases*: Boots too old for wear
that have been used to keep candle-ends in.

47 *chapeless*: Lacking a sheath. The 'chape' was literally
the metal plate on a scabbard that covered the point of
a sword.

48 *points*: Tagged laces used for fastening the hose to the
doublet.

hipped: Lamed in the hip.

49 *of no kindred*: That don't match, that are not a pair.

49–50 *possessed with*: Affected by, suffering from.

50 *the glanders*: A contagious disease in horses, marked by
swellings beneath the jaw and discharge of mucous
matter from the nostrils.

like to: Likely to.

mose in the chine: The word *mose* is not known outside
this passage and is probably corrupt. 'To mourn of the

chine' was to suffer from the final stage of 'glanders', and this is probably what is meant here.

51 *lampass*: A disease of horses in which the fleshy lining behind the front teeth swells and hinders mastication.

fashions: Farcy (a horse disease similar to glanders).

52 *windgalls*: Soft tumours on a horse's legs just above the fetlocks.

sped with: Ruined by.

spavins: Swellings of the leg joints.

rayed: Soiled, befouled.

yellows: Jaundice.

53 *fives*: Strangles (a swelling of the parotid glands).

stark spoiled with: Absolutely wrecked by.

staggers: A horse disease marked by giddiness.

54 *begnawn*: Gnawed at.

bots: A disease caused by intestinal worms.

swayed: Strained. F reads *Waid*.

54–5 *shoulder-shotten*: With a dislocated shoulder.

55 *near-legged before*: Knock-kneed in the front legs.

55–6 *half-cheeked bit*: Bit on which the cheeks (the rings or side pieces attaching the bit to the bridle) had got broken.

56 *headstall*: The part of the bridle covering the horse's head.

sheep's leather: Not so strong as pigskin or leather of cowhide, which were normally used.

57 *restrained*: Drawn tight.

58 *new-repaired*: F has *now repaired*, but the context makes it clear that this operation has been done not once but time and again.

girth: The leather band going round a horse's belly and drawn tight to hold the saddle in place.

59 *pieced*: Mended.

crupper: Strap, normally of leather, ending in a loop which passes under the horse's tail and prevents the saddle from slipping.

of velure: Made of velvet.

60 *two letters for her name fairly set down in studs*: Her two initials handsomely marked on it in studs (probably of brass or silver).

61 *pack-thread*: String.

63 *for all the world caparisoned*: In every respect harnessed, dressed in trappings exactly.

64 *stock*: Stocking.
   kersey: Coarse woollen cloth.

65 *boot-hose*: Over-stocking which covers the leg like a jack-boot.

66 *list*: Strip of cloth.
   the humour of forty fancies: This must be an allusion to some kind of fashionable affectation, but precisely what it was no one knows.

66–7 *pricked in't*: Pinned to it.

69 *odd humour pricks*: Strange whim that incites.

78 *all one*: One and the same thing.

79–83 *Nay, by Saint Jamy . . . many*: This jingle is printed as prose in F.

80 *I hold you*: I bet you.

87 *I come not well*: I don't arrive opportunely? (Petruchio has noticed the look of displeasure on Baptista's face.)

88 *you halt not*: Taking *come* in the literal sense of 'walk', Baptista points out that Petruchio's entrance has been unceremonious.

90 *Were it not better*: F reads *Were it better*, which does not make very good sense.

92 *Gentles*: Gentlefolk, gentlemen.

94 *wondrous monument*: Strange portent.

95 *Some comet*: Comets were regarded as omens of disaster. Cf. *Julius Caesar*, II.2.30–31:

> When beggars die, there are no comets seen;
> The heavens themselves blaze forth the death of princes.

   prodigy: Omen.

98 *unprovided*: Unprepared, improperly dressed.

99 *habit*: Dress, outfit.
   estate: Rank, social status.

101 *occasion of import*: Matter of consequence, important reason.

105 *Sufficeth*: It is enough that.

106 *digress*: (1) Go out of my way; (2) deviate from my promise.

110 *wears*: Is passing, wears on.

111 *unreverent*: Disrespectful, unseemly.

115 *Good sooth*: Yes indeed, truly.
    ha': Have (colloquial).

117 *wear*: Wear away, use up. The allusion is bawdy.

122 *lovely*: Loving.

123–5 *He hath some meaning in his mad attire . . . church*: These words, which give the impression that Tranio is about to follow Petruchio, were almost certainly written for Hortensio in the original version of the play. There can be little doubt that the part of Hortensio has been rather clumsily excised from this scene and that his words have not very appropriately been given to Tranio.

126 *event*: Upshot, outcome.

127 *But, sir, to love*: F reads *But sir, Loue*, which does not make sense. Some editors change this to 'But to her love' which certainly makes the meaning much clearer. The abrupt beginning of this speech, together with Tranio's remaining onstage after his previous remarks, and with the presence of Lucentio, who is not included in F's entry at the beginning of the scene and who has not said a word hitherto, all point to cobbling. There is every indication that something has been cut between Baptista's exit and the beginning of this speech.

127–8 *to love concerneth us to add | Her father's liking*: It is essential for us to win her father's good will and join it to her love for you.

131 *It skills not much*: It doesn't matter much, it makes no difference.

138 *steps*: Movements, actions.

139 *to steal our marriage*: To make a secret marriage.

140 *let all the world say no*: Even though it meets with universal opposition.

143 *watch our vantage*: Look out for a favourable opportunity.

144 *overreach*: Dupe, get the better of.

145 *narrow-prying*: Inquisitive.

146 *quaint*: Crafty, scheming.

147 *Enter Gremio*: The very short space of time allowed for the marriage — a mere twenty lines — adds to the evidence that the dialogue between Tranio and Lucentio has been heavily cut.

148 *came you*: Have you come.

149 *As willingly as e'er I came from school*: Like much that Gremio says, this expression was a proverbial one.

150 *And is the bride and bridegroom coming home*: Shakespeare often uses the singular form of the verb when the subject is two singular nouns. Cf. 'Hanging and wiving goes by destiny' (*The Merchant of Venice*, II.9.83).

151 *a groom indeed*: A really rough individual just like a servingman.

156 *a fool*: A gentle innocent (term of pity, as often in Shakespeare).

157 *Sir Lucentio*: In Shakespeare's day foreigners belonging to the gentry were often addressed as *Sir*. Lucentio, like Vincentio at IV.2.106, is regarded as a foreigner because he comes from Pisa.

158 *Should ask*: Asked, came to ask. *Should* is sometimes used by Shakespeare to denote a reported statement: cf. *As You Like It*, III.2.167–8, 'But didst thou hear without wondering how thy name should be hanged and carved upon these trees?'

159 *by gogs-wouns*: By God's wounds (a common oath).

161 *again to take it up*: To take it up again.

162 *took him*: Struck him, gave him.

164 *Now take them up*: Here *them* refers to the bride's dress. Petruchio is explaining his conduct by saying that he suspected the bending priest of trying to interfere with Katherina's underwear — cf. Grumio's remarks to the Tailor at IV.3.154–9. Such a suspicion would have some plausibility for an Elizabethan audience, since it was customary after the marriage ceremony for the young men present to rush forward and pluck off the elaborate emblems made of ribbons that the bride wore on

her dress, and also to remove her ribbon garters.

164 *if any list*: If anyone cares to (an obvious threat to any who sought to follow the custom described in the previous note).

165 *rose up again*: F reads *rose againe* which is unmetrical. Another way of curing the defect is by reading 'arose again'.

166–82 *Trembled and shook . . . minstrels play*: These lines are printed as prose in F.

167 *cozen*: Cheat, deceive (by some irregularity that would make the marriage invalid).

169 *He calls for wine*: At the conclusion of the marriage service in Shakespeare's time a cup of muscadel (see note below) with cakes or sops in it was drunk by the bride, the bridegroom and the company.

171 *muscadel*: A sweet wine. Petruchio leaves none for anyone else.

174 *hungerly*: Sparsely, having a famished undernourished look.

180 *rout*: Company, crowd of guests.

184 *think*: Expect.

190 *Make it no wonder*: Don't be surprised.

202 *not stay*: Not content to stay.
    how you can: How you may.

203 *horse*: Horses. 'Horse', the old form of the plural, was still common in Shakespeare's time.

204–5 *they be ready – the oats have eaten the horses*: The horses are fresh (ready to gallop) because they have had more oats than they could eat.

210 *You may be jogging whiles your boots are green*: Be off while your boots are fresh (proverbial expression for getting rid of an unwelcome guest).

212 *a jolly*: An arrogant, overbearing.

213 *That take it on you at the first so roundly*: Since you assume authority so unhesitatingly from the outset.

214 *content thee*: Compose yourself, keep your temper.

215 *what hast thou to do*: What business of yours is it, what right have you to interfere?

216 *stay my leisure*: Wait till I'm ready.

223 *domineer*: Feast riotously.

226 *for*: As for.

227 *Nay, look not big, nor stamp, nor stare, nor fret*: These words are almost a concealed stage direction to Katherina – it is what she should be doing – but Petruchio, affecting not to see her, speaks them angrily to the rest of the company.

big: Angry, threatening.

229–31 *She is my goods, my chattels, she is my house . . . any thing*: Much of this echoes the Tenth Commandment. Petruchio wittily accuses the company of coveting Katherina.

233 *I'll bring mine action on the proudest he*: I'll take legal proceedings against the proudest man.

238 *buckler*: Shield, defend.

240 *Went they not*: If they had not gone (subjunctive).

244 *is Kated*: Has caught the 'Kate' (as though it were the name of a disease). Cf. Beatrice's remark: 'God help the noble Claudio! If he have caught the Benedick, it will cost him a thousand pound ere 'a be cured' (*Much Ado About Nothing*, I.1.81–3).

245–6 *wants | For to supply*: Are not here to fill.

247 *there wants no junkets*: There is no lack of delicacies.

249 *room*: Place, seat.

250 *bride it*: Play the bride.

IV.1

F marks no Act division at this point, though the move to Petruchio's house in the country is the first real change in the location of the action since the play proper began. Shakespeare makes it abundantly plain in Grumio's first speech that the move has taken place and that this house is a very different place from Padua. Even the weather is on Petruchio's side.

1 *jades*: Vicious worthless horses.

2 *foul ways*: Dirty roads.

3 *rayed*: Dirtied.

5 *a little pot and soon hot*: Grumio is quoting a well-known proverb which means that little men soon grow angry. That Grumio was imagined by Shakespeare as

a little man is also evident from his reference to *a taller
man than I* (9) and from Curtis's calling him *you three-
inch fool* (23).

7 *come by*: Get, find.

11 *so coldly*: Like one benumbed with cold.

16–17 *fire, fire, cast on no water*: This is a reference to the catch

> Scotland's burning, Scotland's burning,
>   See yonder! See yonder!
> Fire, fire! Fire, fire!
>   Cast on water! Cast on water!

Grumio, unlike Scotland, wants to burn.

18 *hot*: Angry, violent.

20 *winter tames man, woman, and beast*: This is an allusion
to the proverb 'Winter and wedlock tame both man
and beast'. Grumio significantly adds woman to the
list.

23 *I am no beast*: By naming himself third, Grumio has
equated himself, and therefore his fellow-servant
Curtis, with the beasts. Hence Curtis's rejoinder.

24–5 *thy horn is a foot, and so long am I at the least*: The
inevitable retort – Grumio says that he is big enough
to have made Curtis a cuckold.

26 *complain on*: Complain about.

28 *hot office*: Duty of fire-making.

32 *Do thy duty, and have thy duty*: Do thy duty and take
thy due.

36 *Jack boy, ho boy*: An allusion to a catch which begins

> Jack boy, ho boy, News:
> The cat is in the well.

36–7 *as wilt thou*: As you could wish.

38 *cony-catching*: Trickery, evasion (perhaps with reference to Grumio's fondness for catches).

41 *rushes strewed*: The strewing of fresh rushes on the floor
was an essential part of the preparation for a guest.

42 *fustian*: Coarse cloth made of cotton and flax.

43 *Jacks*: (1) Men-servants; (2) leather drinking-vessels.
44 *Jills*: (1) Maid-servants; (2) metal drinking-vessels.
   the carpets laid: On tables and chests rather than on the floor, which was strewn with rushes.
52 *ha't*: Have it (colloquial).
56 *feel*: Experience, suffer.
57 *sensible*: (1) Capable of being felt; (2) easily understood.
59 *Imprimis*: First, to begin with (Latin).
61 *Both of*: Both on.
64 *crossed*: Interrupted.
67 *bemoiled*: Covered with mud and dirt.
73 *of worthy memory*: Worthy of remembrance, that ought not to be forgotten.
74 *unexperienced*: In ignorance of them.
76 *more shrew*: More of a shrew (*shrew* could be applied to either sex).
78 *But what*: But why.
80 *slickly*: Smoothly, sleekly.
81 *blue coats*: Normal uniform of servants.
82 *of an indifferent knit*: Of a reasonable pattern, not too showy.
82–3 *curtsy with their left legs*: As a token of submission – to put the best foot first was a sign of defiance.
84 *horse-tail*: Horse's tail.
   kiss their hands: To kiss one's own hands was a mark of respect to a superior.
87–8 *to countenance*: To grace, to honour.
91 *calls*: This is the second person singular. Shakespeare, who wrote his words to be spoken, not read, often avoids the '-est' form.
93 *credit*: Honour, do credit to. Grumio, of course, takes the word in the other sense of 'provide credit for'.
102 *spruce*: Lively, brisk.
103 *All things is ready*: *All things* is thought of as a collective equivalent to 'everything'.
105 *Cock's passion*: A corruption of 'by God's Passion'.
111 *logger-headed*: Thick-headed, stupid.
115 *peasant swain*: Country bumpkin.

whoreson: Literally, 'son of a whore', but commonly used as a term of contempt and reprobation.

malt-horse drudge: Slow heavy horse, used to grind malt by working a treadmill.

119 *all unpinked*: Entirely without their proper ornamentation. To 'pink' leather was to decorate it by punching out a pattern on it.

i'th': In the (colloquial).

120 *link*: Blacking made of the material of burnt torches, or 'links', as they were called.

121 *sheathing*: Being fitted with a scabbard.

126 *Where is the life that late I led*: This is the first line of a song that is now lost, and *Where are those* appears to be the continuation of it. The existence of the song is known, because an answer to it, entitled 'Dame Beauty's Reply to the Lover late at Liberty', was published in Clement Robinson's *A Handful of Pleasant Delights*, 1584. The song would be appropriate to Petruchio's newly married state.

127 *Where are those –*: F reads *Where are those?*

128 *Food, food, food, food*: F reads *Soud, soud, soud, soud.*, which makes no sense whatever. Food, however, is exactly what Petruchio wants, and if it were spelled 'foud' in the manuscript, as it well may have been, the mistake is easily intelligible, since the letter 'f' and the 'long s' (ʃ) closely resembled each other.

129 *when, I say*: Common expression denoting impatience.

131 *It was the friar of orders grey . . . way*: These lines are the beginning of another lost ballad. The friar in question is a Grey friar or Franciscan.

133 *Out*: An expression of anger.

134 *mend*: Make a better job of.

135 *Some water here*: Washing of the hands before meals, especially important at a time when people ate with their fingers, was carried out at table in Shakespeare's England.

Enter one with water: The direction is placed at this point in F and there is no need to move it, as many editors have done, four lines down to make it follow

Petruchio's second demand.

137 *my cousin Ferdinand*: This looks like a loose end, for
     the cousin never turns up.

143 *beetle-headed*: Thick-headed. A 'beetle' is a heavy
     wooden mallet.

     flap-eared: With heavy pendulous ears.

144 *stomach*: Appetite.

145 *give thanks*: Say grace.

149 *dresser*: Kitchen-table on which food was prepared.

151 *trenchers*: Wooden platters used for serving up meat.

152 *heedless joltheads*: Careless blockheads.

153 *I'll be with you straight*: I'll be after you, I'll chastise
     you.

     Exeunt Servants hurriedly: F provides no direction here
     but one is plainly needed both as a consequence of
     Petruchio's threat and so that the Servants can *Enter
     severally* at 164.

154 *disquiet*: Upset, in a temper.

155 *well*: Good, satisfactory.

158 *For it engenders choler*: For the belief that overcooked
     meat produced an excess of choler, and so stimulated
     anger, see *The Comedy of Errors*, II.2.67–8, where
     Dromio of Syracuse begs his master not to eat dry
     unbasted meat, 'Lest it make you choleric, and purchase
     me another dry basting.'

160 *of ourselves*: By nature.

162 *mended*: Put right.

163 *for company*: Together.

164 *severally*: One by one.

166 *He kills her in her own humour*: He outdoes her (and so
     masters her) in her own special line of tantrums.

169 *Making a sermon of continency to her*: Giving her a lecture
     on the virtues of moderation and restraint.

170 *rates*: Scolds, lays down the law.

     that: So that.

174–97 *Thus have I politicly begun my reign . . . to show*: This
     speech, addressed direct to the audience, is central to
     the play, because in it Petruchio explains his plan for
     taming Katherina and, at the same time, through the

image of the falcon, gives his estimate of her character.
174 *politicly*: Prudently, like a clever statesman.
begun my reign: This is an allusion to the idea that the
wife was the husband's subject. Cf. V.2.145–6, *Thy
husband is thy lord . . . thy sovereign.*
176–82 *My falcon now is sharp and passing empty . . . obedient*:
The methods used in the training of a wild hawk or
haggard, as she was called, in order to make her 'meek,
and loving to the man', are thus described by a contemporary of Shakespeare:

All hawks generally are manned after one manner, that is to
say, by watching and keeping them from sleep, by a continual
carrying of them upon your fist, and by a most familiar
stroking and playing with them, with the wing of a dead fowl
or such like, and by often gazing and looking of them in the
face, with a loving and gentle countenance, and so making
them acquainted with the man. (Gervase Markham, *Country
Contentments* (1615), 4th edition (1631), pp. 36–7)

176 *sharp*: Sharp-set, famished.
passing: Extremely.
177 *stoop*: Fly to the lure.
full-gorged: Allowed to feed her fill.
178 *looks upon*: Regards, takes notice of.
lure: Apparatus used by falconers to recall their hawks,
being a bunch of feathers attached to a cord, within
which, during its training, the hawk finds its food.
179 *man my haggard*: Tame my wild hawk.
181 *watch her*: Keep her awake.
these kites: Those falcons.
182 *bate and beat*: Flutter and flap their wings.
189 *hurly*: Commotion.
intend: Pretend, try to make out.
190 *reverend*: Reverent, respectful.
191 *watch*: Stay awake.
193 *still*: Constantly.
194 *to kill a wife with kindness*: To 'kill with kindness' was

a proverbial phrase for harming someone by excessive and mistaken indulgence. Petruchio is using it ironically for to 'give her a taste of her own medicine'.

197 *charity to show*: To show public spirit. The rhyme 'shrew/show' indicates how 'shrew' was pronounced.

IV.2

3 *she bears me fair in hand*: She deceives me in a very convincing fashion.

4–8 *Sir, to satisfy you in what I have said . . . Love*: F distributes these lines wrongly, giving 4–5 to Lucentio, 6 to Hortensio, 7 correctly to Bianca and 8 to Hortensio. For a possible explanation of how the confusion may have arisen see the note to III.1.46–56.

4 *to satisfy you in*: To convince you of.

5 *Enter Bianca, and Lucentio as Cambio*: F reads *Enter Bianca.* – a consequence of the mistaken attribution of the previous speech to Lucentio.

8 *that I profess*: That which I practise.
The Art to Love: Ovid's witty poem the *Ars Amatoria*, in which love is presented as a science.

11 *Quick proceeders*: Apt students. The allusion is to 'proceeding' from BA to MA – cf. *master of your art* at 9.

15 *wonderful*: Surprising, incredible.

18 *scorn*: Scorns. The verb agrees with the antecedent *I* instead of with the relative *that*.

20 *cullion*: Base fellow, rascal.

23 *entire affection to*: Pure unalloyed love for.

24 *lightness*: Wantonness, loose behaviour.

31 *fondly*: Foolishly.
withal: With.

34 *how beastly*: In what animal fashion.

35 *Would all the world but he had quite forsworn*: Hortensio spitefully wishes that Cambio were Bianca's only suitor. It does not occur to him that she could ever think of marrying the apparent menial.

37 *a wealthy widow*: The sudden mention of this new character, of whom there has not been a word so far, is another sign that the part of Hortensio has undergone some cobbling.

38 *which*: Who (the two words are often interchanged in
    Shakespeare).

39 *haggard*: Wild intractable hawk – used metaphorically
    here for a light woman. Cf. *Othello*, III.3.257, 'If I do
    prove her haggard', meaning 'unfaithful'.

43 *In resolution*: With fixed purpose, fully determined.

45 *'longeth to*: Belongs to, suits with.

46 *ta'en you napping*: Caught you in the act (of billing and
    cooing).

53–8 *Ay, and he'll tame her ... chattering tongue*: Tranio knows
    far more about Hortensio's plans than Hortensio has
    just told him. This passage is yet more evidence that
    the part of Hortensio has been much altered.

57 *tricks eleven and twenty long*: Tricks of exactly the right
    kind. The allusion is to the game of cards called 'one-
    and-thirty' that Grumio refers to at I.2.32.

58 *charm*: Use a magic spell in order to silence (cf. I.1.206).

60 *dog-weary*: Dog-tired, worn out.

61 *An ancient angel*: A fellow of the good old stamp. An
    angel was a gold coin, worth ten shillings (50p), carrying
    as its device the archangel Michael and the dragon.
    Biondello may also be thinking of the Pedant as the
    angel who has come in answer to his prayer.

62 *Will serve the turn*: Who will serve our purpose.

63 *marcantant*: Biondello's version of *mercatante*, Italian
    for 'merchant'.

67 *trust my tale*: Believe my story.

71 *let me alone*: Rely on me.

73 *farrer*: Farther. F reads *farre*, which editors render as
    'far', but *farrer* makes better sense and is supported by
    Shakespeare's use of this old form of the comparative
    in *The Winter's Tale* (IV.4.426–8), where Polixenes tells
    Florizel, in the F text:

> we'll bar thee from succession;
> Not hold thee of our blood, no, not our kin,
> Far than Deucalion off . . .

77 *What countryman*: Where do you live?

79   *careless of*: Regardless of.

80   *that goes hard*: That's a serious matter.

81–7 *'Tis death for any one in Mantua . . . proclaimed about*:
     Tranio's story looks to be borrowed from Shakespeare's
     own *The Comedy of Errors*, I.1.17–20.

83   *stayed*: Held up.

84   *For private quarrel*: On account of personal dissension.

86   *'Tis marvel*: It's strange. Two constructions are involved
     here. Tranio begins to say 'It's strange you haven't
     heard', but then changes abruptly to another way of
     putting it, as people often do in speech.
     but that you are newly come: But for the fact that you
     have only just arrived.

87   *about*: Up and down the city.

88   *than so*: Than you think.

89   *bills for money by exchange*: Bills of exchange, promis-
     sory notes.

95   *Pisa renownèd for grave citizens*: A repetition of I.1.10.

101 *As much as an apple doth an oyster*: A well-known
     phrase.

102 *and all one*: Just the very same.

107 *credit*: Reputation.
     undertake: Assume, take on you.

109 *Look that you take upon you as you should*: See that you
     play your part properly.

112 *accept of*: Accept.

113 *repute*: Consider, think of.

115 *make the matter good*: Put the plan into effect.

117 *looked for*: Expected.

118 *pass assurance of*: Settle, make a binding promise of.

IV.3

     F marks the beginning of this scene as the opening of
     Act IV, heading it *Actus Quartus. Scena Prima*. See the
     headnote to IV.1.

2   *The more my wrong*: The greater the injustice done to
     me.

5   *Upon entreaty have a present alms*: Have only to ask and
     they receive alms immediately.

9   *meat*: Food in general.

11 *spites*: Mortifies, vexes.

13 *As who should say*: As if to say, as though he were saying.

44 *present*: Immediate.

15 *some repast*: Something to eat.

16 *so*: So long as, provided that.

17 *a neat's foot*: The foot of an ox.

19 *choleric*: Productive of anger, prone to make one irascible.

20 *broiled*: Grilled, cooked over the coals.

22 *I cannot tell*: I don't know what to say.

26 *let the mustard rest*: Don't worry about the mustard.

32 *the very name*: The mere name, the name and nothing else.

36 *sweeting*: Darling, sweetheart.
   all amort: Down in the dumps, sick to death (French, *à la mort*).

37 *what cheer*: How is it with you?
   as cold as can be: As cold a reception, as poor entertainment, as can be imagined (quibbling on the other sense of *cheer*).

43 *all my pains is sorted to no proof*: All my labour has been in vain, has been taken to no purpose; *pains* is always singular in Shakespeare.

45 *poorest*: Slightest, most insignificant.

46 *mine before*: The ellipse of the verb 'be' is common in Shakespeare, otherwise 'mine be 'fore' would be an attractive reading.

48 *to blame*: Too blameworthy, too much at fault. This use of *to blame* as though it were 'too blame' was common in Shakespeare's day. Cf. the Nurse's reproof to Old Capulet, 'You are to blame, my lord, to rate her so' (*Romeo and Juliet*, III.5.169).

51 *do it*: May it do.

52 *apace*: Quickly.

54 *as bravely*: In as splendidly dressed a manner.

56 *ruffs*: Articles of neckwear elaborately fluted and stiffly starched.
   farthingales: Hooped petticoats.

57 *bravery*: Finery.

58 *this knavery*: Tricks of dress like those, that sort of trumpery.

59 *stays*: Awaits.

60 *ruffling*: Swaggering, gay.

62–140 *Lay forth the gown . . . Ay, there's the villainy*: Some interesting parallels to this attack on fashions in dress are to be found in *Life in Shakespeare's England*, ed. J. Dover Wilson, Penguin edition (1968), pp. 161–73.

63 *HABERDASHER*: F heads this speech *Fel.*
bespeak: Order.

64 *moulded on*: Modelled on, shaped like.
porringer: Small basin from which soup, porridge and the like were eaten.

65 *A velvet dish*: A dish made of velvet.
lewd and filthy: Elizabethan equivalent of 'cheap and nasty'.

66 *cockle*: Cockle-shell.

67 *knack*: Knick-knack, silly contrivance.
toy: Piece of nonsense.
trick: Bauble, practical joke.

69 *fit the time*: Suit the fashion.

75 *endured me say*: Suffered me to say.

76 *best you stop*: It were best for you to stop.

82 *custard-coffin*: Crust of pastry in which a custard was baked.

83 *in that*: Because, inasmuch as.

86 *Exit Haberdasher*: F gives the Haberdasher no exit, but now that the business of the cap is over there is no reason for his remaining.

87 *masquing stuff*: Clothes that look suitable for use in a masque. Strange and elaborate costumes were a feature of the masque.

88 *demi-cannon*: Large gun with a bore of about six and a half inches. The sleeve in question is of the leg-of-mutton variety that became popular around 1580. It was often slashed as well as being padded and stiffened with embroidery – hence Petruchio's subsequent attacks. Men's dress, it should be added, was equally elaborate.

91 *censer*: The usual explanation of this rare word – that
   it was a fumigator, consisting of a brazier with a perfor-
   ated lid to emit the smoke of burning perfumes – is
   not very satisfactory in this context, but until a better
   is found it must serve.

92 *a devil's name*: In the name of the devil.

94 *bid*: Past tense.

96 *Marry, and did*: Indeed I did.
   be remembered: Recollect.

97 *mar it to the time*: Ruin it for ever.

98 *hop me*: Hop, I say.
   kennel: Gutter, surface-drain of a street.

99 *hop without*: Lose. Cf. *Henry VI, Part II*, I.3.133–5:

   > Thy sale of offices and towns in France,
   > If they were known, as the suspect is great,
   > Would make thee quickly hop without thy head.

100 *make your best of it*: Do what you like with it.

102 *quaint*: Artfully made, elegant.

107 *nail*: A measure of length for cloth, being one sixteenth
    of a yard.

108 *nit*: Egg of a louse. There is no need to assume from
    these abusive terms, as some editors have done, that
    the part of the tailor was played by a small man or by
    a boy. Petruchio is practising the rhetorical art of
    diminution, encouraged, no doubt, by the common
    proverb 'Nine tailors make a man'.

109 *Braved*: Defied, challenged.
    with: By.

110 *rag*: (1) Tattered bit of cloth; (2) shabby person.
    quantity: Scrap.

111 *bemete*: Measure (with a quibble on 'mete out punish-
    ment').

112 *As thou shalt think on*: That you will think twice about.

121 *faced*: (1) Trimmed with braid, velvet or some other
    material; (2) impudently confronted, bullied.

123 *braved*: (1) Provided fine clothes for; (2) defied, set
    yourself up against.

126 *Ergo*: Therefore, consequently (term much used in logic).

129 *The note lies in's throat*: (1) The note tells a black lie; (2) the musical note is in his throat, meaning 'the words come from his mouth'.

130–31 *loose-bodied*: (1) Loosely fitting; (2) of the kind worn by 'loose bodies', meaning 'harlots'.

132–3 *bottom of brown thread*: Ball of brown thread. The *bottom* was really the core or bobbin on which thread was wound.

135 *compassed*: Cut so as to fall in a circle.

137 *trunk sleeve*: Large wide sleeve.

139 *curiously*: (1) Carefully, accurately; (2) elaborately. Petruchio takes the word in the second sense, of course.

141 *bill*: (1) The *note* of 127; (2) bill of indictment, accusation.

143 *prove upon thee*: Establish by fighting you. The allusion is to trial by combat. Cf. *Richard II*, IV.1.44–8:

> Aumerle, thou liest. His honour is as true
> In this appeal as thou art all unjust;
> And that thou art so there I throw my gage
> To prove it on thee to the extremest point
> Of mortal breathing.

145 *an*: If.

145–6 *in place where*: In a fit place, in the right spot.

147 *for thee straight*: Ready to do battle with you at once.
    bill: (1) Note; (2) kind of pike or halbert used by watchmen.

148 *mete-yard*: Measuring rod.

149 *God-a-mercy*: God have mercy!

150 *odds*: Advantage, superiority (probably with a quibble on the odds and ends left over from a garment which were the tailor's perquisites).

153 *take it up unto thy master's use*: Take it away and let your master make what use he can of it.

154–5 *Take up my mistress' gown for thy master's use*: See note on III.2.164.

155 *use*: Sexual purposes.

156 *conceit*: Idea, notion, innuendo.

157 *think for*: Imagine.

163 *Take no unkindness of*: Don't imagine there is any ill-will in.

166 *mean habiliments*: Poor clothes.

167 *proud*: Puffed up.

170 *peereth in*: Can be seen peeping through.

174 *painted*: Richly coloured.
    contents: Pleases, delights.

176 *furniture*: Outfit, dress.
    array: Attire.

178 *frolic*: Be merry.

180 *To Grumio*: Not in F, but Petruchio would never give an order of the kind that follows to Katherina.

184 *dinner-time*: Between eleven o'clock and noon.

186 *supper-time*: Between half-past five and half-past six. Petruchio and Katherina are substantially agreed, if on nothing else, that it takes about four hours to get to her father's.

188 *Look what*: Whatever, no matter what.
    think to do: Intend to do, think of doing.

189 *still crossing*: Always contradicting, constantly thwarting.
    let't alone: Forbear, take no further action about the matter.

192 *so*: Apparently, according to what he has said. This line leads on very neatly to the opening of IV.5, the next scene in which Petruchio and Katherina appear.

IV.4

0 *Enter Tranio as Lucentio, and the Pedant, booted, and dressed like Vincentio*: F reads: *Enter Tranio, and the Pedant drest like Vincentio*. For the addition of the word *booted*, meaning 'wearing riding boots', see the second note to 17.

1 *please it you*: May it please you.

2 *what else*: Of course.
    but: Unless.

4 *Near*: Nearly.

5 *Where we were lodgers at the Pegasus*: F prints this as
the first line of Tranio's speech – the result of a careless alignment of the speech-prefix in the manuscript,
or, perhaps, to indicate that the line is to be spoken by
the Pedant and Tranio simultaneously as a sign of their
complicity.
  at the Pegasus: The winged horse of classical mythology
was a popular inn-sign in Shakespeare's London.

6 *hold your own*: Play your part well.

9 *schooled*: Instructed in his part.

10 *Fear you not him*: Don't be worried about him.

11 *throughly*: Thoroughly, properly.
   advise: Instruct, caution.

12 *right*: Real, true.

16 *looked for*: Expected.

17 *Th' art a tall fellow, hold thee that to drink*: You're an
able chap, take that to get yourself a drink.
   Enter Baptista, and Lucentio as Cambio: F reads *Enter
Baptista and Lucentio: Pedant booted and bare headed*.
As the Pedant is already onstage at this point, it looks
as though this direction may well be something left
over from an earlier version in which the scene began
here.

18 *Set your countenance*: Look like a grave father.

21 *stand*: Be, show yourself.

23 *Soft*: Gently, just a moment.

24 *having come*: I having come. The omission of the noun
or pronoun on which a participle depends is fairly
common in Shakespeare. Cf. 'Coming from Sardis, on
our former ensign | Two mighty eagles fell' (*Julius
Caesar*, V.1.79–80).

26 *weighty cause*: Serious matter.

28 *for*: Because of.

30 *to stay him not*: In order not to keep him waiting.

32–3 *to like | No worse than I*: To be no less satisfied than I.

35 *With one consent*: In entire agreement.
   bestowed: Matched, married.

36 *curious*: Over-particular in a matter of business,
niggling.

45 *pass*: Settle upon.

46 *done*: Settled.

48–50 *Where then do you know best . . . with either part's agree-
      ment stand*: Where, in your opinion, may we best be
      betrothed and such legal arrangements be made as will
      be agreeable to both parties?

52 *Pitchers have ears*: This proverb, which Shakespeare uses
   again in *Richard III*, II.4.37, puns on the *ears* or handles
   by which water-vessels were lifted, and means 'there
   may be listeners'.

53 *hearkening still*: Still watching his opportunity.

54 *happily*: Haply, perchance.

55 *an it like*: If it please.

56 *lie*: Lodge.

57 *pass*: Settle.

58 *He winks at Lucentio*: This is not in F but is clearly
   demanded by Biondello's remark at 74.

59 *scrivener*: Notary, one publicly authorized to draw up
   contracts.

60 *slender*: Slight, insufficient.

61 *pittance*: Fare, diet.

62 *hie you*: Get you, hurry off.

63 *straight*: Immediately, straightway.

68 *Enter Peter, a Servingman*: This direction is based on
   F, which reads *Enter Peter*. Although Peter says nothing,
   his purpose is almost certainly to indicate to Tranio,
   by a gesture, that the meal is ready.

70 *One mess is like to be your cheer*: One dish is likely to
   be your fare.

76 *'has*: He has.

78 *moralize*: Explain the meaning of.

79 *safe*: Safely out of the way.

80 *deceiving . . . deceitful*: Sham . . . sham.

86 *command*: Service.

89 *assurance*: Legal settlement.
   Take you assurance: Make sure.

89–90 *cum privilegio ad imprimendum solum*: This Latin inscrip-
      tion, frequently found on the title-pages of books
      printed in Shakespeare's time, meant originally 'with

the privilege for printing only', but it was later taken
to mean 'with the sole right to print', which is the significance Biondello has in mind here. There is a pun on
printing in the sense of 'stamping one's own image on
a female by getting her with child'.

91 *some sufficient*: Enough, the right number required by
law.

92 *that you look for*: That which you long for.

99 *against you come*: In preparation for your coming.

100 *appendix*: Appendage (meaning Bianca).

103 *I'll roundly go about her*: I'll approach her without ceremony.

104 *It shall go hard if Cambio go without her*: Cambio is not
going to lose her if he can possibly help it.

IV.5

The location of this scene, established in the first two
lines, is somewhere on the road between Petruchio's
house and Padua. No Elizabethan audience would
trouble its head over whether the travellers are in that
Long-lane, mentioned by Petruchio at IV.3.181, or
whether they are somewhere further along the main
road, walking up a hill to rest their horses. The audience would know that the characters must be on foot,
because horses did not appear on the Elizabethan stage.

7 *list*: Please, choose.

8 *Or e'er*: Before ever.

14 *rush-candle*: Candle of feeble power made by dipping
a rush in grease.

20 *And the moon changes even as your mind*: A nice touch
showing that Katherina has lost neither her spirit nor
her sense of humour.

23 *go thy ways*: Go on, carry on (used as a term of appro-
bation).

25 *against the bias*: Against its natural inclination. The bias
is the weight lodged on one side of the wooden ball,
or bowl, used in the game of bowls, in order to make
it swerve when rolled.

27 *where away*: Where are you going?

29 *fresher*: More youthful.

31 *spangle*: Brightly adorn.

35 *'A*: He (colloquial).

36 *the woman*: So F, though most editors prefer to follow
   F2 and read *a woman*. The allusion is, however, to the
   theatre, where the part of the woman was played by a
   boy. Petruchio, says Hortensio, is assigning the old man
   the woman's role in the little play he is staging. Cf.
   Coriolanus, II.2.93–5:

   > In that day's feats,
   > When he might act the woman in the scene,
   > He proved best man i'th'field.

38 *Whither away, or where*: This is the reading of F2; F
   has *Whether away, or whether*. Since *where* was a
   contracted form of 'whether', the mistake is easily
   understood.

41 *Allots*: The old plural.

47 *green*: (1) Green in colour; (2) fresh, new, youthful.

54 *encounter*: Manner of address, greeting.

61 *father*: Father-in-law. Petruchio is rather stretching the
   meaning.

62–3 *The sister to my wife, this gentlewoman, | Thy son by
   this hath married*: Neither Petruchio nor Hortensio,
   who adds his assurance at 74, can possibly know this
   since it has not yet happened. Moreover, Hortensio has
   every reason to think it never will, because Tranio, who
   for him, as for Petruchio, is Lucentio, joined with him
   in forswearing Bianca for ever. Although these discrepancies are likely to go unnoticed in the theatre, they do
   point, nevertheless, to the same kind of cobbling that
   is evident in the conduct of so much of the sub-plot.

64 *of good esteem*: Of good reputation, highly respected.

66 *qualified*: Endowed with good qualities.
   beseem: Befit.

71 *or is it else*: Or else is it.

72 *pleasant*: Merry, facetious.
   break a jest: Play a practical joke.

76 *jealous*: Suspicious.

77 *put me in heart*: Encouraged me.

78 *froward*: Difficult, refractory.

79 *untoward*: Unmannerly, unforthcoming.

V.1

F marks no Act division at this point, but since the
action has now moved back to Padua, where it will
remain for the rest of the play, this is obviously the
right place for the last Act to begin

0 *Enter Biondello, Lucentio as himself, and Bianca. Gremio
is out before*: So F, except that it fails to indicate that
Lucentio is no longer in disguise. The very unusual
direction *Gremio is out before*, which has all the appearance of an afterthought, means that Gremio comes on
first, and the rest follow after a brief interval. Why he
is waiting for Cambio (see 6) is never made clear, but
his failure to notice him when he does come on is
accounted for by the fact that Lucentio is not now *in
the habit of a mean man* (II.1.38).

4 *I'll see the church a your back*: I'll see the church at your
back, meaning 'I'll see you safely married'.

7–8 *Sir, here's the door, this is Lucentio's house . . . market-
place*: These two lines are a strong indication that for
the part of the action that takes place in Padua one
of the main doors leading on to the stage is thought of
as the entrance to Lucentio's house and the other as
the entrance to Baptista's house.

10 *You shall not choose but*: You must.

11 *your welcome*: A welcome for you.

12 *some cheer is toward*: Some good cheer is to be expected.

13 *Pedant looks out of the window*: This stage direction has
been adapted from a similar one in Gascoigne's
Supposes, where in the corresponding scene (IV.3)
Dalio, the cook in the house of Dulipo (Tranio),
'cometh to the window, and there maketh them answer'
when the true father of the hero turns up. The window
in question was probably above the stage-door that
served as the entrance to Lucentio's house.

17 *withal*: With.

23–4 *To leave frivolous circumstances*: To have done with

pointless talk, to cut the cackle.

27 *from Mantua*: F reads *from Padua*, which does not make very good sense since they are in Padua. A much better comic effect is produced by letting the Pedant forget his role for a moment and give the name of the place he has really come from.

32 *flat*: Downright, bare-faced.

34–5 *'a means to cozen*: He plans to cheat.

35 *under my countenance*: By pretending to be me.

37 *God send 'em good shipping*: May God grant them a good voyage (a proverbial phrase for wishing someone good luck).

38 *undone*: Ruined.

40 *crack-hemp*: Rogue deserving to be hanged, gallows-bird.

41 *I hope I may choose*: I trust I may suit myself, meaning 'be allowed to go on my way'.

56 *offer*: Dare, have the effrontery.

58 *fine*: Richly dressed.

59 *copatain hat*: Sugar-loaf hat.

60 *good husband*: Careful economical manager.

65 *habit*: Appearance.

66 *what 'cerns it you*: How does it concern you, what business of yours is it?

67 *maintain*: Afford.

69 *Bergamo*: This town, some 25 miles to the north-east of Milan, is an improbable place for a sailmaker to live, but it is exactly the right place for Tranio to come from, since it was the traditional home of Harlequin, the facetious servant of the Italian *Commedia dell'arte*.

82 *an officer*: A constable.
Enter an Officer: Not in F though required by the dialogue and the action.

84 *forthcoming*: Ready to stand his trial when required.

89–90 *cony-catched*: Cheated, swindled, made the victim of a confidence-trick.

96 *dotard*: Drivelling old fool.

97 *haled and abused*: Dragged about and wrongfully treated.

99 *spoiled*: Ruined.

101 *Exeunt ... as fast as may be*: There is a parallel to this
picturesque bit of description in *The Comedy of Errors*,
IV.4.144, where F's direction reads *Exeunt omnes, as
fast as may be, frighted*.

106 *counterfeit supposes*: False suppositions caused by the
exchange of identities. There is an obvious reference
here to Gascoigne's *Supposes*.

bleared thine eyne: Deceived your eyes.

107 *Here's packing, with a witness*: Here's plotting, and no
mistake.

119 *I'll slit the villain's nose*: The slitting or cutting-off of
the nose was a recognized form of revenge. Cf.
Othello's words about Cassio, 'I see that nose of yours,
but not that dog I shall throw it to' (*Othello*, IV.1.142–3).

123 *go to*: Come, don't worry.

128 *My cake is dough*: I have failed. See note to I.1.108.

129 *Out of hope of all*: With no hope of anything.

141 *Better once than never, for never too late*: Petruchio has
rolled two proverbs into one: 'Better late than never'
and 'It is never too late to mend'; *once* here means
'sometime'.

V.2

F heads this scene *Actus Quintus.*, disregarding the
change of location that has occurred a scene before and
leaving the last Act rather thin.

0 *Enter Baptista ... banquet*: F reads *Enter Baptista,
Vincentio, Gremio, the Pedant, Lucentio, and Bianca.
Tranio, Biondello, Grumio, and Widdow: The Seruingmen
with Tranio bringing in a Banquet*. Tranio, it will be
noticed, is mentioned twice, while Petruchio, Katherina
and Hortensio are not mentioned at all. A direction
such as this can hardly be the work of the author and
it would certainly not have passed muster in the theatre.

banquet: Dessert of fruits, sweetmeats and wine, served
after supper.

1 *long*: Late, after a long time.

agree: Harmonize.

3 *scapes*: Escapes.

overblown: Gone by, that have blown over.

4–5 *My fair Bianca, bid my father welcome ... thine*: Lucentio is giving the banquet at his house, to which they have all adjourned after enjoying the wedding-feast at Baptista's.

5 *kindness*: The feelings proper to kinship, goodwill.

8 *Feast with*: Feast on.

9 *close our stomachs up*: Put the finishing touches to our meal. Cheese is normally used for this purpose today but our ancestors had different ideas.

13 *affords this kindness*: Offers this as the natural thing.

14 *kind*: Affectionate, kindly. Petruchio is thinking of Katherina.

16 *fears*: (1) Is afraid of (the sense in which Petruchio uses it); (2) frightens (the sense in which the Widow takes it).

17 *Then never trust me if I be*: I can tell you I am not.

18 *sensible*: Judicious, discriminating.
sense: Meaning.

20 *He that is giddy thinks the world turns round*: People are prone to attribute their misfortunes to others. The saying was proverbial.

21 *Roundly*: (1) Outspokenly; (2) glibly.

22 *Thus I conceive by him*: That's the state I think he's in.

23 *Conceives by me*: The obvious quibble.

24 *conceives her tale*: Interprets her remark.

25 *mended*: Rectified.

31 *mean*: Petty, trivial.

32 *I am mean, indeed, respecting you*: I am moderate in behaviour by comparison with you.

33 *To her*: Have at her, assail her.

35 *marks*: A mark was worth 13*s*. 4*d* (67p).
put her down: (1) Get the better of her; (2) have sexual relations with her – the sense Hortensio gives the phrase. There is a similar quibbling exchange between Don Pedro and Beatrice in *Much Ado About Nothing*, II.1.259–62.

36 *office*: Employment.

37 *like an officer*: Like one who does his duty.

39 *butt together*: Butt each other. F reads *But together*, which
many editors change to 'butt heads together' in order
to prepare the way for Bianca's retort. This, however,
makes the line unmetrical and is not strictly necessary
since the use of the head is implicit in the act of butting.
Shakespeare employs the same analogy between young
people exchanging witticisms and cattle butting each
other in *Love's Labour's Lost* (V.2.251–2), where
Longaville tells Katharine:

> Look how you butt yourself in these sharp mocks.
> Will you give horns, chaste lady?

40 *Head and butt*: Head and tail; *butt* here means 'bottom'.
   hasty-witted body: Quick-witted person.

41 *your head and butt were head and horn*: Your butting
   head was a horned head (a reference to the cuckold's
   horns).

45 *bitter*: Shrewd. F reads *better*.

46–7 *Am I your bird . . . as you draw your bow*: The reference
   is to the Elizabethan method of fowling with bow and
   arrows. The target had to be a sitting one; therefore,
   if the bird moved to another tree or *bush*, the fowler
   had to follow.

49 *prevented*: Forestalled, escaped from.

52 *slipped*: Unleashed.

54 *swift*: Prompt, quick.

56 *your deer does hold you at a bay*: Your deer (with a quibble
   on 'dear') shows fight and holds you off. A stag is said
   to be *at bay* when it turns on the dogs and defends itself
   with its horns.

57 *hits you*: Gives you a shrewd blow, catches you on the
   raw.

58 *gird*: Taunt, gibe.

60 *'A*: He (colloquial).
   galled me: Scratched me, given me a surface wound.

61 *did glance away from*: Ricocheted off.

63 *in good sadness*: In sober earnest.

65 *for assurance*: To make sure.

72 *of*: On.

75–6 *That will I. Biondello,* | *Go*: F reads *That will I.* | *Goe*
      Biondello, which is metrically unsatisfactory. The trans-
      position of the two words *Biondello* and *Go* puts the
      metre right while leaving the sense unaltered.

77 *I'll be your half*: I'll go half-shares with you in the risk
      and the profit of betting that.

81 *How*: Really? (expression of surprise).

84 *I hope better*: I have better expectations.

97 *The fouler fortune mine, and there an end*: The worse
      my luck, and that's that.

98 *by my holidame*: By all I hold sacred, by my halidom
      (Holiness).

101 *conferring*: Chatting.

102 *deny*: Refuse.

103 *Swinge me them soundly forth*: Beat them soundly, I tell
      you, and make them come hither.

105 *wonder*: Miracle.

106 *bodes*: Portends, presages.

108 *awful*: Commanding due respect.
      right supremacy: Supremacy that deserves the name.

110 *fair befall thee*: Good luck to you, congratulations to
      you.

114 *as she had never been*: As if she had never existed, out
      of all recognition.

117 *obedience*: So F, but the repetition of the word is suspi-
      cious. It has probably been caught by the compositor
      from the end of the previous line.

127 *a hundred crowns*: F reads *fiue hundred crownes*, though
      Lucentio's bet, made at 74, was only for one hundred.
      The best explanation of the mistake is C. J. Sisson's;
      he thinks that the manuscript read 'a hundred', which
      the compositor took as 'v hundred'.

128 *laying*: Laying a bet, wagering.

135 *unkind*: Harsh, in a manner contrary to nature.

138 *blots*: Disfigures, destroys.
      meads: Meadows.

139 *Confounds thy fame*: Ruins your reputation.
      shake: Shake to pieces.

141 *moved*: Annoyed, in a bad temper.

142 *ill-seeming*: Unpleasant to look at.

    thick: Turbid.

143 *none so dry*: No one no matter how dry, no one however dry.

147 *maintenance; commits*: F reads *maintenance. Commits*, which many editors change to 'maintenance commits', assuming that it is in order to maintain his wife that the husband *commits his body | To painful labour*. In this edition the punctuation of F is substantially adhered to, because it brings out a general contrast between the life of the husband and the life of the wife, the one exposed to the dangers of the world, the other safe at home.

148 *painful*: Hard, toilsome.

149 *watch*: Be on guard through, be on the alert through.

158 *foul*: Wicked.

159 *graceless*: Depraved, sinful.

160 *simple*: Foolish, unintelligent.

161 *offer*: Begin, declare.

165 *Unapt to*: Unfit for.

166 *conditions*: Qualities, temperaments.

168 *unable*: Weak, impotent.

169 *My mind hath been as big as one of yours*: My inclination has been as strong as that of either of you.

170 *heart*: Courage.

    haply: Perhaps, maybe.

171 *bandy*: Exchange (as a ball is hit to and fro in tennis).

173 *as weak*: As weak as straws.

174 *That seeming to be most which*: Seeming to be that in the highest degree which.

175 *vail your stomachs*: Lower your pride.

    it is no boot: It is of no avail, there is no help for it.

176 *And place your hands below your husband's foot*: There may well be a reference here to some traditional act of allegiance, but the basic idea is clearly set out in the Homily entitled 'Of the State of Matrimony', where wives are advised to submit to their husbands

in respect of the commandment of God, as St Paul expres-
seth it in this form of words: *Let women be subject to their
husbands, as to the Lord; for the husband is the head of the
woman, as Christ is the head of the church.* Ephes. v (Sermons
or Homilies (no date), pp. 553–4)

178 *do him ease*: Give him satisfaction.
180 *go thy ways*: Well done.
    ha't: Have it, meaning 'have the prize', 'be acknow-
    ledged as the winner'.
181 *a good hearing*: A nice thing to hear, a pleasant spec-
    tacle.
    toward: Docile, tractable (the exact opposite of
    'froward').
184 *sped*: Done for, defeated.
185 *the white*: The white ring at the centre of the target
    (with a quibble on the name Bianca, Italian for white).
186 *being*: Since I am. Petruchio, like a successful gamester,
    goes off while his luck still holds.

PENGUIN SHAKESPEARE

AS YOU LIKE IT
WILLIAM SHAKESPEARE

WWW.PENGUINSHAKESPEARE.COM

When Rosalind is banished by her uncle, who has usurped her father's throne, she flees to the Forest of Arden where her exiled father holds court. There, dressed as a boy to avoid discovery, she encounters the man she loves – now a fellow exile – and resolves to remain in disguise to test his feelings for her. A gloriously sunny comedy, *As You Like It* is an exuberant combination of concealed identities and verbal jousting, reconciliations and multiple weddings.

This book includes a general introduction to Shakespeare's life and the Elizabethan theatre, a separate introduction to *As You Like It*, a chronology of his works, suggestions for further reading, an essay discussing performance options on both stage and screen, and a commentary.

Edited by H. J. Oliver

With an introduction by Katherine Duncan-Jones

General Editor: Stanley Wells

PENGUIN SHAKESPEARE

CYMBELINE
WILLIAM SHAKESPEARE

WWW.PENGUINSHAKESPEARE.COM

The King of Britain, enraged by his daughter's disobedience in
marrying against his wishes, banishes his new son-in-law. Having fled
to Rome, the exiled husband makes a foolish wager with a villain he
encounters there – gambling on the fidelity of his abandoned wife.
Combining courtly menace and horror, comedy and melodrama,
Cymbeline is a moving depiction of two young lovers driven apart by
deceit and self-doubt.

This book includes a general introduction to Shakespeare's life and the
Elizabethan theatre, a separate introduction to *Cymbeline*, a chronology
of his works, suggestions for further reading, an essay discussing
performance options on both stage and screen, and a commentary.

Edited with an introduction by John Pitcher

General Editor: Stanley Wells

PENGUIN SHAKESPEARE

MEASURE FOR MEASURE
WILLIAM SHAKESPEARE

WWW.PENGUINSHAKESPEARE.COM

In the Duke's absence from Vienna, his strict deputy Angelo revives an ancient law forbidding sex outside marriage. The young Claudio, whose fiancée is pregnant, is condemned to death by the law. His sister Isabella, soon to become a nun, pleads with Lord Angelo for her brother's life. But her purity so excites Angelo that he offers her a monstrous bargain – he will save Claudio if Isabella will visit him that night.

This book includes a general introduction to Shakespeare's life and the Elizabethan theatre, a separate introduction to *Measure for Measure*, a chronology of his works, suggestions for further reading, an essay discussing performance options on both stage and screen by Nicholas Arnold, and a commentary.

Edited by J. M. Nosworthy

With an introduction by Julia Briggs

General Editor: Stanley Wells

read more

PENGUIN SHAKESPEARE

THE MERCHANT OF VENICE
WILLIAM SHAKESPEARE

WWW.PENGUINSHAKESPEARE.COM

A noble but impoverished Venetian asks a friend, Antonio, for a loan to impress an heiress. His friend agrees, but is forced to borrow the sum from a cynical Jewish moneylender, Shylock, and signs a chilling contract to honour the debt with a pound of his own flesh. A complex and controversial comedy, *The Merchant of Venice* explores prejudice and the true nature of justice.

This book includes a general introduction to Shakespeare's life and the Elizabethan theatre, a separate introduction to *The Merchant of Venice*, a chronology of Shakespeare's works, suggestions for further reading, an essay discussing performance options on both stage and screen, and a commentary.

Edited by W. Moelwyn Merchant

With an introduction by Peter Holland

General Editor: Stanley Wells

PENGUIN SHAKESPEARE

A MIDSUMMER NIGHT'S DREAM
WILLIAM SHAKESPEARE

WWW.PENGUINSHAKESPEARE.COM

A young woman flees Athens with her lover, only to be pursued by her would-be husband and her best friend. Unwittingly, all four find themselves in an enchanted forest where fairies and sprites soon take an interest in human affairs, dispensing magical love potions and casting mischievous spells. In this dazzling comedy, confusion ends in harmony, as love is transformed, misplaced and – ultimately – restored.

This book includes a general introduction to Shakespeare's life and the Elizabethan theatre, a separate introduction to *A Midsummer Night's Dream*, a chronology of Shakespeare's works, suggestions for further reading, an essay discussing performance options on both stage and screen, and a commentary.

Edited by Stanley Wells

With an introduction by Helen Hackett

General Editor: Stanley Wells

PENGUIN SHAKESPEARE

MUCH ADO ABOUT NOTHING
WILLIAM SHAKESPEARE

WWW.PENGUINSHAKESPEARE.COM

A vivacious woman and a high-spirited man both claim that they are determined never to marry. But when their friends trick them into believing that each harbours secret feelings for the other, they begin to question whether their witty banter and sharp-tongued repartee conceals something deeper. Schemes abound, misunderstandings proliferate and matches are eventually made in this sparkling and irresistible comedy.

This book includes a general introduction to Shakespeare's life and the Elizabethan theatre, a separate introduction to *Much Ado About Nothing*, a chronology of Shakespeare's works, suggestions for further reading, an essay discussing performance options on both stage and screen, and a commentary.

Edited by R. A. Foakes

With an introduction by Janette Dillon

General Editor: Stanley Wells

PENGUIN SHAKESPEARE

ROMEO AND JULIET
WILLIAM SHAKESPEARE

WWW.PENGUINSHAKESPEARE.COM

A young man and woman meet by chance and fall instantly in love. But their families are bitter enemies, and in order to be together the two lovers must be prepared to risk everything. Set in a city torn apart by feuds and gang warfare, *Romeo and Juliet* is a dazzling combination of passion and hatred, bawdy comedy and high tragedy.

This book includes a general introduction to Shakespeare's life and the Elizabethan theatre, a separate introduction to *Romeo and Juliet*, a chronology of his works, suggestions for further reading, an essay discussing performance options on both stage and screen, and a commentary.

Edited by T. J. B. Spencer

With an introduction by Adrian Poole

General Editor: Stanley Wells

PENGUIN SHAKESPEARE

TIMON OF ATHENS
WILLIAM SHAKESPEARE

WWW.PENGUINSHAKESPEARE.COM

After squandering his wealth with prodigal generosity, a rich Athenian gentleman finds himself deep in debt. Unshaken by the prospect of bankruptcy, he is certain that the friends he has helped so often will come to his aid. But when they learn his wealth is gone, he quickly finds that their promises fall away to nothing in this tragic exploration of power, greed and loyalty betrayed.

This book includes a general introduction to Shakespeare's life and the Elizabethan theatre, a separate introduction to *Timon of Athens*, a chronology of Shakespeare's works, suggestions for further reading, an essay discussing performance options on both stage and screen, and a commentary.

Edited by G. R. Hibbard

With an introduction by Nicholas Walton

General Editor: Stanley Wells

PENGUIN SHAKESPEARE

TWELFTH NIGHT
WILLIAM SHAKESPEARE

WWW.PENGUINSHAKESPEARE.COM

Separated from her twin brother Sebastian after a shipwreck, Viola disguises herself as a boy to serve the Duke of Illyria. Wooing a countess on his behalf, she is stunned to find herself the object of his beloved's affections. With the arrival of Viola's brother, and a trick played upon the countess's steward, confusion reigns in this romantic comedy of mistaken identity.

This book includes a general introduction to Shakespeare's life and the Elizabethan theatre, a separate introduction to *Twelfth Night*, a chronology of his works, suggestions for further reading, an essay discussing performance options on both stage and screen, and a commentary.

Edited by M. M. Mahood

With an introduction by Michael Dobson

General Editor: Stanley Wells

PENGUIN SHAKESPEARE

THE TWO GENTLEMEN OF VERONA
WILLIAM SHAKESPEARE

WWW.PENGUINSHAKESPEARE.COM

Leaving behind both home and beloved, a young man travels to Milan to meet his closest friend. Once there, however, he falls in love with his friend's new sweetheart and resolves to seduce her. Love-crazed and desperate, he is soon moved to commit cynical acts of betrayal. And comic scenes involving a servant and his dog enhance the play's exploration of how passion can prove more powerful than even the strongest loyalty owed to a friend.

This book includes a general introduction to Shakespeare's life and the Elizabethan theatre, a separate introduction to *The Two Gentlemen of Verona*, a chronology of Shakespeare's works, suggestions for further reading, an essay discussing performance options on both stage and screen, and a commentary.

Edited by Norman Sanders

With an introduction by Russell Jackson

General Editor: Stanley Wells

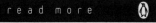

PENGUIN SHAKESPEARE

THE WINTER'S TALE
WILLIAM SHAKESPEARE

WWW.PENGUINSHAKESPEARE.COM

The jealous King of Sicily becomes convinced that his wife is carrying the child of his best friend. Imprisoned and put on trial, the Queen collapses when the King refuses to accept the divine confirmation of her innocence. The child is abandoned to die on the coast of Bohemia. But when she is found and raised by a shepherd, it seems redemption may be possible.

This book includes a general introduction to Shakespeare's life and the Elizabethan theatre, a separate introduction to *The Winter's Tale*, a chronology of Shakespeare's works, suggestions for further reading, an essay discussing performance options on both stage and screen, and a commentary.

Edited by Ernest Schanzer

With an introduction by Russ McDonald

General Editor: Stanley Wells

Read more in Penguin

PENGUIN SHAKESPEARE

The taste of Easton tantalized her senses, intoxicating and arousing all at once in a double dose of what Portia remembered from their passionate encounter the night of the tropical storm.

A night she hadn't spoken of since then.

His hand palmed her back and he drew her closer until they were chest to chest. With a will of their own, her fingers crawled up his hard-muscled arms to grip his wide shoulders.

She'd slept with him. She knew the full extent of his appeal, so she couldn't figure out why a simple kiss could turn her so inside out. Okay, not a simple kiss, because nothing with Easton was ever uncomplicated.

Still, how could her body betray her so, especially after what he'd said about not wanting children? As quickly as that thought hit her, she shut it down again. She'd ached to be in his arms for so long, she was a total puddle of hormones in need of an outlet.

In need of him.

Now.

* * *

His Secretary's Little Secret
is part of The Lourdes Brothers of Key Largo duet—
In the wilds of Florida, two wealthy brothers meet
the women who will capture their hearts!